Sex Addiction

Sex Addiction

A Critical History

Barry Reay, Nina Attwood and
Claire Gooder

polity

The right of Barry Reay, Nina Attwood, Claire Gooder to be identified as
Author of this Work has been asserted in accordance with the UK Copyright,
Designs and Patents Act 1988.

First published in 2015 by Polity Press

Polity Press
65 Bridge Street
Cambridge CB2 1UR, UK

Polity Press
350 Main Street
Malden, MA 02148, USA

ISBN-13: 978-0-7456-7035-5
ISBN-13: 978-0-7456-7036-2(pb)

A catalogue record for this book is available from the British Library.

Library of Congress Cataloging-in-Publication Data

Reay, Barry.
   Sex addiction : a short history / Barry Reay, Nina Attwood, Claire Gooder.
    pages cm
   Includes bibliographical references and index.
    ISBN 978-0-7456-7035-5 (hardback : alk. paper) – ISBN 978-0-7456-
7036-2 (paperback. : alk. paper) 1. Sex addiction. 2. Sex addiction–
History. I. Attwood, Nina. II. Gooder, Claire. III. Title.
   RC560.S43R42 2015
   616.85′833–dc23
                         2014045194

Typeset in 10.5 on 12 pt Sabon
by Toppan Best-set Premedia Limited
Printed and bound in the UK by CPI Group (UK) Ltd, Croydon, CRO 4YY

For further information on Polity, visit our website: politybooks.com

Contents

Figures

Mental health professionals often take the symptoms of structured disorders at face value. They create treatment centers and techniques that cater to particular disorders. Psychiatric researchers devote their careers to studying particular disorders and journals arise to publish their results. Support groups emerge to reinforce the reality of the symptoms. Disorders become aspects of social movements that invest in, create, and reinforce the reality of the conditions. Sociologists, however, need to study how these disorders come to be socially defined as real, rather than accept the taken-for-granted notion that diagnostic measures reflect natural entities.

Allan V. Horwitz, 2002

Chapter 1
Introduction

In America, if your addiction isn't always new and improved, you're a failure.

Chuck Palahniuk, 2002[1]

Daddy's Secret Cedar Chest (2013) is for the 'children of sex addicts'. An unnamed boy discovers a huge box in Daddy's bedroom (the cedar chest of the book's title) full of magazines and DVDs with 'pictures of women with no clothes on!' The dad (we are not told why he has his own bedroom unless Mummy's bedroom is called Daddy's bedroom too) also spends too much time with his computer in his home office. 'Everything Daddy did was a secret.' The boy tells his mother, and his parents argue about his father's 'habit'. The boy becomes unsettled – 'I was feeling scared.' He has bad dreams: 'A big hairy lady monster was crawling out of the humongous cedar chest. She stood up on her big hairy legs and opened up her big empty black hole of a mouth.' In the dream this rather clumsy metaphor swallows his father. The boy's concerned mother takes him to a therapist. Daddy moves out to seek help for his 'habit' and then returns home to an improved family environment. The big hairy lady monster and the chest have gone.[2]

Why have we come to a stage in our history and culture where it is even conceivable that 'children ages 6 to 12' might have to be told 'that they are not alone in their suffering, that help is available to them, and...that they did not cause their parent's sex addiction'?[3]

The aim of the book that follows is to trace the history of a new sexual concept, a modern sexual invention called sex addiction, and its sufferer the sex addict. Though we will discuss definitional complexities in due course, the sex addict has usefully been described as 'a person who is obsessed with some type of sexual behavior, and whose behavior is compulsive and is continued despite significant adverse consequences'.[4] Aviel Goodman characterized it to the readers of the *Journal of Sex & Marital Therapy* as 'simply the addictive process being expressed through sex, the compulsive dependence on some form of sexual behavior as a means of regulating one's feelings and sense of self'.[5]

The idea's beginnings are somewhat imprecise. One possible origin at a practical level was in the self-help or recovery culture of the 1970s (we will discuss the link between sex and alcohol addiction later). Sex and Love Addicts Anonymous grew out of a local Alcoholics Anonymous support group in Boston in 1976 and other national sexual-addiction recovery fellowships were utilizing the Twelve-Step programme by the late 1970s and early 1980s. Sex Addicts Anonymous (1977) had its headquarters in Minneapolis; Sexaholics Anonymous (1978) was centred in Simi Valley, California; while the New York and Los Angeles Sexual Compulsives Anonymous was operational by 1982 as were gay and bisexual sexually compulsive support groups in New York.[6]

We know that a linkage between sex and addiction was informally entertained in popular culture in the late 1950s and 1960s. Pulp fiction during that period included Don Elliott's *Love Addict* (1959) and Curt Aldrich's *Love Addict* (1966) (see Figure 1). The latter was about a promiscuous man so the term 'addict' referred to lust rather than affection.[7] But it was William Donner's *The Sex Addicts* (1964) that can actually claim first usage of the precise words 'sex addict' in the correct context (see Figure 2). It was about a couple of womanizers on a cruise ship: 'It's the way he is...Compulsive. He can't stay with a woman more than a single night, he says. At least, not if others are available...He's slept with almost nine hundred women.'[8] One friend observed

Figure 1 Curt Aldrich, *Love Addict* (1966). Author's collection.

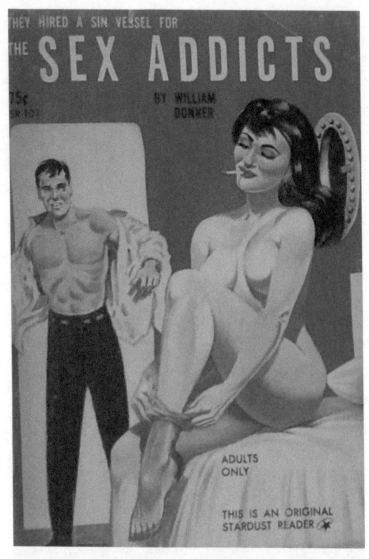

Figure 2 William Donner, *The Sex Addicts* (1964). Author's collection.

of the other, 'You're compulsive. You've got a monkey on your back', and suggested analysis. Later the man, who was close to his nine hundred, admitted 'Monkey on my back is right. Only I'm a sex addict, not a drug fiend.'[9]

Pulp fiction aside, we also know that homosexual psychotherapy patients were referring to 'sex heads' – in the sense of addicts – in the 1960s: 'I'm not only a pot head...I'm a sex head...it's completely eaten into everything.' In short, the term may have arisen independently at a more grassroots level.[10] When we later discuss the intellectual origins and viability of the concept, it is worth recalling this evidence for its humble origins.

Conceptually, as we will see, Lawrence Hatterer and Stanton Peele in the US and Jim Orford in Britain played roles in the malady's history. The New York sex therapist Avodah Offit mentioned 'sex addicts' in 1981 (immediately after a discussion of nymphomania and hypersexuality), citing a link between sex and the release of endorphins: 'Thus sex, in addition to whatever else it does, may actually reduce pain and promote euphoria in much the same fashion as small doses of the morphinelike drugs. The sex addict, then, may literally be a junkie, in one sense.'[11] However, the actual term 'sex addiction' is most clearly associated with the work of the US psychologist Patrick Carnes and his book *The Sexual Addiction* (1983), republished as *Out of the Shadows: Understanding Sexual Addiction* (1983). Carnes's centrality, for better or for worse, will become clear in the pages that follow.

The idea of sexual addiction enjoyed varied reception in these early years, and there was already an indication that endorsements might vary. It appeared in the 'Current Trends' section of the journal *Medical Aspects of Human Sexuality* in 1985.[12] A comment in the *British Journal of Sexual Medicine* in 1986 by a Chicago psychiatrist indicated both that the concept had arrived and a certain amount of scepticism about its usefulness:

> the theory of sexual addiction as an illness is so wide a net that it has the danger of being used on the one hand as an excuse to cover or continue a whole range of inappropriate or law-breaking sexual behaviours, and on the other it is a catch-all that has scooped up normal sexual behaviours as well.[13]

It was included momentarily in the American Psychiatric Association's *Diagnostic and Statistical Manual* DSM-III-R in 1987, but was absent from all subsequent editions, a struggle that we will return to later in this book.[14] Psychologists discussed in the same year whether the complaint was best termed sexual addiction, hypersexuality, compulsive sexual behaviour or (their preference) sexual impulsivity.[15] It was mentioned in a 1988 text on disorders of sexual desire, but without elaboration and minus its own chapter, in a book that devoted more attention to *lack* of sexual desire than to its excesses.[16] It came to the attention too of the famous John Money, emeritus professor of medical psychology and professor of pediatrics at the Johns Hopkins University and Hospital, though not with the notice that addictionologists might have sought:

> Sexual addiction...is a newly coined term for a disorder as fictitious as thirst addiction, hunger addiction, or reading addiction...Sexual addictionology does not address the specificity of addiction. Instead it decrees that the only non-addictive form of sexual expression is lifelong heterosexual fidelity and commitment in monogamous marriage. Everything else is the gateway of sin through which exits the broad road to sexual depravity, degeneracy and addiction. Within addictionology, the wheel of degeneracy has made a full turn![17]

Certainly the notion of perceived, out-of-control sexual behaviour moved from a situation in 1972 where hypersexuality was proclaimed 'a rare phenomenon' to the moment in the late 1980s when a relatively early publication in the addictionology genre, Charlotte Davis Kasl's *Women, Sex, and Addiction* (1989), began with reference to the 'epidemic proportion of addictive behavior in this country'.[18] The bestselling therapist Anne Wilson Schaef echoed Kasl dramatically: 'Sexual addiction is a progressive disease and...results in destruction and early death for addicts and often those with whom they are involved. Sexual addiction is of epidemic proportions in this society and is integrated into the addictiveness of the society as a whole.'[19] However, this may merely have indicated a split between professional psychiatry and the enthusiasm of popular medicine. The New Jersey psychiatrists who edited the state-of-the-art statement on desire disorders in 1988 said of sexual addiction that they had not 'encountered clinically more than a handful of such cases in the past decade'.[20] Yet they also noted the 'popular appeal' of the concept and hinted at a potential clientele:

> There are, however, numerous individuals who are on the high end of the desire continuum – who are sexually enthusiastic with little provocation, who never seem to become satiated, and who engage in high frequencies of both self- and partner stimulation. These individuals tend to be admired or envied rather than diagnosed![21]

Sexual addiction played a part in the issues-based, sexuality studies reader *Taking Sides* (1989) but as part of a debate – a 'controversial issue' rather than an established problem – in the clashing-views format, with Carnes's uncritical acceptance of the disorder pitted against a highly critical counterargument, 'The Myth of Sexual Addiction', by two sociologists, Martin Levine and Richard Troiden.[22] Janice Irvine (another sociologist) summarized this early history in 1995: 'Claimsmakers for the sex addiction diagnosis have...achieved a reasonable level of success thus far.'[23] Its consolidation thereafter would prove more impressive.

The historiographical starting point for what follows in this book is indeed Irvine's 1995 argument that sex addiction was a social construction, a product of late twentieth-century cultural anxieties.[24] She was not the first critic to put this case. Levine and Troiden had similarly argued that 'The concepts of sexual addiction and compulsion constitute an attempt to repathologize forms of erotic behavior that became acceptable in the 1960s and 1970s.'[25] The principal facilitators in this making, these early critics argued, were an addiction discourse (gambling, alcohol) that leant itself almost seamlessly to sexual matters; a strange and momentary combination of conservative Christian and radical feminist social purity; and the initial impact of AIDS in the 1980s that so dramatically intensified such sexual apprehensions. The rapid spread of the concept was aided by its imprecision: 'Claims about what constitutes sex addiction are so vague...that they can potentially include large numbers of the population.'[26]

Sex addiction's success as a concept lay with its medicalization, both as part of a self-help movement in terms of self-diagnosis, and as a rapidly growing industry of therapists on hand to deal with the new disease. And the media also played a vital role: TV, the tabloids, and the case histories of claimed celebrity victims all helped to popularize this newly invented term. As Irvine wrote, 'The power of sex addiction lay not in the number of sufferers but in the expansion of this particular narrative of sexual disease.'[27]

Irvine and her fellow sociologists were writing and researching in the 1980s and early 1990s. By the time her article appeared, the sexual addiction specialists had their own journal, *Sexual Addiction & Compulsivity: The Journal of Treatment and Prevention* (founded in 1994), and Carnes and his team were treating health professionals, primarily doctors, accused of sexual misconduct and referred by regulatory boards and health programmes (half the group were adjudged to be sex addicts).[28] Carnes's Golden Valley Health Center in the Twin Cities (Minneapolis–Saint Paul) in Minnesota had treated over 1,500 alleged addicts from 1985 to 1990, around 10 per cent of whom were ministers of the church.[29] As a claimed disorder, sexual addiction achieved endorsement with its own section (by Goodman) in the third edition of *Substance Abuse: A Comprehensive Textbook* (1997) and mention in the seventh edition of the influential psychiatric text, *Kaplan & Sadock's Comprehensive Textbook of Psychiatry* (2000), used by generations of medical students and practitioners. 'In the author's view sex addiction is a useful concept heuristically because it can alert the clinician to seek an underlying cause for the manifest behavior.'[30] The next edition of *Kaplan & Sadock* in 2005 had a chapter on sex addiction by none other than Patrick Carnes.[31]

Moreover, Irvine's 'sexualized society' was on the eve of what Linda Williams has described as 'on/scenity', capturing pornography's everyday visibility and presence – in huge volume – in the early twenty-first century, where sex became central to everyday discourse and representation, termed variously pornographication or pornification, 'striptease culture', a hypersexual society, mainstreaming sex or the 'sexualization of culture'.[32] Feona Attwood has nicely captured this cultural turn as 'the proliferation of sexual texts' and we will see that sexual addiction was very much one of those texts.[33]

Irvine's media was also a media without the power of the Internet and the ubiquity of Internet sex.[34] In 1997, as a joke on an Internet bulletin board, a New York psychiatrist invented IAD or 'Internet Addiction Disorder' and found that it was immediately taken seriously as a syndrome.[35] He was tapping into a zeitgeist. Kimberly Young, a psychologist from the University of Pittsburgh, had already raised the possibility in 1996, and announced 'Internet Addiction: The Emergence of a New Clinical Disorder' in the pages of the new journal *CyberPsychology & Behavior* in 1998, which would go on to be cited in 342 different publications.[36] When the contributors to the *Handbook of Clinical Sexuality for Mental Health Professionals* (2003) wrote their section on sexual compulsivity, they focused on 'online sexual compulsivity'.[37] Both Jennifer Schneider and Robert Weiss featured cybersex in their chapters in the 2004 *Handbook of Addictive Disorders*.[38] Carnes's entry on sexual addiction for *Kaplan & Sadock's Comprehensive Textbook of Psychiatry* (2005) referred to cybersex as the 'Crack Cocaine of Sex Addiction'.[39] The entry on sex addiction in the sexuality studies textbook *Our Sexuality* (2008) was paired with a think-piece 'Cybersex Addiction and Compulsivity: Harmless Sexual Outlet or Problematic Sexual Behaviour?'[40]

A critic of the diagnostic value of sexual addiction, the Denver family therapist Tracy Todd, wrote that 'More and more people are showing up at my door with it branded on their foreheads. "I learned it from a talk show", one man told me...Clients arrive with a wealth of information obtained from the Internet.' He was clearly impressed, though concerned, at the speed with which the label was 'gaining popular attention and acceptance'.[41] And this was only 2004.

The technological sexual temptations faced by the sex addict in 1990 were the VCR and phone sex. By the 2010s the addictionology timeline of sexual access had expanded to include chat rooms, porn sites, Craigslist, Facebook, Twitter, Sexting, GRINDR and many other sites and applications. Smartphones had replaced laptops.[42] The afflicted have their own aids to counter temptation: the iRecovery app for iPhone or iPad, a kind of digital workbook with links to networks of support and charts to monitor progress, and the rather alluringly illustrated Android app on Google Play called 'Overcoming Sex Addiction' (see Figure 3).[43]

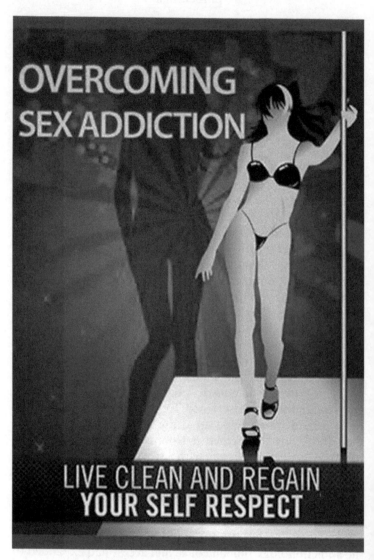

Figure 3 'Overcoming Sex Addiction': Android app on Google Play. Reproduced by permission of KoolAppz.

If sex addiction was a response to cultural anxiety, then, a historical construction, what of its history since Irvine's 1995 intervention? What happened to its early-hinted social opportunism and diagnostic amorphism? Did the combination of therapeutic self-interest and popular cultural endorsement persevere? We know that by 2010 sex addiction had another variant, 'hypersexual disorder', but what of the histories in between and thereafter?

Sexual addiction was part of a wider addiction discourse. 'In common parlance we now extend addiction to relate to almost any substance, activity or interaction', Hatterer wrote in 1982: 'People now refer to themselves as being addicted to food, smoking, gambling, buying, forms of work, play and sex.'[44] As early as the end of the 1980s, Stanton Peele, a specialist in the area of alcohol and drug abuse, was warning against what he termed the addiction treatment industry. Although his work in the 1970s had contributed to the expansion of the concept of addiction, he was critical of the misappropriation of his ideas in the decade that followed. He was concerned about the move from alcoholism counselling to therapy for sexual addiction and the sheer expansion of the variety of such newly defined diseases – his book was called *Diseasing of America* (1989). It seemed as if 'each American must have at least one such disease and, in addition, must know of many other people who altogether have a score of other diseases. It is hard to escape the conclusion that ownership of an emotional-behavioral-appetitive disease is the norm in America.'[45] Sex addiction's link to other dependencies was clear from the start, as outlined in an interview with a rare creature, a lesbian sex addict:

> I didn't realize that I was a sex addict until I stopped drinking and doing drugs. I was in Alcoholics Anonymous (AA) at the time. I realized that I had to stop having sex or I would start drinking again. I was using sex with men to avoid dealing with my sexual feelings about women. I decided to go to Sexual Compulsives Anonymous (SCA).

The poor woman was obviously addicted to addiction:

> Yes, I've spent my whole life juggling my addictions to stay alive. I went to Overeaters Anonymous (OA) first for bulimia

> ...Then I was sent to AA by OA. For years I substituted one
> addiction for another. I've been addicted to alcohol, drugs,
> sex, food, caffeine, cigarettes, shopping, and gambling.[46]

By the start of the new millennium, Eva Moskovitz was
noting America's obsession with the psychological: 'Today
Americans turn to psychological cures as reflexively as they
once turned to God.'[47] Addiction had become identity. She
listed the choice of support groups meeting during the course
of a week at one Colorado church in 1990: Cocaine Anonymous, Survivors of Incest, Alcoholics Anonymous, Debtors
Anonymous, Codependents of Sex Addicts Anonymous,
Adult Children of Alcoholics, Sex and Love Addicts Anonymous, Adult Overeaters Anonymous, Codependents Anonymous, Self-Abusers Anonymous.[48] The numbers she gave
were impressive. Forty per cent of adult Americans were
attending recovery meetings, around 75 million people. There
were more than 3 million such groups in the USA, including
6,000 for sex addicts, and 260 different Twelve-Step programmes.[49] These numbers are dwarfed by the estimates of
those who actually suffered from such disorders, which
Moskovitz took from the websites of the organizations
involved in trying to treat them: 20 million alcoholics, 20
million gamblers, 30 million overeaters, 25 million sex
addicts, 15 million compulsive shoppers, and the 80 million
codependents of all of the preceding. If those estimates were
accurate (a huge if), these addicts would have comprised
nearly 70 per cent of the entire 2001 US population![50] From
a transatlantic perspective Frank Furedi called it therapy
culture, where addiction became a fetish, with all the powerlessness, vulnerability and passivity associated with that
state.[51]

The other crucial setting for the early history of sex addiction was the rise of madness in America, and the roles both
of the American Psychiatric Association's *Diagnostic and Statistical Manual of Mental Disorders* (DSM) and the pharmaceutical companies in this turn to mental disorder. The DSM,
the 'Psychiatric Bible' that has been criticized for creating
mental disorder where it does not exist, can, as one commentator has expressed it, 'in effect usher diseases in and
out of existence with the stroke of a pen'.[52] Homosexuality

famously was excised from DSM-II in 1974.[53] Disinhibited Social Engagement Disorder (a child's over-familiarity with unfamiliar adults) and Restless Legs Syndrome (an urge to move the legs) are but two interesting examples of newer inventions.[54] (One enterprising neurological unit in Italy has discovered a case of pathological gambling, hypersexuality, impotence and restless legs syndrome, all in the one patient.[55]) It is noticeable that the move has been to include rather than exclude (sex addiction's experience notwithstanding): the DSMs have increased their tally of mental illnesses from 180 in 1968 to over 350 in 1994, and DSM-5 (2013) has maintained that upper level.[56]

Hence the histories of other psychiatric complaints are crucial when we consider sex addiction, especially given the relationship between the DSM and the pharmaceutical companies. 'Once upon a time, drug companies promoted drugs to treat their diseases', a former editor in chief of the *New England Journal of Medicine* has observed: 'Now it is often the opposite. They promote diseases to fit their drugs.'[57] There is an impressive list of ailments whose diagnoses and treatment have increased exponentially in recent decades in what has been termed the medicalization of society (or, less elegantly, 'disease mongering'): Bipolar Disorder, Attention Deficit Hyperactivity Disorder (ADHD), Autism, Posttraumatic Stress Disorder (PTSD) (added to DSM in 1980 as a diagnosis for the complaints of war veterans but then extended to describe victims of sexual abuse and domestic violence), Social Phobia and Major Depressive Disorder (MDD).[58]

Sociologists and cultural historians of medicine and psychiatry have outlined the ingredients for the expansion of a syndrome – whereby, say, what was considered mere shyness could, in less than a decade, become the widespread mental disorder 'Social Anxiety Disorder'.[59] First, the illness was named: for example, DSM-III's 300.23 Social Phobia, later DSM-5's 300.23 Social Anxiety Disorder (Social Phobia).[60] Then it needed a drug (or the drug needed it), in this case the SSRIs (selective serotonin reuptake inhibitors) and the pharmaceutical companies to market both the ailment and its supposed cure. In the US the naming in the symptom-based DSM provided the medical legitimacy for insurance claims, and coverage, where appropriate, through Medicaid and

Medicare; in short, the funding for treatment. Herb Kutchins and Stuart Kirk have dubbed DSM endorsement 'the psycho-therapist's password for insurance coverage'.[61] Then there was the role of patient advocacy (consumers who already thought they knew what their ailment was) and self-help groups, therapists of various sorts, including the primary care physicians with prescribing powers (far more numerous than psychiatrists), other agents with access to possible sufferers (teachers have played a role in brokering ADHD), open-ended tests to locate the complaint, celebrity confessions, sufferers' memoirs, self-help guides, research institutes and projects, new specialist journals, and constant promotion by a less-than-critical media.[62] (It will all become very familiar.) Christopher Lane's careful psychiatric history *Shyness: How Normal Behavior Became a Sickness* (2007) analysed this process.[63] Similarly Allan Horwitz and Jerome Wakefield's *Loss of Sadness* (2007) has demonstrated the transformation of sadness (an everyday social response) into an epidemic of depressive disorder.[64] The facilitators and processes – the 'diagnostic inflation' – are almost identical.[65] And this was in an environment accepting of the ubiquity of untreated mental maladies, where such disorders were taken as a cultural com-monplace, what Horwitz has called 'a shared culture of medi-calized mental disorders'.[66] If health policy researchers were to claim in 2005 that in the course of their lives nearly half of all Americans would meet the criteria for a DSM-IV dis-order, it is scarcely surprising that sex might become part of this national inclusion.[67]

In her history of Alcoholics Anonymous and what she has termed the 'recovery movement' Trysh Travis outlined the various layers, levels or components of this culture: the addicts themselves or those in recovery, their organizations (Alcoholics Anonymous and similar groups), a 'vast network' of clinics, treatment centres, what she described as 'profes-sional therapeutic entities', and finally a 'subculture' of memoirs, novels, handbooks, and TV and Internet discussion dealing with addiction and recovery.[68] Unsurprisingly, for sex addiction is part of Travis's recovery movement (though not integral to her account), our book will be traversing similar territory.

Where we differ, however, is with Travis's refusal to take a position, her studied neutrality on recovery (recall that she was dealing with alcohol rather than sex addiction).[69] Let us be clear about our approach. We are cultural historians, not clinicians, but we have read the clinically related literature – as contemporary history – and remain unpersuaded of the existence of this supposed malady. Why we are so sceptical will become clear by the end of the book. Though it is essentially mythical, creating a problem that need not exist, sex addiction has to be taken seriously as a phenomenon. It is a socio-psychological discourse that has taken hold on the public imagination – and proven an influential concept in academic circles too. What follows is a critical examination of the power of the idea and its cultural and (short) historical context.

Chapter 2
Beginnings

Although sex addiction has undoubtedly been around for centuries, it is only over the past few years that we have started to fully understand it.

Paula Hall, 2013[1]

The documentation of excessive sexual desire and conduct by sexologists of the nineteenth and early twentieth centuries has been the usual starting point for proponents of the sex addiction concept – when they have found it necessary to sketch out its history, or are not assuming that it has always existed (as with the epigraph to this chapter). 'There is a long history of characterizing behaviorally enacted excesses of sexual behaviors as "hypersexual"', Martin Kafka has written, citing the famous Richard von Krafft-Ebing to support the case that his new category was 'consistent' with an extensive clinical heritage.[2] Kafka's proposal in 2010 for the inclusion of 'hypersexual disorder' in the 'Sexual Disorders' section of DSM-5 had a brief paragraph, 'Historical Overview of "Excessive" Sexual Behaviors', that contained references to works by Benjamin Rush (1812), Krafft-Ebing (1892), Havelock Ellis (1905) and Magnus Hirschfeld (1948). They, he claimed, were the 'precursors' to the 1960s and 1970s sex researchers – Clifford Allen (1962), Albert Ellis and Edward Sagarin (1965) and Robert Stoller (1975) – who dealt with the 'protracted promiscuity' that Kafka saw as a type of hypersexuality: Don Juanism or satyriasis in males and nymphomania in women.[3] In Kafka's article – and he was not alone there – these were scholarly references, without elaboration or discussion, to provide authority and depth to a justification for a new psychiatric category. (Havelock Ellis, for instance, actually had nothing to say on the subject.[4]) But how close were these sexual phenomena, Kafka's 'excessive sexual behaviors', to sex addiction or hypersexuality? Rather than merely using these earlier sexologists and psychiatric clinicians as scholarly paraphernalia, it is worth spending some time to consider what it was that they were actually saying.

It is true that 'irresistible hypersensuality' and 'hypersexuality' are among Krafft-Ebing's names for the condition of excessive sexual desire. But his essential category was 'hyperaesthesia' or 'pathologically exaggerated sexual instinct', what he called the 'abnormal excitability of the imagination'.[5] And he had many other terms to describe this sexual state ('abnormally increased sexual desire', 'psycho-sexual extravagances', 'excessive libido', 'pathologically exaggerated sex life', 'priapism', 'satyriasis') and for those who suffered from it ('Don Juans', 'nymphomaniacs').[6] Moreover, a history of excessive sexual desires and behaviour is not the same as a history of sex addiction. This sort of conflation risks misrepresenting evidence to serve a particular narrative. The meanings of sexual categories that we take for granted today – heterosexuality, homosexuality and lesbianism – have dissolved when considered historically. Acts and desires are not transhistorical.[7] Societal notions of normative and transgressive sexual behaviour have changed over time, and appreciating the complexities of specific historical, social and cultural contexts allows for a more nuanced understanding of the kinds of sexual classifications that are the subject of this book. Kafka's twenty-first-century 'increase in intensity and frequency of normophilic sexual behaviours that are associated with significant adverse consequences' was very different to nineteenth- and early-twentieth-century nosology.[8]

Krafft-Ebing's cases of sexual hyperaesthesia were small in number, varied in scope and differed markedly between men and women. The manifestations of irresistible hypersensuality in men were acts of sexual violence and crime, and it was to those more serious cases that he paid attention. He acknowledged milder forms of hypersexuality but said that such sufferers were 'not afflicted with a pathological sexual condition'.[9] Krafft-Ebing's three male cases of hyperaesthesia involved a man who tried to force both his ward and his own child to have sex with him at gunpoint, a teacher at a girls' school who masturbated while teaching in class, and another whose high sex drive resulted in pederasty and bestiality (or, more specifically, 'employment of the tongue of a dog').[10] The three cases of satyriasis included a man whose sexual episodes ended in assault and rape attempts, another who attempted rape, committed incest and bestiality, and one who had had sex as many as fifteen times in a twenty-four-hour period and forced his wife to have sex with men and animals while he watched.[11]

The pioneering sexologist Iwan Bloch (not mentioned by Kafka) also discussed 'sexual hyperaesthesia' in his *Sexual Life of Our Time* (1908): 'The abnormal increase in the sexual impulse (sexual hyperaesthesia, satyriasis, nymphomania) begins at the point in which the normal sexual impulse is exceeded; and that point is subject to wide individual variations, according to the age, race, habits, and external influences.'[12] He considered hyperaesthesia more frequent in men (satyriasis) than women (nymphomania), but varied in its duration. His claim that the disorder was 'accompanied by a greater or less diminution of responsibility, or even by complete lack of responsibility' had a semblance to the claims of modern sex addiction, but his recommendations to wear cooler clothing and use colder bedding at night to quell lascivious thoughts were a reminder of a very different historical context.[13] Like Krafft-Ebing, Bloch focused his (brief) discussion on the severer forms where sexual desire and the attendant 'reaction on the part of the genital apparatus' attained such a degree

> that the man (or woman) may really be 'sexually insane', and, like the wild animals, rush at the first creature he meets of the opposite sex in order to gratify his lust; or he may be overpowered by some abnormal variety of the sexual impulse, so that he seizes in sexual embrace any other living or lifeless object, and in this state may perform acts of paederasty,

bestiality, violation of children, etc. In these most severe cases we can always demonstrate the existence of mental disorder, general paralysis, mania, or periodical insanity...as a cause.[14]

This does not quite conform to present-day notions of sex addiction – except perhaps in the wilder fantasies of the talk show. His reference to women who consulted gynaecologists as often as possible because of the 'sexual excitement' they got from the speculum suggested an emphasis on the physical sexual female response very different from today's female love and sex addicts, whose compulsions are usually seen more in terms of relationships than raw sex.[15] The discussion of satyriasis and nymphomania was limited. Bloch's focus was rather on its opposite: sexual anaesthesia or 'sexual loss of appetite'.[16]

These claimed antecedents were highly gendered in their perceptions of sexual compulsion. Krafft-Ebing was a proponent of the oft-mentioned, nineteenth-century belief that 'woman has less sexual need than man' and, accordingly, that evidence of 'predominating sexual desire' in women aroused 'suspicion of its pathological significance'.[17] 'The normal, untainted wife guided by ethical reasons knows how to conquer herself' when faced with 'unrequited love' outside the marriage.[18] Those who could not restrain themselves and sought sex outside of marriage were 'pathological', demonstrating 'an utter want of understanding of the bearings and consequences of the scandalous behaviour, jeopardizing the honour and dignity of wife and family'.[19] Krafft-Ebing differentiated such cases from nymphomania because 'the illicit intercourse was of a strictly monogamic character'.[20] Yet he treated such disorders with the same psychological and behavioural seriousness as he did with the men and their sex crimes. We would see things rather differently today.

The difference gender played in evaluating the severity of the disorder was one of the more revealing aspects of the sexological literature. The male sex crimes already detailed were of course serious 'and of great importance for the criminal court', especially because, as Krafft-Ebing claimed, 'the individual so affected can scarcely be held mentally responsible'.[21] But these male cases were at the criminal end of the hypersexual spectrum. He did not medicalize (to the same

degree) or criminalize those men whose behaviour fell short
of sex crimes. The implication of female sexual infraction was
far greater than for men, well before any actual sex crimes
were committed.

> Chronic conditions of nymphomania are apt to weaken public
> morality and lead to offenses against decency. Woe unto the
> man who falls into the meshes of such an insatiable nympho-
> maniac, whose sexual appetite is never appeased. Heavy neu-
> rasthenia and impotence are the inevitable consequences.
> These unfortunate women disseminate the spirit of lewdness,
> demoralize their surroundings, become a danger to boys, and
> are liable to corrupt girls also, for there are homosexual nym-
> phomaniacs as well.[22]

It is true, then, that nineteenth-century sexology has docu-
mented and discussed the concept of excessive sexual desire
and behaviour – though to a very limited extent. Modern
addictionologists have had some justification for including it
in their brief historical résumés. But in the earlier period it
was largely characterized as sexual criminality in men and
moral corruption in women. Its rarity – as we will also see
in the case of twentieth-century nymphomania – was key.
There was no sign of the epidemic proportions favoured in
later, twentieth-century, sexual addictionology. David Ley has
similarly warned against picking and choosing from the
annals of sexology in an effort to validate the concept of sex
addiction. Krafft-Ebing's work did catalogue hyperaesthesia,
satyriasis and nymphomania, but he also said that masturbation led to social and moral degeneration.[23] Benjamin Rush,
the American physician and signatory to the Declaration of
Independence, invoked by Kafka and others as an early docu-
menter of excessive sex, did indeed write that such appetites
were 'both a disease of the body and mind'.[24] But he also
believed that too much sex and masturbation could create
impotence, blindness, vertigo, epilepsy, loss of memory and
death. For Rush the causes of the disease included rich food,
intemperance and idleness, and his recommended treatments
comprised marriage, a simple diet, temperance, constant
employment and cold baths.[25] In the case of unrequited love,
the remedy was 'bleeding and blistering'.[26]

Intriguingly, the early psychoanalyst Wilhelm Stekel was not among the authorities cited by Kafka, though his work *Bi-Sexual Love*, published first in 1922, contained a section on the Don Juan figure in male sexuality and a whole chapter on satyriasis and nymphomania.[27] His extended discussion of individual cases included those who might well have been claimed as precursors to sex addicts: an inventor who kept a second house to receive his women and who never passed a day without possessing 'some woman – any woman – in addition to his wife'; the clerk whose every waking thought was of women – 'I feel as if something within me has taken possession of my soul driving me on from one adventure to another'; and the beautiful married woman who was unable to resist temptation – 'She is easily the victim of any man who comes near her...a woman who does not know how to say "no".'[28] Yet Stekel's heterosexual hypersexuality was different to sex addiction:

> One would think that a man who devotes his whole life to women, who dreams day and night only of new conquests, who considers every woman worth while when opportunity favors him, a man for whom no woman is too old, or too ugly, if he desires her, that such a man would be far removed from any homosexual trend. Yet the contrary is the fact and the greater my opportunity to study the 'woman chaser' the stronger my conviction becomes that, back of the ceaseless hunt, stands the longing after the male.[29]

For Stekel, who believed in a natural bisexuality, hypersexuality indicated homosexual rather than heterosexual desire. The womanizer's contempt for women and his constant reaffirmation of his masculinity masked his hidden homosexual desires; his quest for 'new and untried gratifications' stopped short of the same-sex sexual acts that he secretly longed for but denied in his paraded disgust for any hint of homosexuality.[30] Thus, wrote Stekel, 'His search is endless because he is truly, though secretly, attracted by the male. His sexual goal is man.'[31]

Similarly for the 'Messalina type', Don Juan's female equivalent, perpetually in pursuit, and never satisfied because their hunger for men was really unacknowledged desire for their own sex: 'Nymphomania shows the same homosexual basis as satyriasis.'[32] Stekel's treatment of such cases, through psychoanalysis, was to get his patients to recognize their underlying homosexualities – not quite the goal of modern-day, sex addiction therapists.

Albert Ellis and Edward Sagarin's 1964 study of nymphomania, one of the more substantial and better-known works on the topic that Kafka did refer to, actually demonstrated the rarity of 'true' nymphomania.[33] The issue of gender remained central to definitions of compulsive sex: 'What is often termed nymphomania is *usually* promiscuity, relatively well controlled, probably highly selective, and of a nature that would be considered relatively normal if found in almost any male in our society. Aside from their having several lovers, the promiscuous woman and the nymphomaniac have little in common.'[34] Although the characteristics of the true nymphomaniac were lack of control, continuous need, compulsivity and self-contempt – terms similar to the languages of modern sex addiction – the condition was so rare that despite their many years in sex research and clinical practice they had never encountered a single case.[35] Their book *Nymphomania* was effectively about female promiscuity.

As Carol Groneman has argued in her history of nymphomania, there was no straightforward narrative but rather 'multiple ways, at particular moments in time, in which doctors and their patients understood certain expressions of sexual desire as disease or disorder'.[36] Groneman has charted this history through its roots in organic disease to when it became a psychological disorder, and into its more modern incarnations. Treatments varied according to the claimed causes: surgical (tumour removal, clitorodectomy), hormonal, psychoanalytical and psychological. Psychology brought an even longer list of possible causes: narcissism, masochism, thwarted maternal instincts, childhood repression, incestuous attraction, latent homosexuality and frigidity.[37] And throughout this history, as with sex addiction after it, the eternally unanswerable question remained: how much is too much sex? Groneman was alert to the historical range of sex once considered to be hypersexual for women – masturbation, oral, post-menopausal, pre- and extra-marital – that was less contentious by the 1970s. Changes in the sexual culture of the 1960s and 1970s meant that nymphomania could no longer be defined by the intensity of sex drive or the number of partners. The sex therapist Avodah Offit wrote of psychiatrists scrambling to 'comprehend the new, sexually aggressive woman', the 'hypersexual trend among women'.[38] Emphasis then shifted from the frequency of the sexual act to its meaning. The new 'criterion for excess', the new pathology, became sex without love or affection.[39]

The biggest claims to continuity between modern sex addiction and the historical existence of excessive sexual desire – though they are certainly not the ones that the proponents of sex addiction have had in mind – are the instability of definitions and the mythmaking that accompanied them. Where 'true' nymphomania and satyriasis were discussed, the emphasis was on their extreme rarity and their physical as well as psychological origins. Even when medical specialists published work on these states, they ended up discussing not the 'true' forms but the more common 'selective promiscuity' that, as the word 'selective' implied, suggested some premeditation and self-control.[40] Such was (and is) the public fascination with sexual excess that cheap paperbacks on nymphomania and satyriasis were published in the early 1960s with the aim of 'educating' about these 'harsh truths' – again despite their rarity.[41] Thus the reframing of promiscuity as extreme medical disorder and the role of sensationalized publishing to buttress it were where the greater similarity with today's sex addiction and its inclusivity rested.

If anything, sex addiction has continued on from nymphomania in functioning as a metaphor for the fears, fantasies and anxieties surrounding male and female sexuality.[42] Despite the relief that some individuals have claimed to derive from its currency, Janice Irvine has argued that 'sex addiction is a deeply problematic metaphoric system...Its languages site deviance in the individual physical body, reinscribe stereotypic ideas of gendered sexuality, and expose deep cultural anxieties about sex.'[43]

It is rather ironic that Kafka used the work of Alfred Kinsey's team in his background discussion of an 'operational definition' for hypersexuality, turning to Kinsey's figures for the total sexual outlets (that is, orgasms) of the 'underworld' (that is 'deviant') section of his male population sample. The total sexual outlet of around half this subgroup was at least

seven orgasms a week, exactly the threshold for Kafka's definition of hypersexual desire in adult males.[44] We say ironic
because Kinsey's mid-twentieth-century sex research marked
a significant departure in the discussion of sexual desire 'disorders'. His work challenged the notion that any sexual
behaviour should be judged normal or abnormal, arguing
that any such categorization was moral rather than scientific.
Setting aside modern evaluations of his professed objectivity,
Kinsey's perspective on excessive sexual desire and behaviour
is what is of interest here. The idea that someone could have
too much sex was nonsensical in Kinsey's view:

> Psychologic and psychiatric literature is loaded with terms
> which evaluate frequencies of sexual outlet. But such
> designations as infantile, frigid, sexually under-developed,
> under-active, excessively active, over-developed, over-sexed,
> hypersexual, or sexually over-active, and the attempts to rec-
> ognize such states as nymphomania and satyriasis as discrete
> entities, can, in any objective analysis, refer to nothing more
> than a position on a curve which is continuous. Normal and
> abnormal, one sometimes suspects, are terms which a particu-
> lar author employs with reference to his own position on that
> curve.[45]

'The most significant thing about this curve…is its continuity', Kinsey claimed. 'No individual has a sexual frequency
which differs in anything but a slight degree from the frequen-
cies of those placed next on the curve.'[46] For Kinsey, the terms
'normal' and 'abnormal' threatened scientific objectivity,
were morally framed and were always relative to the observer.
LeMon Clark cited this line of reasoning in his article on
satyriasis, 'The Insatiable Male', published in the popular
magazine *Sexology* in 1963. Referring to Kinsey's male subjects aged between fifteen and forty and averaging more than
twenty-one orgasms per week, Clark questioned whether
having sex at this frequency was any more 'abnormal' than
limiting such activity to once a month or less. None of these
men should be classed as having satyriasis 'if they obtained
a sense of relief following a climax, and for a time were able
to direct their energies towards something else'.[47] While
Clark, unlike Kinsey, believed the condition of satyriasis
existed, he followed Kinsey in arguing that there was a very

broad spectrum of normal. The article's byline read: 'Is there such a thing as male "nymphomania" – is one man's "normal frequency" another man's disease?'[48]

In what was really a prophetic insight of developments to come in the later twentieth and early twenty-first centuries, Kinsey argued that it was the attempt to medicalize and pathologize difference that was the problem. It was the reaction of individuals to perceived aberrations – not the aberrations themselves – that needed studying:

> The real clinical problem is the discovery and treatment of the personality defects, the mental difficulties, the compulsions, and the schizophrenic conflicts which lead particular individuals to crack up whenever they depart from averages or socially accepted custom, while millions of other persons embrace the very same behaviour, and may have as high rates of activity, without personal or social disturbance.[49]

He noted further that postulating the incidence of 'sexual irregularities' across the general population from the basis of clinical presentation was an inaccurate measure.[50] If the behaviour did not upset you, you did not go to a clinic. The problem, therefore, was not the behaviour itself, but how it was being interpreted. There were no 'deviants' without 'deviance'.[51]

This more sex-positive approach to excessive sexual desire was likewise followed by others in the field of sexology (though Kinsey was of course a zoologist, not a sexologist as such). The magazine *Sexology*, published in the US from 1933, fielded letters from concerned readers on all manner of sexual issues, including nymphomania and satyriasis. Specialists also wrote feature-length articles on these disorders from time to time, but with relative infrequency and no more fanfare than the rest of the cornucopia of sexual subjects they covered. When Mrs B. G. from Texas wrote to the journal in 1952 to complain that sex once a day was not enough to satisfy her, the reply was: 'How often are any of us fully and positively satisfied about, or with anything?' Mrs B. G. was 49 years old, had been married for 32 years, was faithful to her husband, but missed the days when they had sex 'several times a night'. The editors mentioned the term 'nymphomania', but avoided any further medicalization in their reply. 'Sex is natural', they said: 'There are all sorts of beliefs about what is normal or abnormal in sex, or moral and immoral.' They recommended that she masturbated, restrained her expectations of her husband, and tried to be as happy as she could in the situation.[52] When Mrs B. W. from Nevada complained in 1960 that her husband was 'highly over-sexed', they replied that 'individuals have varying sex needs and abilities and coordination is necessary for husbands and wives'. They implored her 'to realise that each of you must compromise in order to achieve as happy a sexual partnership as possible'.[53]

Discourses of sexual excess overlapped in an untidy manner; it was not a case of one worldview replacing another. A 1949 *Sexology* article, 'What Causes Nymphomania?', rehearsed Bloch half a century earlier: the possible physical causes (brain tumours, hormonal imbalances); the main symptoms ('excessive sensitiveness of the vulva'); and possible psychological causes ('in the patient's mind', congenital insanity). It discussed women who 'react passionately to the insertion of speculums', women who ask to have their clitorises removed, and the 'many instances' where 'sterility is the price paid for the satiation of the sexual cravings of the nymphomaniac'. But in the fashion of the magazine's more measured overall tone it claimed that many normal women had been suspected of being afflicted merely due to a 'healthy desire for sexual intercourse', 'the same as an ordinary healthy man'; 'just because amorous women are usually not supposed to broach the subject of their sexual desire so openly as men, they have no doubt often been harshly misjudged as nymphomaniacs'.[54] Twelve years later – in 1961 – another letter to the editor received a mixed reply when Mrs W. G. of New York asked for information about nymphomania. She was given a dictionary definition ('a woman who has almost insatiable sexual desires'), told that the cure depended on the cause ('if the cause is some local irritation or inflammation in the region of the clitoris or vagina, removal of this may give great relief'), informed that 'actually not too much is known about this condition' and then advised to see a doctor, preferably a psychiatrist![55]

Apart from the name 'hypererotism', which he preferred to 'satyriasis' and 'nymphomania', and his amusing description of the hypererotist as 'a set of genital organs with a person attached to it', Magnus Hirschfeld added almost nothing to the nosology of 'excessive sexuality' with his citing of the cavalry officer who wanted marital sexual intercourse eight times a day and the woman whose marriage lasted six weeks because her sexual demands on her husband limited him to an hour's sleep each night.[56] The impression given in a mere eight pages of his posthumously published 538-page book *Sexual Anomalies* (1948) was of a rare condition that was difficult to define.[57] Compared to the attention that he devoted there and elsewhere to homosexuality, transvestism and sadomasochism, his interest in excessive sexuality seemed slight. Clifford Allen (1962), another of Kafka's cited authorities, was equally cursory in his textbook summary of the 'psychosexual disorder'. 'Sexual hyperperversion' (his name) was discussed mainly in terms of the heightened desire of the tubercular and those suffering from brain disease, mania, schizophrenia and epilepsy.[58] He thought hyperperversion rare in men and rarer in women ('a wish-fulfilling fantasy').[59] It is difficult to see how his account could be of any real relevance to modern notions of sex addiction or hypersexuality.

The histories of nymphomania, satyriasis and excessive sexual desire were ambiguous, then. Definitions were never clear or stable, actual incidence was rare, and case studies were of exaggerated and limited examples. Stekel's patient histories, referred to earlier, were of just three people, including a man who practised a 'very curious form of infantile sexuality', lying in his own faeces and masturbating in an 'orgy of filth'.[60] Stephen Levine's reconsideration of nymphomania, on the eve of the impact of sex addiction, stressed its rarity and provided instances of one woman who for nearly thirty years had 'masturbated herself to orgasm between 30–100 times per day', another who 'begged her husband to claw at her vaginal walls', and a clerk, in her mid-twenties, who 'roamed the streets and had intercourse in cars or alleyways with strangers'.[61] Offit's 'Nymphomania Reconsidered' revealed that she had treated only one such case – there are 'so few true nymphomaniacs – perhaps there are none' – a beautiful woman who picked up a different man every night for fifteen years and who had approached the sex therapist not because she wanted to change her lifestyle but because

she 'didn't have orgasms with everyone!'[62] A 1980 case study
of satyriasis – again 'a rare complaint' – was of a man who
was referred for psychiatric evaluation after he was detained
rubbing up against women at a race course. He claimed to
have sex with his wife two or three times a day and would
also masturbate, using what the psychiatrist termed 'quite
elaborate aids' – a vacuum cleaner and an inflatable doll, as
well as a rope and chain. He had a recurring erotic dream in
which he was 'miniaturized to enable him to explore the
vaginas of his female acquaintances'.[63] This unusual, fantasti-
cal, shrinking man belongs more on the pages of the novelist
Nicholson Baker than in the annals of sex addiction.[64]

Krafft-Ebing and other pioneers of sexology were classify-
ing and recording, for the first time, the varieties of human
sexual behaviour. It was clear in the terminology used (psychopathia, perversion) that a myriad of acts and desires were
deemed abnormal or perverted. For example, Krafft-Ebing
noted one patient's impulse to perform oral sex on his wife
as 'perverse' and referred to the 'pathological love of married
women for other men'.[65] This is not to say that the sexological enterprise was a wholly negative exercise in stigmatiza-
tion. In the case of same-sex desires, the creation of the
nomenclature and category of homosexuality (if 'inverted'
and 'contrary to nature') meant an identity or label at that
early stage of development and sense of community for those
previously isolated and troubled by their desires.[66] That
homosexuals were also denoted perverts was the double-
edged sword. But the point is that the cultural context is
all-important in understanding how ideas like hypersexuality
were and are understood. The nineteenth-century man who
committed incest, rape and bestiality and the nineteenth-
century woman having her single adulterous affair are not
the equivalents of Robert Stoller's twentieth-century 'cryp-
toperversions' of Don Juanism and nymphomania and the
twenty-first-century sex addict.[67]

What this prehistory of excessive sexual desire indicates is
not so much the validation or existence of a real medical
condition but rather a range of terminology used to denote
historically contingent breaches of normative sexual, gender
and moral codes: what in 1973 Eugene Levitt (with reference to nymphomania) called a 'muddy semantic situation'

involving a 'stigmatic word'.[68] Levitt argued for discontinuing the term 'nymphomania' not only because it was 'full of value judgments and male chauvinistic prejudices' but also because of lack of actual research on the topic, 'an ominous absence that suggests a chronic problem in defining the phenomenon'.[69] He was at pains to distinguish it from drug and alcohol dependency: 'Such extreme implications seem totally inapplicable to any form of female sexual behavior.'[70]

The one thing that these experts agreed on was the rarity of the disorder. A study of sixty doctors in California in the 1960s, cited by Levitt, found that of the nearly 14,000 estimated patient sexual complaints only 0.15 per cent – in other words, 15 in 10,000 – involved nymphomania or satyriasis. (In contrast: lack of orgasm, frigidity and impotence formed 37 per cent of the calculated total cases.)[71] A few further articles continued to claim either the scarcity of the phenomenon or the lack of data concerning it – even as they attempted to explain those very behaviours and desires.[72] As late as 1973, then, excessive desire for intercourse (whatever that was) was far from the everyday problem of modern addictionology. Virginia Sadock's claim that sex addiction dated back to 'classical times' and was derived from satyriasis ('male sex addiction') and nymphomania ('female sex addiction') was highly misleading.[73]

Where does sex addiction come in? While indelibly associated with Patrick Carnes by the 1980s, it did have earlier origins, both cultural and conceptual. In his 1945 work *The Psychoanalytic Theory of Neurosis*, Otto Fenichel stated that 'the great majority of neurotics have gross and manifest sexual disturbances' of both the hypo and hyper varieties, and that 'severe cases of "sexual addictions"' did exist.[74] For the psychoanalyst Fenichel such sexual behaviour derived from original neuroses; thus the motivations for hypersexual behaviour were narcissistic (to use Fenichel's term) rather than sexual. He mentioned the words 'sexual addictions' only once, but had more to say about 'love addicts', no doubt because the focus on non-sexual attachments better aligned with the favoured Freudian theories of infantile experiences, fear of abandonment and so on. In Fenichel's reasoning, all addictions were 'unsuccessful attempts to master guilt, depression or anxiety by activity'.[75] Victor Eisenstein wrote in 1956 of sex becoming 'an addiction rather than the spontaneous culmination of the tendency to love'. But this was a fleeting reflection in a brief discussion of hypersexuality in marriage, which he saw (like Fenichel) as the 'manifestation' of many psychiatric disorders rather than 'a clinical entity' in itself.[76] Morey Segal's 1960s psychoanalytic observations on impulsive sexuality referred to 'an avidity for object addiction' amidst its Freudian theorizing about parental loss, ego integration, infantile regression and orality.[77] The Californian psychologist Stanley Willis was arguing in 1967 that sexual promiscuity could have addictive properties, 'a kind of addictive dependence in which all-too-brief nirvanic release sets in motion a vicious cycle which is likely to get more and more compelling and less and less satisfying'.[78] In terms of theory, the British clinical psychologist Jim Orford was one of the first (in 1978) to make a conceptual link between addiction – normally associated with alcohol and drugs – and sex. Though he actually used the terms 'hypersexuality' and 'excessive sexuality', he was extending consideration of dependence and 'excessive appetite behavior' beyond drugs to gambling (which would become his academic speciality) and 'sexual behavior which is compulsive or excessive' (which would not).[79] Ironically, he felt that the concept of hypersexuality would find little favour with the permissive spirit of the times, 'the general relaxation of sexual inhibitions'; a prediction that could not have been more misplaced.[80]

The early work of the psychologist Stanton Peele certainly included love and relationships (though not sex in particular) among the addictions. Peele's book *Love and Addiction* (1975) (written with Archie Brodsky) claimed that the interpersonal dependency that some people had for each other was 'not *like* an addiction, not something analogous to addiction; it *is* an addiction. It is every bit as much an addiction as drug dependency.'[81] In an article entitled 'Interpersonal Heroin', published a year prior to the book's publication, Peele and Brodsky had represented this idea with a photograph of a man's arm with lipstick marks in lieu of a drug addict's needle marks.[82] Peele's work advocated a broadened theory of addiction; he wanted to make addiction 'a viable concept once again'.[83] The difference between Peele and others working with an expanded definition of addiction was that he did not

believe in addiction (including to alcohol and drugs) as a
chemical reaction or physiological dependency. For Peele,
addiction was 'an *experience* – one which grows out of an
individual's routinized subjective response to something that
has special meaning for him – something, anything, that he
finds so safe and reassuring that he cannot be without it'.[84]
'Anything that people use to release their consciousness can
be misused.'[85] Peele might have eschewed the disease or
medical basis of addiction but his language often contradicted
this intent: 'Addiction can be considered a pathological habit';
'It is a malignant outgrowth, an extreme, unhealthy manifestation, of normal human inclinations.'[86] Somewhat confus-
ingly this 'outgrowth' was also the 'norm': 'Addiction is not
an abnormality in our society. It is not an aberration from
the norm; it is itself the norm.'[87] His view of addiction was
certainly inclusive and he was one of the first to connect love
(and by implication sex) with addiction. 'Interpersonal addiction – love addiction – is just about the most common, yet
least recognized, form of addiction.'[88] Although Peele would
later decry the appropriation of his expanded addiction
theory in what he called 'the diseasing of America', he clearly
laid some serious groundwork for what followed in the
history of the concept of sex addiction (and continues to be
cited as doing so).[89]

However, the actual expression 'sex addict' had appeared
for the first time in academic usage (recall the pulp fiction of
the 1960s) in 1974 in the work of Lawrence Hatterer, a psychiatrist at Cornell University Medical School, who published
a two-page discussion paper claiming that a culture of instant
gratification was contributing to addictive personalities.[90]
One of the examples he gave was the sex addict.

When Hatterer used the term 'sex addict' in 1974 he was
also invoking those other process or behavioural addictions
that would become all too culturally familiar as the century
ended:

Addicts are not just skid-row alcoholics or heroin users. The
mother who avoids family conflict by swallowing a tranqui-
lizer or can't socialize till she has a drink; the father who drops
his paycheck at the track or in a poker game; the insecure
teenager who gulps food as a defense against unpopularity;

the compulsive shopper; the working girl whose sex life is a series of empty encounters – all are showing addictive traits.[91]

In Hatterer's definition of addiction, actions performed for temporary escape became addictive 'when a person does them excessively, impulsively, and compulsively'.[92] The trigger for the 'sex addict' might have been 'an array of porno magazines'; 'Life for the addict is a powerful network of stimuli, reminding him of the compulsive urge to drink, gamble, take drugs, have sex.'[93] The language of Hatterer's short article anticipated the rhetoric of the 1980s and 1990s: 'Addiction, because it offers an illusive escape from seeking real remedies to life's problems, is a chronic, crippling disease each of us must fight against. It *can* be overcome.'[94]

Yet it was Hatterer's book *The Pleasure Addicts* (1980) that can lay claim to being the foundational text of sex addictionology. This curiously neglected work – which began life in 1969 as a television script called 'Hooked People: Food, Sex, and Drug Addicts', and which drew on many years of work with those Hatterer identified as addicts, including a 'three-year audiotaped study of the therapy of a sex addict' – elaborated on sex as part of what he termed 'the addictive process', encouraged by a society that promoted and revelled in varieties of excess.[95] In fact his therapy, including the linkage of certain forms of sexual behaviour to addiction, stretched back to the 1950s and 1960s with his treatment of 'homosexual illness' in *Changing Homosexuality in the Male*, published in 1970.[96] While there is no way of knowing from the published versions of his case notes exactly how early he was using the language of sexual addiction, we can be certain that it was employed by the late 1960s at the latest. *Changing Homosexuality* referred to 'addictive homosexuality', of men whose lives were 'sex, sex, and more sex', who were consumed by 'sexual preoccupation and practice...like an alcoholic', of 'addictive homosexual sex', 'addictive hypersexualized living' and an 'addictive sexual pattern'.[97]

Rick showed a determination to rid himself of the destructive aspects of his homosexual addiction. He agreed for the first time in his life to work at changing his pattern. Hours of repetitive interpretations finally showed him how he had, like a chronic alcoholic, become so addicted to sexual activity that he used it to solve every problem, as his sole means of dealing with anger, anxiety, depression, and failure.[98]

Most of these men, like Rick, were homosexual (Hatterer's area of specialization at that time), but there were heterosexuals too 'who are as addicted to sex as any homosexual'.[99]

In contrast to the invariably superficial case studies of 'sex addiction' in later addictionology, Hatterer's *Changing Homosexuality* and *Pleasure Addicts* provided detailed, explicit and extensive psychoanalytic summaries from recorded sessions at New York's Payne Whitney Psychiatric Clinic; the tapes formed part of the therapy as the patient was asked to listen to and comment on their contents 'away from the emotionally charged context of a psychiatric encounter'.[100] It is the power of what Hatterer described as these 'internal monologues of...addicts in states of addictive crisis' that makes his work such compelling reading.[101]

Hatterer also anticipated something that we will discuss later: the pornographic elements of sex addiction discourse. Of the four case histories (alcohol, drugs, food and sex) in *Pleasure Addicts*, Tom the homosexual/heterosexual sex addict's was easily the most explicit: 'that was what I needed...some guy's mouth wrapped around my dick'; 'She was getting wetter and wetter and moving all over my tongue and lips. She loved it! And her ass ...' [102] One publisher told the author of *Pleasure Addicts* that the case study of the sex addict was 'really just porno'.[103] Hatterer justified this explicitness in his analysis of the tape extracts and patient history:

> Tom's taped monologues constantly revealed his addictiveness. His hours of memories and free associations were saturated with sexuality; in fact almost every action, feeling, fantasy, and impulse was sexualized. He was compulsively driven to one form or another of sexual interaction with the world around him. Even his language had become highly eroticized. He had reached the point of coping with every pressure, conflict, failure, insecurity, anxiety, or depressive reaction, by turning to a sexual act or fantasy.[104]

The psychotherapist wanted his readers to know his patients before he embarked on his analysis of their addictions.

Hence his 'Portraits of Addicts' was the prelude to a candid discussion of identifying and treating addicts, admitting to the experimental nature of the therapeutic process and not denying setbacks – 'I, like others, often failed with the chronic and multiply addicted.'[105] He discussed the unreliability of the addicts' narratives, the complicity of family and loved ones, the pleasures that seemed to outweigh the pain ('Addiction is itself the excessive use of pleasure to remove pain') and the relative invisibility of the 'disease' ('he submits to it without admitting it exists').[106] He admitted that his work had mostly been with upper- and middle-class whites and acknowledged the plight of poorer, 'inner-city addicts' who were additionally faced with the task of mere survival.[107]

Hatterer is not beyond critique. We will return later to the role of homosexuality in his perceived addictive process. However, when we later encounter the banality of twenty-first-century addictionology it is worth remembering that Hatterer has demonstrated that it was not always so. It is curious that he has been ignored in the addictionologists' own history.

When the new Internet tool Google Ngram Viewer plots the usage of the terms 'sex addiction', 'hypersexuality', 'nymphomania' and 'satyriasis' in books in English from 1800 to 2008, it tells only part of the story (see Figure 4). We are now able to provide more detail. 'Satyriasis' and 'nymphomania' were strongly identified with the long nineteenth century but have proven remarkably resilient in modern culture, if Ngram is a rough guide. However, they, as we have seen, are not synonymous with 'sex addiction'. 'Hypersexuality' was essentially a twentieth-century word that enjoyed increased usage as the century progressed, reinforced, no doubt, by its adoption – post-sexual addiction – as an alternative for that diagnosis: the word remained the same but its meanings, we have seen, changed. What is not in doubt is the trajectory of 'sexual addiction'. It begins around 1980 and overtakes usage of all the other terms. This is the history that we are now concerned with.

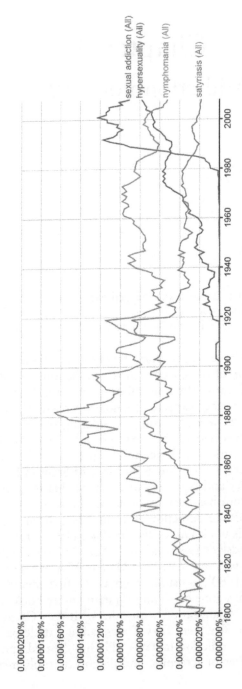

Figure 4 Sex addiction terms on Google Ngram. Google and the Google logo are registered trademarks of Google Inc., used with permission.

Chapter 3
Addictionology 101

Patrick Carnes is the acknowledged expert in a field that until recently didn't exist.

Promotional quote for Patrick Carnes, 1983[1]

Although we have argued that others can lay claim to being the originators of the concept of sex addiction, it is Patrick Carnes who is most often described as its leading proponent – 'guru', 'pioneer', 'expert', 'founder', 'crusader', 'leader'. These labels are not surprising considering the prominence that Carnes has had in the creation and promotion of the syndrome. Carnes himself acknowledged Jim Orford's role.[2] We have argued too for the importance of Stanton Peele and Archie Brodsky and especially of Lawrence Hatterer, but it is true that Carnes has been involved at almost every stage in the history of sex addiction. Carnes has proven the most influential. His book *Out of the Shadows* (1983), rather than Peele and Brodsky's *Love and Addiction* (1975) or Hatterer's *Changing Homosexuality in the Male* (1970) and *The Pleasure Addicts* (1980), is usually seen as the first sex addiction text, and he has gone on to publish many more books as sole author or in collaboration with others.[3] It was Carnes who featured when *The New York Times* ran an article on excessive sex as an addiction in 1984.[4] He has created and influenced a number of screening and diagnostic tools including the Sex Addiction Screening Test (SAST), the Sexual Dependency Inventory (SDI) and PATHOS, the brief assessment tool for clinicians. He established the Certified Sex Addiction Therapist (CSAT) programme, which is offered at the International Institute for Trauma and Addiction Professionals (IITAP), an institute that he also founded. He was editor-in-chief of *Sexual Addiction & Compulsivity: The Journal of Treatment and Prevention*, the journal of the Society for the Advancement of Sexual Health (SASH), formerly the National Council of Sexual Addiction and Compulsivity (NCSAC). He was the creator of the Gentle Path Treatment Programs for sexual addiction and founder of Gentle Path Press. His name occurs 165 times in P. J. Carnes and K. M. Adams's edited sex addiction text *Clinical Management of Sex Addiction* (2002).[5]

Many of Carnes's disciples have gone on to forge careers specializing in sexual addiction: authors and therapists whose names will reoccur in this book, including Robert Weiss, Stefanie Carnes (Patrick's daughter), Jennifer Schneider and Alexandra Katehakis. SASH now bestows a Carnes Award for those considered to have made a significant contribution to the field of sexual addiction. Previous winners include Schneider (1998), Weiss (2008) and Katehakis (2012).

Sex addictionology is the study and treatment of sex addiction or, as Patrick Carnes has called it, 'the science of addiction'.[6] This chapter unpacks sex addictionology, how sex addiction has been defined, built and reinforced through the industry of therapists and therapy-speak; in workbooks for addicts and partners, and textbooks for clinicians; through websites, and social networking services such as Twitter and Facebook. Our concern in this chapter is essentially an introductory presentation of sex addiction discourse. Although there are voices of dissent, including much of what follows in other chapters, we try to set those aside for the moment for ease of presentation. This chapter takes sexual addiction at face value. It is primarily concerned with those who have created, embraced and fashioned sex addiction – and its variants, more of which later – as a concept, a disease, a malady.

Sex addiction has been defined as when a person exhibits sexual behaviour or thoughts that they or someone else (partner, family, friends) finds problematic, and by their inability to stop this conduct which, in itself, indicates loss of control. In the opening to his foundation text *Out of the Shadows* Carnes said that the realization of addiction comes when 'the consequences are so great or the pain is so bad that the addict admits life is out of control because of his or her sexual behavior'.[7] SASH defines sex addiction as 'a persistent and escalating pattern or patterns of sexual behaviors acted out despite increasingly negative consequences to self or others'.[8] The diagnosis is often made by addicts themselves, or by their loved ones. The range of what constitutes such acts or desire is endless; each individual decides what *they* feel is problematic sex. Of course, they are guided in such decisions through the questions asked in the self-tests, the examples given in the workbook vignettes, the media coverage of celebrity sex addicts, the messages contained in therapy websites, and social or cultural ideas about appropriate sexual behaviour.

In 2014, for example, those who consult the IITAP website SexHelp.com seeking an answer to the question 'Am I a sex addict?' are asked: 'Are you concerned that you may have an addiction to sex and/or pornography? Do you feel you cannot stop once you start…? Do you have a secret life that you do not want others to find out about?'[9] These questions illustrate that the initial focus is on the impact on the person's life, not the specific behaviours that could be causing these problems. It goes on to say

> Sex addition takes many forms. In other words, there are many types of sex addicts and sexual addiction. If your sexual behavior is causing problems in your life – personal or professional, take the free and anonymous online test to determine if sex addiction is a problem. At the end of the test, it will show a graph and give you the 'typical' range and show where your answers score compared to the that [sic] group. If you find that your behavior is problematic, we strongly encourage you to seek help from a qualified, CSAT trained therapist. There are treatment centers that can provide help too. There is help and there is hope![10]

When specific behaviours are delineated, they include compulsive masturbation, pornography, prostitution, simultaneous or frequent affairs, exhibitionism, multiple anonymous partners, voyeurism, unsafe sexual activity, indecent phone calls, phone sex, cybersex, sexual aversion, child molesting, incest, rape and violence.[11] Sometimes these are written as lists, as with Carnes's three levels of sex addiction. Level One behaviours are culturally accepted but are 'devastating when done compulsively': masturbation, heterosexual relationships, pornography and strip shows, prostitution and homosexuality.[12] Level Two behaviours 'warrant stiff legal sanctions' and involve a victim; they include exhibitionism, voyeurism and indecent phone calls.[13] The final level, Level Three, represents those behaviours where 'some of our most significant boundaries are violated', for example child molesting and incest, and rape and violence.[14] The problematic behaviour is characteristically illustrated through case studies where addicts engage in behaviour that leads to their demise. The vignettes are discussed in more detail later.

However, the telltale signs of a problem come from Carnes's ten 'sex addiction criteria': compulsive behaviour; loss of control; efforts to stop; loss of time; preoccupation; inability to fulfil obligations; continuation despite consequences; escalation; social, occupational and recreational losses; and withdrawal.[15] The consequences of sex addiction include 'work problems; broken relationships; emotional/physical health, financial and legal problems...the ugly face of sex addiction'.[16] Carnes has always stressed that addiction has 'nothing to do with "amount" or "number of times" a person has sex or masturbates'.[17]

For diagnosing and treating sex addiction, Carnes used the addiction model developed in relation to substance addiction – alcohol and drugs – and the Twelve-Step therapy model developed for alcoholics by Alcoholics Anonymous (AA). Addiction, according to that model, involved behaviour that was repeated despite adverse consequences, loss of control over the intake of the substance or the engaged in conduct, and an increasing tolerance resulting in greater frequency, quantity or strength of the substance or behaviour. For Carnes, sex addiction was when repeated sexual conduct, with damaging results, led the addict's life to become unmanageable.[18] For Weiss, sex addiction was when people 'use sex and relationships in a repetitive, objectified, and ultimately self-destructive way'.[19]

The underlying basis for Carnes's theory was his early work with sex offenders. His unpublished 1976 paper, 'The Sex Offender: His Addiction, His Family, His Beliefs', claimed, he told readers later, that most sex offenders were suffering from an addiction and that the origins of this addiction lay in the family either as an inherited addiction or as the result of ongoing family dynamics.[20] The 'theoretical assumptions' in the paper formed the basis for programmes and workshops for sex addiction, using the logic that sex addicts 'were not "sex offenders", but suffered from the same pathology'.[21] His programmes incorporated the Twelve Steps of AA and 'general systems theory', which recognized behaviours as self-regulating, habitual, influenced by context and interrelated.[22]

Carnes was not the first one to think about behavioural problems as addictions. Gamblers Anonymous (founded in 1957) and Overeaters Anonymous (founded in 1960), and also modelled on AA, were already addressing behavioural issues in this manner. We have seen that in 1974 Hatterer was warning of 'addictive personalities'.[23] Like Carnes, Hatterer believed that such dispositions were the result of genetic inheritance and family patterns. He also promoted the idea of the co-addict, where one addict married another whose 'needs mesh with their own'.[24] And, like Carnes, Hatterer believed ultimately in overcoming such addictions through distraction, willpower, Twelve-Step programmes and group or family therapy.[25] But it was Carnes who would prove to deal with the perceived problem the most extensively and be considered within the industry as the concept's founder.

Adapting AA's Twelve Steps to his workbooks and residential programmes, Carnes established treatment specifically catering for the new malady. The original Twelve Steps of AA appeared in *Out of the Shadows* alongside Carnes's adaption of the steps for sexual addicts.[26] In fact the steps remained the same, except for minor word changes. Step 1, 'We admitted we were powerless over our sexual addiction – that our lives had become unmanageable', had the phrase 'our sexual addiction' replacing the word 'alcohol'. Step 12 changed 'carry this message to alcoholics' to 'carry this message to others'. The remaining ten steps were unchanged, including retaining the overtly religious references of the original: seven of the Twelve Steps mentioned God or spiritual matters. The Twelve Steps are to be carried out in order. Steps 1–3 give the message that the addict must admit their powerlessness over their addiction and yield to a higher power to address their addiction successfully. Steps 4–10 involve personal reflection, where the addict identifies the problems within themselves, their character, their behaviour, and recognizes how they may have affected others in order to take responsibility for these 'shortcomings', while also asking God to 'remove all these defects of character'. Steps 11–12 are about moving forward through a spiritual awakening to a new life guided by a new set of principles, and encouraging others to live under those moral guidelines.[27]

At the same time that Carnes was promoting the use of Twelve-Step treatment programmes for sexual addiction, addicts had formed groups for support as we have seen: Sex and Love Addicts Anonymous (SLAA), also called the Augustine Fellowship; Sex Addicts Anonymous (SAA); and Sexaholics Anonymous (SA). Each group operated with slightly different guidelines, particularly around defining 'sexual sobriety', but the timing of the creation of these groups indicated that they were part of a developing public discourse around issues of sexual behaviour borne out of the historical and cultural context of the late 1970s. Janice Irvine has observed that while the individuals themselves might have initially applied the addiction discourse to sexual behaviour, 'professionals soon took note. And their participation helped popularize and legitimize the concept.'[28] Carnes certainly took note that 'the simultaneous foundings' of SLAA, SAA and SA 'spoke to the need and readiness for these programs'.[29]

So the label 'sex addiction' and its conceptualization as a disease came into existence initially from the 'addicts' themselves – the ultimate in self-diagnosis. These individuals identified their sexual behaviour as problematic and, already being *au fait* with addiction discourse through AA groups and self-help texts, applied this logic and discourse to their sexual behaviour.[30] And self-diagnosis has continued to be a feature of sex addiction identification and treatment-seeking. As noted earlier, one of the main channels whereby people have entered therapy for sexual addiction is as the result of a self-test where they or someone close to them answers a series of questions to determine whether or not they have a problem.

The window that opens at SexHelp.com when one clicks to take the SAST has a Carnes quote at the top: 'Knowing you are a sex addict doesn't mean you are bad or perverted or hopeless. It means you may have a disease, an obsession from which many have healed.'[31] Before taking the test, the user is being given the framework from which to consider the questions and from which to answer: powerlessness, a disease, an obsession. There is a glimmer of hope for redemption and cure, as well as the inference that the abnormality affects many.

There are a number of self-tests available – in workbooks and online. For example, if you type 'sex addiction test' into Google you are given options for thousands of links to self-tests, with only minor differences between them.[32] Carnes created the SAST and published it in *Contrary to Love: Helping the Sexual Addict* (1989), and it has formed the basis for most of the variously adapted self-tests.[33] In *Contrary to Love* Carnes acknowledged that the test did not cater for women or for homosexual men, and he later 'updated' the 1989 test 'to reflect changes in sexual behavior since the 1980's [sic] and to be of assistance whatever your gender or sexual orientation might be'.[34] The original twenty-five questions were increased to fifty-two. Alongside the SAST, SexHelp.com has a range of other tests and surveys that visitors to the website can take to assess their own or their loved one's behaviour. The Sex Addiction Risk Assessment test (SARA), for example, is a fee-based survey that elicits a 'personalized 23-page report to help you determine your next course of action'.[35] It 'compares your answers with thousands of other sex addicts who have preceded you in treatment. Thus, you have the benefit of comparing your life with the lives of others who share the same problem.'[36] Then there is the Partner Sexuality Screening test (PSS), which involves gathering information from partners of sex addicts as part of Stefanie Carnes's research 'to identify and analyse the impacts sex addiction has on the partners of addicts'.[37] The website explains that by answering the PSS the user benefits by 'knowing you are advancing research in the field of sex addiction' as well as experiencing 'some insights about how your sexuality has been impacted by the addiction' and receiving 'a brief report, free of charge, that outlines areas of your sexuality that may have been impacted by the addiction'. Users are warned that answering the survey involves the risk of raising 'some emotions relating to your experience in this relationship' and they are advised to visit www.iitap.com for a list of certified sex addiction therapists.[38] This is demonstrative of the circular nature of the sex addiction therapy industry: those who already consider the diagnosis of sex addiction find the website, SexHelp.com, administered by Carnes's IITAP organization, then take a survey or test with leading questions, based on Carnes's own research, and through answering these, in some cases, help 'advance the field' of (construct a case for?) sex addiction!

The first three pages of the SAST self-test establish a background for the prospective 'addict'. The first page asks the user to select gender and sexual orientation. The second page moves on to perceptions of behaviour and motivation for taking the test, from 'I have no concerns about my sexual behavior but am curious how I would score' through to 'I know I am a sex addict' and 'I have sought therapy because of my sexual problems.' The third page seeks a reason for the 'addiction': 'Were you sexually abused as a child or adolescent?'; 'Did your parents have trouble with sexual behavior?'; 'Do you often find yourself preoccupied with sexual thoughts?' Once the user has answered these questions there is a final page with a further forty-two questions. The first eighteen focus on how problematic (but unnamed) sexual activities make the person feel. After the initial 'Do you feel that your sexual behavior is not normal?', the remaining questions determine whether that behaviour fits Carnes's ten sex addiction criteria discussed earlier. These are framed in ways such as 'Has your sexual behavior ever created problems for you and your family?', 'Have you made efforts to quit a type of sexual activity and failed?' or 'Is sex almost all you think about?' There are also questions about shame, such as 'Have you felt degraded by your sexual behaviors?' and 'When you have sex, do you feel depressed afterwards?' The last twenty-four questions ask about specific acts. Nine of the twenty-four mention Internet or online behaviour, such as 'Have you purchased services online for erotic purposes (sites for dating, pornography, fantasy and friend finder)?' or the broader 'Has the Internet created sexual problems for you?' Then those tested are asked about sexually explicit material, going to strip clubs or adult stores, bath houses and sex clubs, paying for sex, having casual or anonymous sex, and cheating on a partner. In amongst these are questions about being sexual with minors, being in a physically or emotionally abusive relationship, and engaging in illegal or risky sexual behaviour. Each question only allows for a 'yes' or 'no' answer, and some, such as 'Do you spend too much time online for sexual purposes?' or 'Have you spent considerable time and money on strip clubs, adult bookstores and movie houses?', illustrate the subjective nature of the test, with no guideline given for how much time would be considered 'too much' or how much money 'considerable'.

The SAST questions all fall into a category of ten types or patterns of behaviour that Carnes identified as the ways people 'act out' when they have sexual addiction: fantasy sex; voyeurism; exhibitionism; seductive role sex; trading sex; intrusive sex; paying for sex; anonymous sex; pain exchange sex; and exploitive sex.[39] This list was based on Carnes's analysis of his nearly 1,000-strong sex addict survey (published in *Don't Call it Love*).[40] All of these were seen negatively simply by being put on this list. But what is acceptable sex? From this list we can deduce that committed, monogamous, non-fantasy sex is probably acceptable. One of Carnes's distinctions is preoccupation. Sexual fantasy, for example, is common but becomes problematic when it causes the 'neglect of responsibilities and commitments and by inordinate amounts of time spent in preparation for sexual episodes'.[41] This is the crux of the perceived 'problem' that the logic of sexual addictionology identifies: unacceptable priorities. Instead of prioritizing family, work or social pursuits, the person prioritizes sex. The 'addict' is not fulfilling their role as a productive and helpful citizen. Addicts affected by sexual fantasy face losses of 'intimacy, time, energy and productivity'.[42] Another way of distinguishing healthy sex from addictive sex is that 'sexual addiction always involves exploitation, dissatisfaction, shame, fear, objectification, and a lack of mutual consent. Healthy sex almost always involves the opposite.'[43]

At the completion of the test, the user is presented with a summary of their results and a graph. The summary (for one of the authors of this book) began: 'We have compared your answers with people who have been diagnosed with sex addiction. Your answers HAVE MET a score on a basis of six criteria that indicate sex addiction is present. To help you understand, the graphic below plots your score in relation to the scores of others.'[44] In fact the line graph was somewhat difficult to follow (see Figure 5). Titled 'Number of SAST Core Scale Items Endorsed', it had a non-clinical and a clinical line plotted next to unlabeled x- and y-axes. The y-axis marked percentages from 0.0 per cent up to 20.0 per cent (though it is unclear what these were percentages of) and the x-axis was numbered from 0 to 20 (again it was uncertain what these numbers represented). An arrow pointed to the number 6 on the x-axis and stated 'Most addicts are above 6.'[45] The two graph lines were the inverse of each other, with the non-clinical peaking near the number 2 and steadily declining to 0.0 per cent by number 18. The clinical line

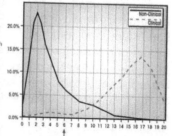

SEXUAL ADDICTION SCREENING TEST

We have compared your answers with people who have been diagnosed with sex addiction. Your answers **HAVE MET** a score on a basis of six criteria that indicate sex addiction is present. To help you understand, the graphic below plots your score in relation to the scores of others.

In addition there are certain subscales to further confirm that a problem exists. The following patterns emerged in your answers:

- A profile consistent with men who struggle with sexually compulsive behavior
- A profile consistent with women who struggle with sexually compulsive behavior
- A profile consistent with homosexual men who struggle with sexually compulsive behavior
- A profile consistent with sex addicts who struggle with sexually compulsive behavior on-line

The SAST measures key characteristics of addiction. The following dimensions of an addictive disorder appeared in your answers:

- Preoccupation: obsessive thinking about sexual behavior, opportunities, and fantasies
- Loss of control: inability to stop behavior despite commitments to self and others and despite problems caused by behavior
- Relationship disturbance: sexual behavior has created significant relationship problems
- Affect disturbance: significant depression, despair, or anxiety over sexual behavior

Number of SAST Core Scale Items Endorsed

YOU SCORED HERE

MOST ADDICTS ARE ABOVE 6

Figure 5 Author screening test, 17 June 2014.

started at 0.0 per cent and rose to a peak of 14 per cent at number 17. If this sounds confusing, it is because it is confusing. But the message, that your score qualifies you to seek further treatment, was clearly received.

Alongside the graph were summarized results from the test. The summary was not personalized. Although one of the authors of this book selected 'heterosexual female' in their test they were given the summary of 'A profile consistent with men who struggle with sexually compulsive behavior', 'A profile consistent with women who struggle with sexually compulsive behavior' and 'A profile consistent with homosexual men who struggle with sexually compulsive behavior', all in the summary of one test. The summary then said, in measuring the 'key characteristics of addiction', that the results show 'the following dimensions of an addictive disorder': 'Preoccupation: obsessive thinking about sexual behavior, opportunities, and fantasies'; 'Loss of control: inability to stop behavior despite commitments to self and others and despite problems caused by behavior'; 'Relationship disturbance: sexual behavior has created significant relationship problems'; and 'Affect disturbance: significant depression, despair, or anxiety over sexual behavior'.[46] At the end of the summary the user was consoled that although they may be 'frightened confused or overwhelmed' now that the test has 'confirmed your fears', the experts 'know how you feel – we've been helping people like yourself since 1983'. The user was then advised to take the anonymous, but fee-based, SARA.

As mentioned at the beginning of this chapter, Carnes dominated the early discourse, cementing sex addiction as a condition, and establishing symptoms, consequences and modes of treatment. However, as sex addiction started to take hold as a concept, and as Carnes gathered a following of therapists and recovering addicts, they started to contribute to the literature; in effect a developing professionalization of sex addictionology. Carnes's influence could be seen in their work, but there was now a plethora of authoritative voices sometimes simply replicating Carnes's ideas, and, in other cases, carving out new specializations.

One way of expanding the reach and developing the sex addiction industry was through incorporating groups beyond

Carnes's focus on the heterosexual male. Carnes and Adams's edited collection *Clinical Management of Sex Addiction* had a section entitled 'Special Populations' which dealt with sex addiction related to cybersex, women, pastors, healthcare professionals, homeless people, gay men and adolescents.[47] Weiss's *Sex Addiction 101* (2013) had separate chapters for women, gay men and teens.[48] (There is apparently still a gap in the market for workbooks dedicated to lesbian sexual compulsives.[49]) But despite the individualized discussions and specialized therapists dealing with these 'others', their work reinforced how all sex addicts were essentially the same, encouraging a sense of cohesion and camaraderie within the addict population, rather than diversity.

Although called 'Females: The Forgotten Sexual Addicts', much of former sex addict, family therapist and author Marnie Ferree's chapter in Carnes and Adams's collection was taken up with explaining the similarities between male and female sexual addicts (range of experiences, ways of acting out, consequences, root causes, process of recovery). Ferree, and authors and therapists such as Kelly McDaniel, Deborah Corley and Alexandra Katehakis, have focused on providing a voice for female sex addicts, with the results including amendments to the SAST, and an edited collection focused on this clientele, *Making Advances: A Comprehensive Guide for Treating Female Sex and Love Addicts* (2012).[50] Although sex addiction had a 'masculine face' and fewer women in treatment, Ferree surmised that 'research may eventually show that females struggle with sexual addiction at nearly the same rate as do males', and that shame and cultural conflict about gendered ideals caused the small numbers.[51] The differences seemed to lie in the perception of the addicts and the judgements placed on them – in other words, on culturally constructed ideas about gender.

Yet the female sex addiction specialists (perhaps unwittingly) reinforced rather than critiqued gender stereotypes. They focused on a woman's need for security, her use of sexual manipulation, or they stressed the prevalence of the love or relationship addict in work discussing female sex addicts.[52] Ferree wrote that while the presentation of sex addiction is similar in men and women, the treatment process is different:

Women need a more relational and slower approach, and
the clinician must take extra care regarding the therapeutic
container. A clinician's setting, energy, wardrobe, touch, and
environment require special consideration. Transference,
countertransference and enactments must be handled with
skill and empathy. The timing of using the thirty recovery
tasks is important, as many FLSAs [Female Love and Sex
Addicts] feel dismissed or misunderstood if the tasks are introduced prematurely or in the absence of a well-established
therapeutic relationship.[53]

Surely these are all considerations for treating male sex
addicts as well. In fact these same issues are outlined in
Weiss's chapter 'Treating Sex Addiction', aimed at clinicians
treating all sex addicts.[54]

Women have also featured in the literature on co-addiction
and codependency, where addiction has spawned co-addicts
and codependents just as the very concept of the co-addict
depends on the existence of the sex addict. Sexual addiction
was a family disease: 'Family members become as sick as the
sex addict, denying the reality of the disease as vehemently
as – or more vehemently than – the addict.'[55] Carnes called
co-addicts 'mirrors of obsession'.[56] Both addict and co-addict
were seen as experiencing fixation, unmanageability and
sexual dysfunction: 'coaddiction is an obsessive illness in
which reaction to addiction causes the loss of self'.[57] Thus
co-addicts have had parallel support groups based on Twelve-
Step principles: Co-SLAA, S-Anon, Codependents of Sex
Addicts (COSA) and Recovering Couples Anonymous (RCA)
(specifically for couples).[58] In theory the co-addict was
assumed to be the partner or spouse of the addict, but support
groups have proved more inclusive, open to 'men and women
whose lives have been affected by another person's compulsive sexual behavior'.[59] S-Anon even created a special subgroup for teenagers – S-Ateen.[60] Carnes's metaphor of
obsessional mirroring applied to the statistics that he used to
bolster the notion of co-addiction. The abuse histories of sex
addicts – sexual (81 per cent), physical (72 per cent) and
emotional (97 per cent) – were almost identical to those of
co-addicts – 81 per cent, 71 per cent and 91 per cent respectively.[61] However, the point about co-addiction is that it has
been heavily associated with women. Mostly it was a hidden

default position, as in the references to family and spouses already quoted. But sometimes the association was more explicit. Men were the addicts: women were the co-addicts. 'While not all sexual co-dependents are women', wrote Douglas Weiss and Dianne DeBusk in 1993, 'the majority are.'[62] And their book provided examples: 'My name is Julie. I'm a woman who loves sex addicts'; 'Hi, I am Becky, and I am a woman who loves and is attracted to sex addicts.'[63] The First Step for women who loved sex addicts was 'We admitted we were powerless over our co-dependency with the sex addict, and that our lives became unmanageable.'[64]

Adolescents' liminal status in society is reflected in the way they have been discussed in the sex addiction literature – exhibiting behaviour that *may* become something significant in adulthood. Although Eric Griffin-Shelley wrote about adolescent sex addicts in 1994, they are now framed as an outcome of the rapidly changing, digital world.[65] They provide a platform for anxieties about 'modern' life and the new challenges that digital technology has brought for sex addiction. In a 2011 interview Patrick Carnes stated, 'Sexual addiction: we're now at a place where we have an epidemic. Where we have two-thirds of our kids watching pornography while they're doing their homework...thirty-four percent of them go on to really pursue that and are at risk for what we call sexually compulsive behavior.'[66] The implication was that the numbers of addicts would increase as the young progressed into adulthood.

Proponents of sex addiction cite large but unverified numbers of those afflicted with the disease. And because of the element of shame attached to non-normative sexual behaviour, those from within the industry have the perfect reason as to why they cannot get precise figures: 'Exact statistics of sexual addiction are hard to determine, due to the taboo nature of the compulsivity.'[67] One critic of the diagnostic definition of sex addiction pointed out that just because individuals perceived their sexual behaviour or fantasies to be 'out-of-control' and sought psychological help for their perceived condition, that was not empirically strong evidence that such a condition existed.[68]

There have been sex therapists who have questioned the very notion of sexual addiction. Domeena C. Renshaw,

professor of psychiatry and director of the Sexual Dysfunction
Clinic at Loyola University, Chicago, wrote in 1991 to advice
columnist Ann Landers at the *Chicago Tribune* that

> the term 'sexual addiction' has become a popular catch phrase
> these past few years. People tend to believe that wildly pro-
> miscuous sexual behavior is an addiction in the way that
> alcoholism is an addiction. This is entirely false. Alcoholism
> involves the abuse of a chemical that categorizes the problem
> as physiological. There is no such component in out-of-con-
> trol sexual behavior.[69]

This letter stemmed from Renshaw's dismay that a woman
came to her clinic requesting assistance for sex addiction on
the basis of advice she had read in Landers's column about
someone else's story of sexual promiscuity. Renshaw's assessment was that the woman in fact suffered from manic-
depressive illness. Renshaw's letter was a critique of the
process of lay diagnoses of sexual addiction. But such diagnosis is central to the sex addiction paradigm, and has been
abetted both by the role of the media in disseminating the
information and by the encouragement for people to medicalize and problematize their own behaviour on the basis of
another person's experiences.

The vague and broad way sex addiction has been defined
has led to ballooning numbers of potential 'addicts' and col-
lapsing distinctions between the sexually abusive and the
sexually unfettered. One workbook equated rape with phone
sex under the broad umbrella of 'sexual self-control problems'.[70] Another author claimed that 'Sex addicts do not
necessarily become sex offenders... Roughly 55 percent of
convicted sex offenders can be considered sex addicts. About
71 percent of child molesters are sex addicts.'[71] And with this
definition of sex addiction as 'engaging in persistent and
escalating patterns of sexual behavior acted out despite
increasing negative consequences to self and others', then it
is surprising that only 55 per cent of sex offenders qualify.
Such a broad definition can include such diverse behaviours
as to be meaningless.

As mentioned earlier, equating sex addiction with substance addiction was a way to promote its 'authenticity and

harmfulness' and constitute it as a real 'disease'.[72] Paula Hall wrote, 'Sex addiction can be viewed as a particularly power- ful mood-altering drug.'[73] And in a text designed to assist therapists treating sexual addiction, psychologist Anne Hast- ings gave the example that 'a sexual addict might miss work in order to pursue a drug-like *sexual trance*' where 'work can seem less important than the "fix" – unless the addict is also addicted to work'.[74] Clinical psychologist Michael Herkov warned that 'seeking help for sex addiction is difficult because your addicted brain wants sexual stimulation and pleasure in much the same way a cocaine addict wants cocaine'.[75] Sex addiction and substance dependence were seen as almost interchangeable. Jennifer Schneider's chapter on sex addic- tion in *The Handbook of Addictive Disorders* (2004) encour- aged therapists to 'extrapolate a framework for the use of the term [sexual addiction] from the DSM-IV's diagnostic criteria for substance dependence'.[76]

Claims of the progressive element of the disease helped intensify assertions of the urgency for seeking treatment. Robert Weiss warned that sex addicts must 'understand the progressive nature of their disease – that their addiction can over time steer their fantasies and behavior in unexpected, unwanted, possibly even illegal directions'.[77] Mark Laaser's book aimed at Christian sex addicts was alarmist in its claims: 'In adulthood the disease grows progressively worse. Ulti- mately, if untreated, its victims will die.'[78] In her book *Escape from Intimacy*, Anne Schaef used the term 'progressive, fatal disease' or 'progressively fatal' eighteen times.[79] Workbooks for addicts and therapists alike pushed the point about the life-threatening consequences of sex addiction. They could be 'life-threatening' in that the parts of life that the addict should hold dear (marriage, job, children, social status) were threat- ened, or in terms of actually causing death. In *Clinical Man- agement of Sex Addiction* one author wrote that 'consequences may include an arrest for solicitation of prostitutes, contract- ing AIDS, a pending divorce, or incarceration for lewd acts'.[80] Hall listed the consequences of sex addiction (on the basis of her own survey) as shame, low self-esteem, losing a relation- ship, loss of employment, wasted time, wasted money, debt, impaired parenting, physical health problems, sexually trans- mitted infections (STIs), mental health problems, suicidal

thoughts, sexual dysfunctions, legal action and press exposure.[81] Hall's table listed actual and potential percentages of
these consequences, though it is unclear how a researcher
could quantify the latter.[82]

According to sex addiction lore it was often an unmanageable consequence that led an addict to therapy: 'Unmanageability is the therapist's ally' and 'severe consequences . . . provide
leverage to help the addict break the addictive cycle'.[83] The
story of one sex addict, 'Tragic Consequences, Great
Rewards', in the personal stories section of *Sex Addicts
Anonymous* outlined the extreme consequences that led the
addict to recovery: their childhood of sexual abuse, an arrest
for solicitation, being robbed and beaten, hospitalization for
depression, contraction of HIV and contemplated suicide.[84]
Contraction of HIV/AIDS has been one of the most dramatic
and frequently used examples in sex addiction workbooks.
Contrary to Love (1989) had an unsophisticated story about
a couple having contracted AIDS as a result of the man's
sexual addiction.[85] Ferree cited the news of a former sexual
partner's death from AIDS as the event that brought her to
her first Twelve-Step meeting.[86] Another addict's story began,
'Even though I risked alienating my children, contracting
AIDS, and losing my husband, I continued to act out sexually.'[87] Weiss pondered, in the preface to his book *Cruise
Control*, 'how many men became infected with HIV because
they are untreated sex addicts who tend to have sex first and
then worry about the consequences later'.[88] As cited in *Clinical Management of Sex Addiction*, the American Society of
Addiction Medicine's *Guidelines for HIV Infection and AIDS
in Addiction Treatment* (1998) encouraged physicians to be
'alert to sexual addictive/compulsive behavior' and stated
that becoming infected or infecting others with HIV is one of
the 'most profound consequences of out-of-control sexual
behavior'.[89] HIV/AIDS became shorthand for the dangers of
non-normative sexual behaviour.

Culturally bound notions of normative sexual behaviour
and desirable lifestyles (marriage, heterosexuality, children
and productive employment) were implicit in the definitions
of sex addiction and were held as both a key to recognizing
the problem (where those aspects of life were compromised)
and an incentive for recovery. They were what Helen Keane

has identified as 'cultural norms and ethical judgments about what people should value and what makes life meaning-ful...The addict is the virtual opposite of the ideal of the rational, productive and self-reliant citizen.'[90] Or as Weiss has expressed it, 'it can be difficult to understand why someone would put their livelihood or family life at risk for the sake of a shallow, two-dimensional online sexual experience or momentary sexual interaction'.[91] Addiction provided expla-nation for the inexplicable.

Workbooks and the Twelve-Step process of sharing experi-ences encouraged addicts to compare notes and seek solidar-ity and familiarity in others' stories. In his first book, *Out of the Shadows*, Carnes explained that its vignettes were 'fic-tionalized composites...carefully designed to be characteri-zations in order to protect individual anonymity. To the degree that they represent any individual [it] is a comment on the commonality of the addicts' experiences.'[92] Such stories have long been part of the fabric of the Twelve-Step recovery programme. Robyn Warhol and Helena Michie have argued that such recovery narratives have established an archetype that provided a sense of cohesion, but that also encouraged people to experience, remember and then share using the same narrative paradigm – to make their story fit the established model.[93] Parallels can be seen with Douglas Mason-Schrock's observations about transsexual narratives and the construction of a 'true' self.[94] The authors of an article about online help for sex addicts felt that 'Reading these stories helps people to feel less isolated with their problem and may assist them in breaking through denial. Many end up seeking face-to-face help as a result of the process.'[95] Stories shared in support groups and outlined in workbooks have been integral to the ongoing conceptualiza-tion and construction of the sex addict.

A workbook vignette requires the reader to identify with the main character. This discursive technique means that the reader starts to conceptualize their experiences in the lan-guage of addiction, and through the lens of the narrative. The characters in these brief stories are described as successful – businesswomen, lawyers, doctors – people with social stand-ing and, by implication, a lot to lose, which bolsters the claim that their behaviour is an addiction or disease rather than the result of choice. They have to be someone with whom the reader identifies, either through similarity or because they have cultural capital. One workbook author questioned the use of physical descriptors in the vignettes, saying, '[i]n a book about addictive love and sex...these details are problematic. They serve to titillate or separate.'[96] But when such characters are described, it is as attractive or powerful. If they had no friends, job-prospects or family, then the consequences associated with sex addiction (loss of family, loss of job, loss of friends) would lose their force. The cameos do not focus on sex offenders or the imprisoned. The case histories were designed to draw the reader in, and for them to identify and sympathize with the character's plight. There had also to be a possibility for redemption; the therapy industry relied on it.[97]

Sex addiction literature has focused primarily on family (environment and biological) and previous abuse as the main causes of sex addiction. Ferree felt that sexual addiction was the result of some form of abandonment, either in childhood or in adulthood 'through divorce, death, parental absence...lack of appropriate nurturing'.[98] Those who believed in sexual addiction looked for these correlations to provide some causal explanation. But their conclusions were drawn from people identifying as addicts, already influenced in perceiving their life experience through the prism of sex addiction. In the introduction to the twentieth-anniversary edition of *Silently Seduced* (2011), Adams wrote that since the book was originally published it had been quoted back to him in therapy sessions and in lectures and that it had 'not only been informative to its readers, but transformative'.[99] Adams said this with pride, and not a hint of critical reflection about how he, and the addiction industry, had shaped and created a language and concept that had then become self-fulfilling.

The scientific fields of neuroscience and genetics have both been used to frame the causes discussed earlier. The genogram process was one therapeutic tool used to uncover what role genetics has played in sex addiction. The fictional couple Dan and Laura who opened *Contrary to Love* (1989) did a genogram and made links between their own sexual dysfunction and that of their family: porn and chemical addictions of siblings; womanizing and alcoholic grandfather; prostitute grandmother; overweight, sexually abusive, alcoholic father; sexually addicted uncle. The 'genogram had done what it always does...clients developed a clearer picture of their family history and of the role that addiction played in their lives. They weren't bad people; rather they had an illness that affected the whole family.'[100] Likewise, the high incidence of multiple addictions was linked to family predisposition: a result of 'family illness' that manifested in a variety of ways. Carnes argued that 'each member [of the family] must use a discipline such as the Twelve-Steps as an ongoing antidote to the addictive process'.[101]

Although genetics still plays a role in explaining sex addiction, neuroscience has surpassed it. When asked to define addiction in 2011, Carnes said: 'Addiction is a brain disease. The brain has become altered.'[102] This illustrated the shift from Carnes's tentative entry into the world of neuroscience in *Don't Call it Love* (1991) – 'breakthroughs in neuroscience are occurring almost daily, but we still have much to learn' – to his position in *A Gentle Path* (2012), where he stated more confidently, 'We also have solid scientific evidence that working a Twelve Step program literally rewires our brains for recovery.'[103] In the world of sex addictionology there must remain hope for recovery, and so neurological issues and genetic predispositions can be overcome with awareness and therapy. Neuroscience is becoming more popular as a way of explaining sex addiction, but it is no more than a new mode to express old ideas.[104] Or as Carnes has put it, neuroscience 'simply helps us to understand the mechanisms of what addicts have been telling us about for years'.[105]

Like neuroscience, the Internet has been woven into sex addiction discourse, playing an increasing role in the twenty-first century. It has provided an *idée fixe* as well as a new medium for disseminating information and promoting the concept of sex addiction. The Internet arrived in the sex addiction literature in the late 1990s as sex addictionologists incorporated the subcategory of cybersex addiction into their new or revised recovery workbooks, with new texts dedicated entirely to the subject.[106] David Delmonico's article 'Cybersex: High-Tech Sex Addiction' (1997) was an early entry in the field.[107] When researching his article, Delmonico bemoaned the 131 hits from his Internet search for the terms 'cybersex and addiction', 'many of which were contrary to promoting recovery from addictive behavior'.[108] In 2014 the same search has generated 66,400 results, indicating an increase in discussion and visibility of the term 'cybersex'.[109] But again, a profusion of information does not necessarily indicate anything more than a canny ability of those in the industry towards excessive output and publicity. And despite claims that the Internet has fundamentally changed sex addiction, the messages remain largely the same.

Concerns about the sexual implications of the Internet have reached hyperbolic proportions, as evidenced in Carnes's 'cybersex revolution'.[110] Weiss has claimed that in the pre-Internet age 3–5 per cent of the adult population struggled with sex addiction, but the Internet had meant 'sexual addiction is both escalating and becoming more evenly distributed among men and women'.[111] In (the pre-Internet) *Contrary to Love* (1989) Carnes had outlined the six phases of sex addiction: initiation, establishment, escalation, de-escalation, acute and chronic.[112] Moving through the stages could be a long, drawn-out process. However, in 2004 Schneider warned 'Progression from the initiation to the acute phase usually takes years, but with the advent of the Internet, the process is often accelerated to months or even weeks.'[113] In an interview from 2011 Carnes explained:

> The Internet is changing everything: it's changing our sexuality; it's changing our culture. No spouse can compete with the Internet…We call it the MESA factor: Machine Enhanced Sexual Arousal. Takes the brain and elevates it to a level that requires so much stimulation that being with just one woman doesn't do it. I hear it from my patients all the time.[114]

As well as increasing the numbers of patients to treat, the Internet provided a platform for greater publicity. It is true that the Internet's 'Triple A Engine' lure of accessibility, affordability and anonymity was outlined as encouraging cybersex addiction.[115] Yet it was recognized that these same traits could be harnessed to help with sex addiction identification and treatment: 'Technology is changing the nature of problems people are having as well as how we treat them.'[116]

The reach of online articles about sex addiction is surely just as large as (if not larger than) that of published authors in the sex addiction genre, considering the way that the Internet is used for accessing information quickly. For example, Michael Herkov has brought sex addiction to a wide audience with his numerous articles posted on PsychCentral.com in 2006.[117] PsychCentral.com is an example of popular access to current ideas and debate regarding psychology. Its Facebook page has 88,798 'likes' and the Twitter account @PsychCentral has 73,512 followers.[118]

In this twenty-first-century, technology-saturated, Western culture, addictionologists must engage with the technology in order for their message to appear current. Introducing Weiss's updated edition of *Cruise Control* (2013), Gentle Path Press editor Corrine Casanova reminisced, 'Back in 2001, we had no idea where technology would take us in the future and how that would specifically impact sex addiction. *Cruise Control* does a great job of showing how recovery is possible in this digital age.'[119] The second edition of *Cruise Control* included a new chapter, 'Technology and the Changing Face of Sex Addiction'.[120] The malleable case studies were also subtly changed. For example, the opening story remained essentially the same: Ed went to the gym to work out and to make contact with men. However, he no longer cruised 'the nearby mall or corporate park restrooms during lunch' but instead 'keeps his smart-phone sex app open at work'.[121] The message is effectively unchanged: sexual addiction will 'take over' a person's life. The Internet and new technologies have not fundamentally altered sex addiction as an idea, but they have added a sense of urgency to the warnings. The Internet has become simply another vehicle for the same concept.

Chapter 4
Cultural Impact

Your girl catches you cheating...Fifty fucking girls? God*damn*
...You try every trick in the book to keep her. You write her
letters. You drive her to work. You quote Neruda. You compose
a mass e-mail disowning all your sucias. You block their e-mails.
You change your phone number. You stop drinking. You stop
smoking. You claim you're a sex addict and start attending
meetings.

Junot Díaz, 2012[1]

It seems an axiom of modern sexual addiction that the ailment
is both widespread and ever increasing. 'Sexual compulsivity
seems more prevalent now than ever', warned the *Handbook
of Clinical Sexuality for Mental Health Professionals* (2003).
Even these rather restrained advisors were somewhat unre-
strained in their estimates that up to 22 million Americans
were addicted to sex in 1998 and that perhaps 40 million had
'online sexual problems' by the year 2000.[2] *The Sex Addiction Workbook* (2003) said 'Although we have no good data
on the prevalence of such problems, they appear to be escalating at an alarming rate, possibly because of the impact of
modern technology, in particular the Internet.'[3] A 2008 article
by a clinician in *Psychiatric Clinics of North America*, with
the obligatory reference to Carnes and the rather negating
use of the words 'possibly' and 'may', claimed that 'Possibly

4 out of 10 adults in United States culture may be sexually compulsive.'[4] One believer was blunter still: 'Like it or not, sexual addiction is a rapidly growing problem, and predicted to be the next tsunami of mental health.'[5]

There is little doubt that much of the hype around sex addiction – either in endorsement or in denial – has been media-driven: 'Duchovny in rehab for sex addiction', 'Are people becoming addicted to sex because of the financial crisis?' and 'Are you addicted to sex?' were just some of the titles in the late 2000s.[6] By the end of 2011 'The Sex Addiction Epidemic' was the cover story in Newsweek, that gauge of the US cultural mainstream.[7] The concept rapidly achieved a taken-for-granted status. The now deceased Cleveland kidnapper and rapist Ariel Castro allegedly blamed his crimes on sex addiction.[8] And police officers have added sexual addiction as a coping mechanism for the trauma and stress associated with their work.[9]

One of the concerning aspects of this familiarization, and we will return to it later, has been the lack of critical inquiry in the reporting, even in quality publications like The New York Times, The Guardian and The Independent. Hence Joanna Moorhead's piece 'Sex Addiction: The Truth About a Modern Phenomenon' that seriously reported a psychotherapist's claims that 10 per cent of the sex addicts she surveyed were under 10 years old when their sex addiction started, and 40 per cent were under 16. This (retrospective) claim for 'how young sex addiction starts' was never questioned.[10]

If The New York Times can be used as a rough guide to educated popular usage, there has been an increasing familiarization with the concept of the sex addict since the early 1990s (Table 1).[11]

Table 1 References to 'sex addict', 'sexual addiction' and 'sex addiction' in The New York Times

Years	No. of references
1971–1980	1
1981–1990	11
1991–2000	87
2001–2009	129

It is worth pausing for a moment to consider the dynamics of the media's role in this habituation, where hardcopy combined with digital delivery and printed stories were reinforced by the moving image. Television, newspapers, magazines and the Internet converged in what became, in effect, the marketing of a concept. News blurred with entertainment in the form of reality TV, chat shows, celebrity culture, documentary and film, while the sex addiction industry itself, the subject of this familiarization, made impressive use of these myriad forms and genres of media delivery. We will see later that the Clinton/Lewinsky affair of 1998 was pivotal in this media merging and that sex addiction featured in the discourse surrounding the scandal. But what we are concerned with here is the public's habituation with a term, a relatively un-interrogated concept with an appeal that resided in its simplicity. What is remarkable is the ease with which 'sex addiction' became part of what Fedwa Malti-Douglas has dubbed (in another not unrelated context) the 'American imaginary'.[12] This process did not have the dramatic intensity of 1998, when, as it has been observed, 'One could literally spend 24 hours a day watching, listening to, and reading about the Clinton scandal.'[13] Sex addiction's media legitimation was a far more protracted affair – a drip, drip rather than John Fiske's event of 'maximum visibility and maximum turbulence' in his 'river of discourses' metaphor for media culture.[14] But it did share some of that late 1990s moment's characteristics, including the unlimited number of sources with rather limited perspectives (a kind of inverse relationship between quantity and quality), and the folding of the distinctions between hard news and entertainment and producer and consumer.[15] Though its genesis preceded such developments, the rise of sex addictionology was arguably facilitated by what has been called the 'collapse of media gatekeeping'.[16] Over time, it would become, like addiction culture generally, to quote Trysh Travis, 'a matter of common sense, a concept so familiar that it seemed to evade – or perhaps not even require – definition'.[17]

Newsweek's cover story, we have seen, was an iconic instant. However, a better example of the phenomenon is its rival *Time* magazine's earlier feature at the beginning of 2011, 'Sex Addiction: A Disease or a Convenient Excuse?', with its follow-up piece on NBC's daily American morning TV, *The Today Show*, and then on the Internet on Today.com. The author of the written piece, John Cloud, started with a time-honoured technique, personalization, as he outlined the case of an individual addict, Neil Melinkovich. If the accompanying photograph of the said addict reposing in bed puzzled the reader, the reason for it soon became evident:

> A difference between an addict and a recovering addict is that one hides his behavior, while the other can't stop talking about it. Self-revelation is an important part of recovery, but it can lead to awkward moments when you meet a person who identifies as a sex addict... within a half-hour of my first meeting Neil Melinkovich... he told me about the time in 1987 that he made a quick detour from picking up his girl-friend at the Los Angeles airport so he could purchase a service from a prostitute. Afterward, he noticed what he thought was red lipstick on himself. It turned out to be blood from the woman's mouth. He washed in a gas-station bath-room, met his girlfriend at the airport and then, in the grip of his insatiability, had unprotected sex with her as soon as they got home – in the same bed he said he had used to enter-tain three other women in the days before.

The feature was by no means an uncritical acceptance of its subject. Cloud noted both the financial and cultural implica-tions of acknowledgement by the *Diagnostic and Statistical Manual of Psychiatric Disorders* (DSM): 'recognition of sex addiction would create huge revenue streams in the mental-health business. Some wives who know their husbands are porn enthusiasts would force them into treatment. Some hus-bands who have serial affairs would start to think of them-selves not as rakes but as patients.' He was ambiguous about definitional aspects of the alleged disease. Martin Kafka's diagnosis of the threshold of hypersexuality at seven or more orgasms a week was problematic; 'by Kafka's definition, vir-tually every human male undergoes a period of sex addiction in his life. It's called high school.' The general tone of the piece was noncommittal: 'they are still trying to address very basic questions. Should we regard out-of-control sexual behavior as an extreme version of normal sexuality, or is it an illness completely separate from it? That question lies at the heart of the sex-addiction field, but right now it's unanswerable.'[18]

The video follow-up on NBC and Today.com was less guarded. 'This disease, this particular affliction is so misunderstood', declared 'sex addict' Melinkovich as he outlined marital infidelities that in his opinion became life threatening. Cloud, the *Time* journalist, seemed less circumspect when in front of the camera, as the segment cut to his explanation of his subject's almost hallucinatory sexual needs: 'The urges were so strong that he was powerless to overcome them.' The anchor's commentary referred briefly (very briefly) to critics, and immediately moved on: 'But medical experts say sex addiction can be a serious problem.' The item then moved to 'Dr Jeff Gardere, Psychologist', a widely known media medical expert, for the stereotypical seconds of authoritative sound and visuals: 'For someone who has a real sexual addiction to the point of their being destructive in their lives there is a major treatment option available and that's checking yourself into an in-patient program that's based on a 12-step-system.' The video was, in other words, sex addiction 101. The addict Melinkovich explained that his recovery was 'a process that will last a lifetime... it just envelops you, it takes your being, when you're in it and you don't think you can get out, it's a very dark place'. Cloud reappeared to state that the sex addicts that he had met reminded him of drug and alcohol dependents in their descriptions of the power of their needs. Then Dr Gail Saltz, a psychiatrist and another well-known TV commentator, clarified that she saw the problem more as compulsion than addiction, 'a compulsive, incredibly overwhelming, urge: I need to do this and it destroys their functioning, that's the operative part.' And the programme ended with Saltz's words: 'you keep doing it and you cannot stop'.[19] The likelihood was that viewers of this item would have been left with the opinion that sex addiction was real, characterized by overwhelming, uncontrollable sexual impulses, and was best conceived and treated as an addiction, like alcoholism. The original *Time* article, while guarded about aspects of the diagnosis, never really questioned its ontology, and, like NBC's *Today*, helped to popularize the concept. An article in the *Columbia Journalism Review* has referred aptly to the manner in which an all-too-common, uncritical journalism has effectively fetishized sex addiction.[20]

Hence the term 'sex addiction' has become firmly entrenched in twenty-first-century popular culture. Season 1 of the UPN sitcom *Girlfriends* (2001) has an episode, 'They've Gotta Have It', that features sex addiction, when one of the principal characters, the lawyer Joan (Tracee Ellis Ross), dates a man who refuses to touch her. When confronted, he says 'I'm a sex addict.' She looks sceptical: 'What man isn't?' The man, Sean, explains: 'I'm a recovering sex addict...Once I get turned on, there's no turning off.' The episode also includes a scene in a sex addiction meeting. Despite the laughs (it was situation comedy), and Joan's friend Lynn (Persia White) registering positive to every item on the sex addiction self-test, and Joan's initial scepticism and recoil at the number of women that Sean had 'slept' with ('almost three hundred'), sex addiction was taken seriously in the episode. As another friend Maya (Golden Brooks) says, 'Do not take that lightly. Michael Douglas is a sex addict...It's real.'[21]

Sex addiction figures similarly in Charlie Sheen's comedy series *Anger Management*, when Charlie gets sexually involved with a recovering addict. Again the malady provokes comedy, heightened no doubt by the actor's own alleged real-life addiction, but its authenticity was never questioned: 'She has a disease...sex addiction.'[22]

From its beginnings, sex addiction seemed perfectly suited to the issue-oriented format of what has been termed the 'first generation of daytime talk shows' (their beginnings coincided).[23] We will see later that Patrick Carnes was appearing on *Donahue* in 1985.[24] The baseball star Wade Boggs claimed that he first realized that he was a sex addict when he watched an episode of *Geraldo* (1989) that dealt with the subject:

> I was watching Geraldo Rivera a couple of weeks ago, and there was a show on about oversexed people, and things like this, and Geraldo had psychologists on there and everything, and they were calling it a disease, and I feel that's exactly what has happened – that a disease was taking over Wade Boggs, and it just did for four years.[25]

Marion Barry, the disgraced mayor of the District of Columbia, was a guest on the *Sally Jesse Raphael* show in 1991, presenting along with other sex addicts: ' "You get caught up in it", said the former mayor,... "The women. This disease is cunning, baffling, powerful. It destroys your judgment." ' The audience responds: 'The audience aaahed.' They intervene: 'What about taking responsibility for your own damn self?' The host glosses: 'Our guests today say they have all brought some measure of shame to themselves and their loved ones.' She warns, adding a frisson to the proceedings: 'Addicts can lie...They're cunning.'[26] Those who did not watch daytime tabloid television could (in this instance) read about the show in *The Washington Post*.[27]

Sex addiction was an ideal topic for a genre that thrived through exploring topical social interest problems at a personal level and which combined audience participation, indeed performance, with guest expertise and facilitated such interaction – almost a mirror image of the conceptual success of sex addiction in wider American society and culture. It dealt with sexual excess, of course, another characteristic of the talk shows. And it was therapy. Jane Shattuc estimated in 1997 that about two-thirds of the talk shows were devoted to psychological matters. A strand of therapeutic discourse was promoted by a medium known for the power of its public therapy.[28]

The topic was still appearing in the later generation of more confrontational talk shows. *Maury* presented a steady offering of sexual addiction themes based on a perceived threat to the family and in keeping with the show's penchant for marital infidelity and teenage sex: 'My Teen Daughter is Addicted to Sex' (1999); 'I Need the Truth – Is My 13-Year-Old Addicted to Sex?' (2004); 'Take the Test! Is My Teen Daughter a Sex Addict?' (2005); 'I'm Addicted to Sex...I Don't Think Our 2 Kids Are Yours!' (2006); 'Young Teen Girls Addicted to Sex and Violence!' (2008); 'My Wife's a Sex Addict...Am I Her Baby's Father?' (2010).[29] Presumably the focus on female sex addicts increased the shock factor in what was often presented as a male-dominated issue.

Ricki Lake featured female sex addicts in 2004, an interesting programme because three of the four admitted to being sex addicts but were defiant about it: 'Yes, I am a sex addict...Hi Ricki, I love your show...I don't think I have a problem.' One woman with more than 700 claimed sexual partners responded that her only problem was that she did not 'get enough'. Another, aged twenty-three and with a total of over 150 male contacts, said 'Yes I am addicted to sex...I've done it with ten guys [in a day], but usually it's five!' Only the fourth admitted to being in any kind of quandary and needing help.[30] Though the first three interviewed women remained unrepentant in a loudly subversive manner (probably to provoke the engagement and controversy required of the genre), the programme was structured so it finished with the addict who was willing to enter therapy.[31] The other principal participants – an 'expert', Catherine Burton (a Texas family and marriage therapist), and a recovered sex addict and memoirist, Sue William Silverman – were there to reinforce the problematic nature of sex addiction, to emphasize that the recalcitrant three were in denial, to advocate therapy and to ensure a master theme of disapproval – reinforced by Ricki Lake's wrinkled nose as she commented 'Clearly she has a problem.' Furthermore, the sex engaged in is presented as addictive, a message that was never challenged: 'I love sex, it's like a drug to me'; 'I have to have it'; 'She likes sex all the time...She eats it, sleeps it, dreams it'; 'My friend Lynette is a very big sex addict. She says that sex is like coffee in the morning for her.'[32] All the tropes of sex addiction were present: the ubiquity of the malady, even in women ('Yes, it's very common...it's not at all unusual'), acknowledging (or not acknowledging) a problem, shame ('You have a lot of shame'), seeking self-worth from men and then feeling bad and immediately requiring another man to provide that sense of identity again, and sexual melodrama ('A road to death').[33]

Phil McGraw's talk show *Dr. Phil* has also included discussion of sex addiction. The 'Suburban Dramas' episode in 2011 featured McGraw's trademark polygraph test: 'Brett says he's addicted to sex, online pornography and talking dirty to other women...Brett insists he's never had a sexual relationship with anyone other than his fiancée. Mandy says she doesn't believe him and wants to know if he's lying.'[34] The 'Secret Life of a Sex Addict' episode in 2013, which had both the critic David Ley and the advocate Robert Weiss as guests, actually came out against sex addiction as the prime explanation of the subjects' woes. Marcos had had more than

3,000 sexual partners (both male and female) in only seventeen years. His wife of nine years, Yvette ('I didn't know he was a sex addict'), was unfaithful too: 'I'm obsessed with hooking up with other men. I cannot maintain monogamy in a relationship with one guy. I have a wandering eye.'[35] However, the experts concluded that sex addiction was the least of their problems. Dr Phil himself listed off a range of possibilities – narcissism, borderline personality disorder, anti-social personality – that might have contributed to what he termed a 'highly dysfunctional family'; 'Sex addiction might wind up on the list but it wouldn't be near the top.' Yet the banner headline was 'Secret Life of a Sex Addict'.[36] The sidebars on Dr Phil's website for the shows included links to sex addiction tests and advice and support centres.

If sex addiction was 'real' in *Girlfriends* and *Ricki Lake*, it was positively surreal in the highly rated, adult animation *South Park*'s sex addiction episode, 'Sexual Healing' (2010), which is merciless in exposing the concept's weaknesses. The nation embarks on a school-wide screening to determine how many elementary schoolchildren are suffering from the disease. They are shown a picture of a naked woman – 'Holy moly, what's that between the lady's legs? It's all bushy ... I've never seen that part of a lady! Do they all got a hedge like that? Do they?' – and then asked what colour was the handkerchief that she was holding? 'Did you see the bush on that lady? What the heck was that?' Those who had not even noticed that there was a handkerchief – 'Fuck no, I wasn't looking at a handkerchief' – are declared to have tested positive for sex addiction and sent off for treatment; 'It was just so big and bushy sir. Why does it look like that?' The results of the survey are proclaimed with confidence: 'In fourth graders, five percent of male students were found to be sex addicts. By sixth grade the number goes up to thirty percent. At high schools, nearly ninety-one percent of male students answered, "What handkerchief?" ... We're facing a sex addiction epidemic in our country.' The fourth-grader Kyle ('Well, I just found out I'm a sex addict. I'm so scared, I haven't even told my mom yet') is the only one to question the concept: 'I mean, maybe this isn't really even a disease.'[37]

When some of the films about sex addiction are examined more closely it soon becomes evident that sex addiction has become a convenient, one might say easy, term to describe what was once termed promiscuous sex. Paul Schrader's film *Auto Focus* (2002) about Bob Crane, the star of the famous 1960s television series *Hogan's Heroes*, a man who traded on his fame to have sex with (and film) hundreds, perhaps thousands, of women before his death in 1978, was immediately classified by an article in *The New York Times* as a film about sex addiction. Crane was a 'sex addict... His sex addiction overwhelmed his career' – even though the term was never used in a film set in a period before the invention of sex addiction.[38] *Auto Focus* is about sexual obsession, the banality of the culture of swinging, the opportunities and transience of celebrity, and the homoeroticism in heterosexual sex.[39] It is a subtle film about sex and addiction that loses any analytical complexity once the two words are combined in that limiting designator 'sex addiction'.[40]

The same could be said of a more recent film, Steve McQueen's *Shame* (2011), which appears to have prompted the earlier-mentioned article in *Newsweek* – an interesting example of the circularity of popular culture – written, significantly, by the magazine's entertainment reporter.[41] *Shame*'s director Steve McQueen and co-screenwriter Abi Morgan have said that the initial idea for the project came from a conversation about sex addiction, that they talked to 'sex addicts' in their preparatory research, that the film's title came from a word frequently used by those addicts, and that it is about a man who used sex in the same manner that others used alcohol. Despite his recognition that it was a 'grey area', the film's main actor, Michael Fassbender, also consulted a 'sex addict' in preparation for his role. Clearly, the creative team thought that sex addiction was genuine – McQueen: 'sexual addiction is real' – and when interviewed invoked several of sex addiction's keywords: 'shame', 'compulsion', 'self-loathing... the shame that these people talk about' and 'lack of intimacy'; 'Brandon is a sex addict. He has problems with intimacy... That's classic sex-addict behavior.'[42] The scene in *Shame* where Brandon purges his pornography collection is a recurring sex addiction trope.[43] The hinted (past or looming) incestuous relationship with his sister in the film was perhaps prompted by the sex addiction literature's suggestion of sexual abuse as a contributor to the malady, though it is not an aspect of the film that has been much discussed. In the printed version of his *Sight & Sound* interview with Nick James, McQueen descended into exaggerated stereotypes that could have come (probably did come) straight from a sex addiction advice book when asked what the tipping point was between promiscuity and addiction: 'When you find that in order to get through a day, someone is on the internet for 20 hours a day or more looking at pornography or having to have a sexual activity at least ten times a day, it's incredible.'[44] His reported discussion in *Newsweek* was positively hyperbolic: 'It's not like alcoholism or drug addiction, where there's some built-in sympathy. It's almost like the AIDS epidemic in the early days. No one wants to deal with you... You're a fiend. That stigma is still attached.'[45]

It is intriguing that *Shame* is far more nuanced than that. Brandon does not spend most of his day on the Internet and does not have ten-times-a-day sex. The terms 'sex addict' or 'sex addiction' never appear in either film or script. The word 'shame' is also absent from the film (apart from its title) and only occurs twice in the script in narrative descriptions: once when the protagonist Brandon (Fassbender) looks in the mirror 'full of shame' after his sister has discovered him masturbating (the mirror-looking does not occur in the film), and then after anonymous sex in a hotel room when 'HOTEL LOVER' pulls on a 'tiny thong' and Brandon 'looks away, fighting back the cold flutter of shame' (the tiny thong and cold flutter are also absent from the moving image rendition).[46] It seems more a film about the contemporary world, the current era of on/scenity referred to earlier, where sex has become quotidian. This is captured perfectly in several sections of the film. One is in the lingering looking that begins and ends the narrative – framing the film – the mutual staring on the subway train that might have led to something more between Brandon and 'PRETTY SUBWAY GIRL'.[47] Another sexually evocative moment occurs when Brandon (and the viewer) gaze upwards to a full-length apartment or hotel window with a naked woman facing outwards, her hands and body pressed against the glass, being fucked from behind. The silence of this watched encounter adds to its distancing.[48] Elsewhere, the noise-scapes of sex (the groans, grunts, gasps, laboured breathing and whispers, the muffled computer porn) are as important as the Bach in the film's soundtrack. It is a masterly filmic portrait of a sexualized society.

Shame is also about the Internet's facilitation of that easy sexualization. The film could almost have been called 'Porno'. McQueen juxtaposes Brandon's boss David's use of the Internet to chat to his son on Skype, retaining everyday family contact, with Brandon's employment of the same medium to access porn and to participate in online sex. Brandon's consumption of online porn is certainly central to several of the movie's scenes.

> Your hard drive is filthy, all right. We got your computer back. I mean, it is, it is dirty, I'm talking like hoes, sluts, anal, double anal, penetration, inter racial facial, man, Cream pie. I don't even know what that is…It takes a really sick fuck to spend all day on that shit:

David's monologue is interrupted by his son, still on Skype, 'Daddy…Daddy'.[49] Later, when Brandon's sister Sissy (Carey Mulligan) opens his laptop she discovers a series of windows, a

> blurred smorgasbord of porn sites, graphic and obscene, their colors reflecting across her face and body. An escalating collage of graphic images, obscene sexual messages and a provocative sexual conversation hanging mid sentence addressed to a live sex chatroom. The images haunting, brutal, from the weird to the sadomasochistic. The open windows, an endless stacking of obscene chatroom conversation, emails posted with graphic sexual photos and live webcam images of every combination of fucking disappearing into the screen in infinite form.[50]

That is in the script. This kaleidoscope of sexual imagery did not make it to the screen. But the live webcam scene survives as a panty-clad beauty beckons Sissy from Brandon's laptop: 'Hey, where's Brandon? Are you Brandon's girlfriend? Do you want to play?…Do you wanna play with my tits? I know Brandon would really like it…And I know exactly what Brandon likes.'[51] In discussion McQueen stated that *Shame* is about 'our relationships with sex and the Internet. It's about how our lives have been changed by the Internet, how we are losing interactions…We've been tainted, it's unavoid-able.'[52] One of the starting points for his interest in the film, he explained in a press conference for the British Film Insti-tute (BFI) London Film Festival in 2011, was the contempo-rary 'accessibility of sexual content'.[53]

Shame is also a film about casual sex in twenty-first-cen-tury New York, where sex is just sex, readily available, and without commitment (Brandon's longest relationship is four months). He engages in a series of escalating, paid and unpaid encounters involving nameless women, a man, and a three-some with two women. The close-ups of wedding rings convey the message that it is not just singles involved in this culture. David (James Badge Dale), who fails and then suc-ceeds in such encounters, is, as Brandon reminds his sister Sissy, married: 'You know he's got a family, right? You know he's got a family?'[54] (Of course uncommitted sex is espe-cially available if you look like Michael Fassbender. One of the film's collusions with the very culture that it is allegedly critiquing is that all of those engaged in such sex, even when it is being paid for, are always so desirable: the script refers to 'PRETTY SUBWAY GIRL', 'PRETTY ASSISTANT', 'ATTRACTIVE WOMAN', 'CUTE NEIGHBOR', 'A stun-ning leggy COCKTAIL WAITRESS', 'HOT GIRLS'.[55])

So *Shame* could also have been called 'Promiscuity', though that would have had an outdated feel and might not have conveyed the intensity and compulsion that McQueen envi-sioned. But whatever the intentions of its makers, it seems more about alienation or ennui than addiction. Brandon's sadness is conveyed, hauntingly, in the window shot after he fails in what might have been committed sex with his col-league Marianne (Nicole Baharie), but the next moment he is engaged in vigorous sex against the same window with an unnamed woman.[56] His suppressed anger, his self-destructive impulses, his sheer desolation, build in brilliant editing – standing in the subway train, in the darkened street, fingering a woman in a bar ('I want to taste you…slip my tongue inside you…just as you come'), tasting his fingers, being beaten by her boyfriend, engaging in gay sex, the threesome, woman kissing woman, prolonged fucking, brutish facial contortions to the point of exhaustion – as the film reaches its climax with Sissy's bloody anguish and Brandon on his knees in torment, in the rain, sobbing. But then the film ends as it had begun with the attractive woman on the subway, the longing looks, the wedding ring. Perhaps it will all begin again. Sukhdev Sandhu came closest in his review in *Sight & Sound* when he described *Shame* as depicting sex addiction as 'a species of anomie'.[57]

Yet much of the coverage of *Shame* has persisted with that restricting 'sex addiction' billing: 'The acclaimed new film *Shame* portrays the harrowing world of sex addicts' (*The Guardian*); 'chilling story of a New York sex addict' (*The Observer*); 'Sex Addiction and the City' (*Newsweek*).[58] Robert Weiss thought it 'a dead-on portrayal of active sex addiction' and worried that some of its scenes might 'trigger a sex addicted client's desire to act out'![59] The classification could even survive content that suggested that *Shame* was about something else or more. Thus Mark Fisher in *Film Quarterly* declared McQueen's creation 'a study of sex addiction' and wrote of 'sex addict Brandon' while he simultaneously referred to 'such an overwhelming sense of affectlessness that it could be about depression as much as sex addiction'.[60]

The incongruity of *Shame* is that the subtlety of its exploration of what its creators have persisted in labelling as sex addiction exposes the limitations of other representations of this supposed complaint – including the shallowness of the concept itself. We do not need sex addiction to explain Brandon's world.

Sex addiction has certainly featured in some forgettable cinema. In Joseph Brutsman's truly awful *Diary of a Sex Addict* (2001) we follow the exploits of sex addict Sammy Horn (yes, Horn), a restaurateur and chef in his fifties (one online reviewer referred to him unkindly as a pensioner), who recounts his exploits to his therapist (Nastassja Kinski) as he takes us through a seemingly never-ending, five-day parade of thrusting sex (Sammy does not believe in foreplay) with improbably beautiful, female sexual partners. Sammy, played by the woeful Michael De Barres, is a kind of Jekyll-and-Hyde character – sexual addiction of the most basic kind – whose saccharine, family-devoted Dr Jekyll ('I love my wife', 'I love my [young] son') is even worse than the sex-addicted Mr Hyde. An IMDb.com reviewer, who described it as a B-grade sexploitation film attempting to 'masquerade as a study of sexual addiction', captured its nature perfectly. But with Rosanna Arquette and Kinski as stars, this softcore pornographic film/video/DVD, best classified as unintentional comedic drama, is still an example of the popular familiarization, if not legitimation, of the concept of sex addiction.[61]

I Am a Sex Addict (2006) is more memorable (see Figure 6). Caveh Zahedi's whimsical, low-budget, 'fictionalized documentary' is about this Woody Allen-like independent filmmaker's long-running obsession with prostitutes. He is a sex addict with honesty, who insists on telling his girlfriends about his problem and musing about the ethics of prostitution: 'I had always considered myself a feminist'. It is never clear how seriously we are supposed to take his addictions – repeatedly asking street prostitutes 'Will you suck me?', grabbing the breasts of massage parlour receptionists and then fleeing, masturbating in the confessional – but the film narrative is framed by Zahedi's attendance at sex addiction meetings and ends with the claim that he is cured.[62]

Figure 6 *I Am a Sex Addict* (2006: Caveh Zahedi). © IFC Films/Photofest.

Thanks for Sharing, a film that was in production when we first began work on this project and out on DVD by the time our book was completed, is certainly a film about sex addiction – undigested, unquestioning sex addictionology straight from Patrick Carnes's *A Gentle Path Through the Twelve Steps* and *Out of the Shadows*, which appear, almost like clumsy product placements, in several scenes in this (for these writers) irritating romantic drama. Set in the context of a sex addiction support group, and starring some well-known names (Tim Robbins, Mark Ruffalo and the singer Pink play the addicts, and Gwyneth Paltrow and Joely Richardson are among their loved ones), the film rehearses all the themes of addictionology. Indeed it follows the format of Alcoholics Anonymous a little too closely with its meetings, sponsors, sponsees, fellowship, sobriety medallions (ambiguously, 'freedom from masturbation and sex outside of a committed relationship'), and frequent references to 'sharing' (hence the film's title), 'one day at a time', 'Friend of Bill' (recovering alcoholic), and invocation of 'a higher power'.[63] The concept of the partner as co-addict also features, with Katie (Richardson) advising Phoebe (Paltrow) that as a partner she consider 'What are *my* issues that *I* have to deal with? After all, I picked an addict.'[64] Alcohol and drug dependency intersect with sex addiction throughout the film to convey the nestling theme discussed elsewhere in this book. Mike (Robbins) is a recovering alcoholic and sex addict. Dede (Pink: Alecia Moore) is in a Narcotics Anonymous programme as well as attending the sex addiction group ('The only way I know how to relate to men is sex').[65] Phoebe's ex-boyfriend was an alcoholic and she is a fitness fanatic with food issues. Neil (Josh Gad) is both a food and sex addict. It seems ironic that Edward Norton, who plays the self-help- and group-therapy-obsessed narrator in the movie version of Chuck Palahniuk's satirical *Fight Club* (1999), was one of the executive producers of *Thanks for Sharing*.

There are hints of a counter-narrative. Neil lies to the group. Phoebe's double mastectomy and recovery from cancer are juxtaposed with Adam's (Ruffalo) rather obsessive five-year sobriety (televisions are removed from hotel rooms to eliminate any likelihood of sexual stimulation). The drug addiction of Mike's son Danny (Patrick Fugit) actually serves to contrast the seriousness of his habit – and ability to overcome it alone – with the triviality of the sexual dependency of the main protagonists and their inability to combat it without group help. The viewer may also wonder what the frotteurism and up-skirt voyeurism of Neil (and uncomfortable sexualized relationship with his mother) and the obvious childhood sexual abuse of Becky (Emily Meade), one of Adam's casual contacts, have in common with the promiscuity of Adam, Mike and Dede.

Then there is the archetypal tension between sex addiction's anti-sex message and the sexualization of elements of its message that will be discussed later in this book. Paltrow's objectification is blatant. A clip of her stripping was used to market the film – one journalistic puff-piece mused whether the clip would promote a fresh outbreak of sex addiction in New York – and her publicity interview on the talk show *Chelsea Lately* managed to focus on her body ('what a vision...thank you for showing your body in this movie because you're naked a lot') while almost totally avoiding any discussion of sex addiction and with only fleeting reference to the actual film that she was ostensibly promoting (see Figure 7).[66]

Figure 7 *Chelsea Lately*, 'Interview with Gwyneth Paltrow', 16 September 2013.

Yet the directorial message in *Thanks for Sharing* is unmistakable: sex addiction is a genuine disease. Adam says 'I have to remind myself every day where this disease could take me.' 'That's the disease. It makes you do things that violate everything that you believe in.' The character Mike puts it more bluntly – 'This disease is a fucking bitch' – and makes it clear early in the film (counter to his son's message) that giving up alcohol was easy compared to shedding his addiction to casual sex. 'This thing is a whole different animal. It's like trying to quit crack while the pipe's attached to your body' (a simile that does not really bear deeper analysis). The seriousness of their malady, 'the darkness', is constantly impressed. Adam's lack of access to a laptop (odd, given his occupation as an environmental consultant: a blocked MacBook Air is specially brought in by an assistant so that he can Skype Phoebe while on a business trip!) is 'saving his life'. 'You think I like not having a television or a laptop? It fucking blows. But guess what? It's saving my life, so I do it.' Dede's counselling would supposedly save her from suicide: 'There's gotta be another way. There has to be, or I'm gonna fucking kill myself.'[67] This sentiment echoes the addictionology language of sex addiction as not only a disease but a progressive and fatal one.[68]

The film's earnestness has convinced commentators who do not share the scepticism of the authors of this book. The movie columnist for the *Chicago Sun-Times* wrote that the film made a 'convincing case' for sex addiction, 'makes you care about sex addicts'.[69] The reviewer for *The Washington Post* thought that the film and its script took seriously the idea that 'sex addiction is a real illness' and showed 'real respect for the power of these programs'.[70] These were surely understatements given that Carnes himself might almost have written the screenplay. Weiss, the founder of the Sexual Recovery Institute in Los Angeles, and Carnes-trained, highly recommended *Thanks for Sharing* to 'therapists interested in what sexual recovery looks like'.[71] The most nauseating instance of the film's endorsement of addictionology is in its closing moments when Billy Bragg's song *Tender Comrade* (1988), a poignant, homoerotic homage to returned, working-class, British soldiers, is played to evoke battle-weary, male camaraderie in the wake of the fight against sex addiction – as if those struggling against sexual urges are in any sense comparable to those engaged in mortal combat.

Even when the references to sex addiction have been humorous or mocking they were still invoking the concept. Victor Mancini, the main character in Chuck Palahniuk's novel *Choke* (2001), is a sex addict who has sex with the female addicts whom he sponsors – in toilets, in a janitor's closet – while meetings are in progress. He never advances beyond the fourth of the Twelve Steps, the listing of his sexual contacts, and he treats sexaholics' meetings as 'a terrific how-to seminar. Tips. Techniques. Strategies for getting laid you never dreamed of. Personal contacts.' 'Plus the sexaholic recovery books they sell here, it's every way you always wanted to get laid but didn't know how.' He hangs about in the recovery section of bookshops to pick up female sex addicts. It is a hilarious novel about casual sex ('her name's Amanda or Allison or Amy. Some name with a vowel in it') that positively revels in its subject matter, but with serious things to say about the addiction industry and American culture. And not just sex with women:

> We don't need women. There are plenty of other things in the world to have sex with, just go to a sexaholics meeting and take notes. There's microwaved watermelons. There's the vibrating handles of lawn mowers right at crotch level. There's vacuum cleaners and beanbag chairs. Internet sites. All those old chat room sex hounds pretending to be sixteen-year-old girls. For serious, old FBI guys make the sexiest cyberbabes.[72]

Its message is the antithesis of everything that believers in the concept of sex addiction hold dear: 'The magic of sexual addiction is you don't ever feel hungry or tired or bored or lonely.'[73] When the film from the novel appeared in 2008, its distributors (in the spirit of Palahniuk) promoted it with gifts of anal beads.[74]

Similarly, John Waters's outrageous comedy *A Dirty Shame* (2004) (see Figure 8), in which a Baltimore suburb is taken over by sex addicts – 'Straight, gay or bi, there's a new sex act just waiting for you. Sex for everybody! Fuck your neighbors joyously... Let's go sexing' – could hardly be said to take the subject seriously.[75] Sex addiction in this film is always the result of concussion, a rather quaint nod in the direction of nineteenth-century, physiological explanations of hypersexuality that modern believers in the malady are hardly likely to endorse. Nor are they likely to be amused by the flippant portrayal of their problem ('I'm a sex addict too. I'm a cunnilingus bottom, and I'm your mother...Let's go down to the Holiday House and fuck the whole bar. Okay, Mom. Let's go sexing!') and their meetings ('My name is Paige, I'm from Roxton and I am a sex addict. My drug of choice...frottage... "Excuse me", I'd say, while I'd grind my crotch into an unsuspecting passenger on a crowded airplane').[76] When asked if he had attended Twelve-Step meetings in preparation for his film, Waters reportedly replied: 'I felt that would have been condescending...But if I were a sex addict, I would definitely go to sex addiction meetings, and for the same reason that they do in this movie – someone's going to slip.'[77]

And yet as Patrick Carnes reportedly observed, 'The fact that pop culture is making jokes about sex addicts is a sign that awareness of the condition is percolating in mass consciousness.'[78]

Figure 8   Selma Blair in *A Dirty Shame* (2004: John Waters). Free desktop wallpaper.

One television series that seems deliberately to have avoided invoking the concept – despite media stories doing it for them – is Showtime's *Californication* (Seasons 1–7, 2007–14). Season 6 began with the main character, womanizing writer Hank Moody (David Duchovny), sent to the wryly named rehab facility 'Happy Endings'. Despite his numerous sexual encounters and the way his sexual behaviour impacts negatively on his life, writing, friends and family, Hank is never described in the series as a sex addict: he is in rehab for his drinking. The absence of the label of sex addict is all the more striking because the actor Duchovny has reputedly been treated for sex addiction. *Californication* is strident in allowing Hank (in line with most of the other characters) his sexual proclivities ('holes is holes') without judgement, though definitely with consequences for the life he thinks that he wants. The characters are framed as creatures of excess, instant gratification, opportunism and a debauched Hollywood lifestyle. Even his fellow rehab inmate, the character listed as 'Tweaker Chick' in the credits (Angela Trimbur), is not described as a sex addict in either the dialogue or the credits, despite her sexual exploits: she shoves Hank's hand down her pants at the end of a group therapy session and then has non-consensual sex with him while he is asleep. Sexually inappropriate and aggressive, 'Tweaker Chick' screams 'I want drugs' as she leaves Hank's room, raising the possibility that she, like Hank, is in rehab for substance abuse, with her sexual behaviour not under scrutiny.[79] When Hank returns to rehab (to sneak drugs in) and sees her again, he good-naturedly says 'hello rapist' as she straddles him, gyrating and pleading 'Feed me some fuckin' inches dude.'[80] The drugs that Hank brings into rehab fuel a sexually charged party. The message seems to be that, given the opportunity, anybody (in or out of rehab) will engage in polyamorous sexual encounters. This is a message about excess and access rather than addiction.

Some material should not be taken seriously. *Dr. Drew's Sex Rehab* (2009), three weeks in the Pasadena Recovery Center under the care of Dr Drew Pinsky, is entertainment rather than treatment, its format, editing, casting and much else determined by the parameters of reality TV, the genre that combines documentary and soap opera, reality and unreality, where viewers look for glimpses of authenticity amidst all the acknowledged, staged fakery.[81] Significantly, *Dr. Drew's Sex Rehab* is a spinoff from *Celebrity Rehab with Dr. Drew* (2008–12). The patients (cast) of porn stars and former porn stars, models and ex-models, a (minor) rock star and a pro-surfer were hardly randomly selected – the women had the same agent and the surfer, allegedly, was paid for product endorsement (which may explain the frequent clothing changes, his mismatching sneakers – 'Interesting shoes' – and the fact that he brought his surfboard with him to the treatment centre!), and were either self-declared non-addicts (the 3,000 women that the rock star slept with were a potential part of any performer's CV) or multiply addicted (sex being the least of their worries). Amber Smith was addicted to antidepressants and opiates. Kari Ann Peniche was a methamphetamine addict. Drummer Phil Varone had a cocaine dependency, as did Nicole Narain, a former Playboy Playmate. Several became almost professional celebrity addicts: Jennifer Ketcham, Peniche and Kendra Jade Rossi would also appear in *Sober House*, Season 2 (2010), and Peniche (again) in *Celebrity Rehab*, Season 3 (2010). Smith had already featured in Season 2 of *Celebrity Rehab* (2008) and Season 1 of *Sober House* (2009). One of those 'treated', Duncan Roy, a gay English film director who had some knowledge of production, wrote later of blatant playing to the camera, that he was concerned that some 'might not be on the show for the same reasons as I was. That they might not have any desire for sexual sobriety. That I might be part of a huge pantomime.'[82] Rossi blogged that when she signed up for the show it was for the money and she did not know what sex addiction was.[83] Varone recalled that his agent phoned and said

> 'OK, we have a supermodel, we have a porn star, we have a Playboy Playmate, we need a rock star.' They need this cast. Do you want to do it? And I said, 'Well to be on television I guess I will.' That's the decision. Those shows are scripted out a certain way.

He did not consider himself a sex addict; he just had access to a lot of groupies and took advantage of it.[84] After the show he produced his own sex DVD, *The Secret Sex Stash*, and commercially manufactured a dildo replica of his penis called the 'phildo': not much shame there.[85]

It is all staged. The *mise en scène* is sexualized in ways totally incongruent with the declared aims of detox. The publicized three weeks of celibacy (including no masturbation), the very public confiscation of sex toys, the ban on digital contact with outside temptations (cell phones, laptops, tablets) only serve to heighten the flirting, sexual innuendo, flaunted cleavages, the very sexualized avoidance of sex by those who include porn stars whom the viewer may well have seen elsewhere engaged in very explicit activity – why else would the producers want such actors![86] Gareth Longstaff has argued that when the former reality TV celebrity Steven Daigle became a porn star, the visual techniques of reality TV merged with those of pornography: 'the mixture of intimacy, liveliness, extreme-close-up, amateur and hand-held camera work, and surveillance imagery associated with the visual rhetoric of both Reality TV and pornography were reworked and repositioned as dual markers of both reality and fantasy'.[87] With the female porn stars in *Sex Rehab* the movement is in the opposite direction, a fascinating example of the intertextual relationship between pornography and sex addiction that we will return to later in the book. Unsurprisingly too, given the presence of those porn stars, there are many emotional 'money shots', those moments of raw feeling – crying, rage – integral to the talk show and reality TV, named by Laura Grindstaff after pornography's famed ejaculatory money shots, visible signs of pleasure rather than grief.[88]

It is perhaps appropriate that reality TV, a media form that our colleagues Misha Kavka and Amy West have characterized as standing outside history to achieve emotional intensity and immediacy, should, in this case, have been promoting a concept (sex addiction) whose proponents, we are arguing, have been so lacking in historical awareness.[89] But the point with this, and other such television, is that it was publicizing the concept. As a blog for the show put it: 'I think after watching this show, a lot of people are going to think, "Am I a sex addict?"'[90]

We have been focusing on the sometimes-dramatic examples of film and television to explain the dissemination of an idea. Yet the quiet insinuation of the concept is perhaps best illustrated by its acceptance by the humble library cataloguer. The Library of Congress established 'sex addiction' as a new subject category in 1989 (revised in 1997) alongside a long list of variants: 'Addiction, Lust'; 'Addiction, Sex'; 'Addictive sex'; 'Compulsive sex'; 'Erotomania (Hypersexuality)', 'Hypersexuality'; 'Lust addiction'; 'Obsession, Sexual'; 'Sexaholism'; 'Sexual Addiction'; 'Sexual compulsiveness'; 'Sexual obsession'.[91] Libraries throughout the world are now able to use these influential Library of Congress subject headings in the cataloguing of their own holdings.

This infiltration may have been unproblematic for nonfiction. It may even be of some utility where sex addiction is a legitimate component of the subject matter of some fictional forms: McQueen's *Shame* and Waters's *A Dirty Shame* appear as 'Sex addiction – Drama' in the University of Melbourne Library Catalog. Murray Schisgal's *Sexaholics* (1995), first performed at the 42nd Street Workshop Theatre in New York in 1997 and now part of ProQuest's Literature Online, is in fact about sexual addiction. The play's two acts are framed by a couple's unlikely off-stage attendance at an addicts' support group after an episode of energetic casual sex:

> These people...They meet a couple of nights a week and they discuss their problems and they help each other, they help each other to stop ruining their lives...The idea is the same for all addicts. And it works. It works because we also have a sickness over which we have no control. For weeks I've been trying to get together the courage to go to a meeting. There's one tonight. If...If you'd go with me ...[92]

John Franc's *Hooked: A Novel* (2011), about a group of male friends visiting brothels, at least contains fleeting reference to the syndrome. But it is more concerning when the term is used to classify any work that contains multiple or non-monogamous sex. Novels as various as Patrick McGrath's *Asylum* (1997) (obsession), Pier Paolo Pasolini's *Petrolio* (1997) (perversity and fascism), Stephanie Merritt's *Gaveston* (2002) (infatuation), Howard Jacobson's *Who's Sorry Now* (2002) (infidelity) and Kathryn Henderson's *Envy: A Novel* (2005) (grief and transgression) have all been catalogued as fiction about sex addiction when they are not about sex addiction at all and the words never appear between their covers other than, perhaps, in the Library of Congress Cataloging-in-Publication Data after the title page.[93]

One of the more intriguing effects of this phenomenon has seen the reclassification of the reprints or newer editions of older classics under the term 'sex addiction' – Djuna Barnes's *Nightwood* (1936), Paul Morand's *Hecate and Her Dogs* (1954, 2009) and Vladimir Nabokov's *Lolita* (1955, 1958) are jarring examples.[94] Our own University of Auckland Library lists the 1995 edition of Philip Roth's controversial *Portnoy's Complaint* (1969) under the subject heading 'Sex addiction – Fiction' despite the fact that sex addiction did not exist in 1969 and Roth does not use the term in the novel. Such retrospective classifications superimpose narratives different to those envisaged by their authors, essentially dehistoricizing these works.[95]

Any literary masterpiece about uncontrolled passion, sexual fixation or unconventional sex is in danger of being classified under the reductive term 'sex addiction'. This was the fate of Oscar Hijuelos's stunningly vibrant *The Mambo Kings Play Songs of Love* (1989). The sexual conquest and longing, the masculine posturing and vulnerability, only part of a Pulitzer Prize-winning novel that was about so much else, was enough for an influential text on addictive disorders to condemn it as a case study of sex addiction; the novel's central character, the philandering musician Cesar Castillo, is a sex addict.[96] Life is effectively squeezed out of the work.

Since Janice Irvine's initial analysis of the place of sex addiction in modern American sexual history, then, the phenomenon has become the default explanation for any kind of promiscuous or obsessive sexual interaction. Jesse Fink, who (we will see later) went on a 'three-year sex binge' with hundreds of women and who wrote about his activity, said that his memoir was promoted as sex addiction against his better judgement. The publisher characterized him as a sex addict but he did not see things in that way and thought the concept, in typical Australian style, 'a crock of shit'. He said that dating four or five women a week in this Internet age was not unusual and certainly not indicative of any addiction.[97]

When Erica Jong published *Fear of Flying* in 1973 – with its famous zipless fucks – her female protagonist Isadora Wing (Jong) may have had 'Nymphomania of the brain' and have been 'a nymphomaniac (because I wanted to be fucked more than once a month)' but she was definitely not suffering from sexual addiction.[98] In 1990, however, Wing, now the central character in Jong's *Any Woman's Blues*, 'a fable for our times' according to its fictitious editor, is indeed 'a woman lost in excess and extremism – a sexoholic [sic], an alcoholic, and a food addict'.[99] The Twelve Steps, AA meetings, frequent references to obsession and addiction are integral to her story:

> Sex was what blotted out the world for me. Sex was my opium, my anodyne, my laudanum, my love. Sex was what I used to kill the pain of life – the pot and the wine were just my avenues to bed. Open your mouth and close your eyes. Open your legs and close your eyes. Open your heart and close your eyes...I lived for sex, for falling in love with love, for breaking (or at least collecting) hearts.[100]

Alcohol addiction and sexual addiction are intertwined in *Any Women's Blues*. 'The Program is like Mary Poppins's elixir: it becomes the specific medicine for whatever ails you. You ask for a cure for sex addiction? You got it.'[101] Wing uses AA as a (not exactly successful) way to battle her sexual obsessions. 'I drew the line at Sexoholics Anonymous. For one mad moment, I thought of going to Sexoholics Anonymous to *meet* men, but I couldn't quite bring myself to. The very notion made my mind giggle.'[102] Irvine rightly referred to this work by a best-selling author as evidence for the popularization of the idea of sex addiction.[103] Works such as Jong's both reflected and facilitated this cultural spread.

However, the story did not finish there, for in 2011, as part of the publicity accompanying the republication of her bestseller, Jong decided retrospectively that *Fear of Flying* had been about sex addiction after all. Both the early Wing and her creator are sex addicts: 'That was my life. I had been a sex addict, a man addict.' Needless to say, in this age of consolidation of the concept, sex addiction was part of the billing. The piece in *The Huffington Post* was called 'Erica Jong on Feminism, Sex Addiction and Why There Is No Such Thing as a Zipless F**k'.[104]

Sex addiction has become part of popular culture. That is why Junot Díaz's character could trot it out as one of his lame excuses in a novel in 2012 in the epigraph to this chapter.

Chapter 5
Sexual Stories

I was a world-famous actor, single, in my early twenties, with money, too much free time, a big libido and a drinking problem. I don't think you need F. Scott Fitzgerald to make my story more clear.

Rob Lowe, 2014[1]

In a press conference for *Shame* Michael Fassbender observed that he, like most people, was introduced to the idea of sex addiction 'through celebrity stories'.[2] Celebrity has certainly played a role in this familiarization. In 2011, for instance, the 'Celebrity Infidelity Examiner' for Examiner.com urged its claimed millions of online readers to attempt their own prognosis of Charlie Sheen's reported sexual activities:

> Is Charlie Sheen...*really* a sex addict, as many people are now beginning to suspect? Only a qualified medical professional can make an accurate diagnosis as to whether or not a person is addicted to sex. But anyone can look at a list of behaviors that are typical of sex addicts, and make an educated guess.[3]

An addiction workbook from the same year suggested that clients familiarize themselves with a case of a celebrity sex addict as a way of broaching the subject with those they envisaged as a support person.[4] A. D. Burks's 2013 memoir of sex addiction got straight into celebrity name-dropping in his introduction when he asked the reader, 'TIGER WOODS, Patrick Dempsey, Kobe Bryant, George Michael, Ted Haggard, Eric Benet, and Jesse James. What do they all allegedly have in common?'[5] The connection with celebrity also works for the spouses of sex addicts. Reese L. Yant's (a pseudonym – supposed to read as 'resilient') memoir of marriage to a sex addict, published in 2012, began with a prologue entitled 'What Sandra Bullock, Tea Leone, Elin Nordegren, and I have in Common'.[6]

Michael Douglas, David Duchovny, Russell Brand, Rob Lowe and of course Tiger Woods are the usual suspects when it comes to celebrity sex addicts (see Figure 9). In Matt Stone and Trey Parker's take on sex addiction in *South Park* the celebrities in the 'Karne [Carnes?] Institute for Sexual Addiction' are Tiger Woods, Ben Roethlisberger (Pittsburgh Steelers quarterback: 'Don't screw girls in the public bathrooms?'), Bill Clinton ('Putting cigars in girls' vaginas'), Charlie Sheen ('Watching internet porn all day, every day'), David Duchovny ('Mr Duchovny, please stop jerking off!'), David Letterman ('having sex with employees') and Michael Douglas.[7]

Figure 9 'I Booked Myself into a Sex Addict Rehab Clinic.' Tom Scott cartoon, 2010. Reproduced by permission of Tom Scott.

But we could extend the list exponentially, and it will
certainly be longer by the time this book goes to press.
David Ley's disbelieving inventory includes South Africa's
president Jacob Zuma, France's International Monetary
Fund head Dominique Strauss-Kahn, and the former gover-
nor of New York Eliot Spitzer.[8] All were accused by the
media of being sex addicts. But we could add many others,
in whose cases, sometimes without the slenderest of evidence, let alone any attempt at clinical justification, sexual
activity of various kinds and intensity is lazily classified
as sex addiction: the Boston Red Socks baseball star Wade
Boggs in 1989, the 1990s mayor of the District of Columbia Marion Barry, the Italian politician Silvio Berlusconi,
US Congressman Christopher Lee, the *Happy Days* actor
Scott Baio, the gay TV host and wedding planner David
Tutera, the US Congressman Anthony Weiner and the
boxer Mike Tyson.[9] Arsenal and Germany's celebrity foot-
baller Mesut Özil was a sex addict because he had dinner
with a former Miss Venezuela.[10] As we write, Abel Ferrara's
film *Welcome to New York* (2014), starring Gérard Depardieu as an obvious Strauss-Kahn stand-in, is described as a
'sex addiction film' and Depardieu as portraying a 'sex
addict'.[11]

Take Tyson's memoirs, billed by the *New York Post* as
'From Champ to Drug and Sex Addict'.[12] There is a lot of
sex in the book, mainly of the kind discussed later where
success brings sexual access.

> Once I started, I couldn't stop. I got too self-indulgent. I'd
> have ten women hanging out in my hotel room in Vegas.
> When I had to go down for the press conference, I'd bring
> one down and leave the rest in the room for when I was fin-
> ished. Sometimes I'd get naked and put the championship belt
> on and have sex with a girl. Whenever there was a willing
> partner, I wanted to do it...After a while I put together a
> Rolodex of girls in different cities. I had my Vegas girls, my
> L.A. girls, my Florida girls, my Detroit girls. Oh, man, why
> would I want to do that?
>
> I just went totally off the track...training hard and party-
> ing just as hard as I was training – drinking, fucking, and
> fighting with these women all night.[13]

Yet reputed sex addiction actually plays only a minor part in Tyson's story: his main dependencies were alcohol and drugs (cocaine principally). It was his anger-management counsellor Marilyn Murray who first suggested treatment for sex addiction given the boxer's sexual promiscuity and general attitude to women. Tyson attended the exclusive Wonderland rehabilitation facility in Los Angeles, which facilitated contact with a sex addiction therapist at Venice Beach who took him to thrice-weekly Sex Addicts Anonymous (SAA) meetings there.[14] In retrospect Tyson said that he had never considered himself to be a sex addict – 'Being the champ, I thought that having sex with all those women was just a perk' – but claimed benefit from the group therapy: 'I was getting a lot of life skills from those meetings.'[15] His memoir carries the traces of his therapy and certainly uses the imagery of addiction:

> Having all those girlfriends while I was married was like a drug in itself. And if I needed some more, I'd just walk down the street and women would throw themselves at me. I was a slave addicted to the chaos of celebrity. I wished I could stop it but I couldn't.[16]

'Pussy was like a drug to me. When I was trying to get pussy, there was no one more desperate than me on the face of the planet.'[17] 'I felt like I was in a hole and the more people I fucked the more despair I felt.'[18] 'I was using sex to get intimacy.'[19] 'My whole life I was looking for love from my mother.'[20] But there are grounds for reader scepticism about the champion's commitment: 'One of the ways to break a sexual addiction, at least for me, was to be broke. If I didn't have any money, that shit wasn't fun anymore.'[21]

So it is curious that the evidential base for much reporting is very dubious and that some of the alleged addicts seem to have been in rehabilitation for alcohol or drugs rather than sex. This is in fact the case for two of the earliest alleged instances of celebrity sex addiction. Both Michael Douglas and Rob Lowe were admitted to the Sierra Tucson rehabilitation facility, which offered therapy for alcohol and sex addiction, although both have claimed that they were getting treatment just for alcohol abuse.[22] Lowe claimed in his autobiography that despite being admitted to rehab for drinking issues the press, the *National Inquirer* in particular, reported that he was a sex addict. Well known for his sexual (mis)adventures when younger, Lowe never once medicalized his past or referred to himself as having sex addiction – as this chapter's epigraph suggests. The press reports annoyed him 'because the sex addicts in the center have *much* more interesting stories and treatments than my group of drinkers did'.[23] Douglas may also have suffered at the hands of the press but was less forthright in defending himself – something that only fuelled the making of the myth. An article in *The Times* in October 1992 claimed that Douglas's then-wife Diandra discovered him in bed with another woman and 'sent him to a sexaholic clinic'. The article went on to make the bold claim that 'In these past few days Michael Douglas may have done for sex addiction what Princess Diana did for bulimia months ago.' Neither went on record about suffering from their respective disorders. 'But the actor's deafening silence after tabloid newspapers reported that he had checked into a clinic for sexaholics and substance abusers has drawn attention to a previously taboo topic.' This same article noted that Lowe was 'another celebrity grateful to therapy for pulling him out of a cycle of drink and sex'.[24]

The 1998 impeachment of President Bill Clinton – what has become known in shorthand as the Clinton/Lewinsky affair – may have not been primarily about sex but it seemed to be, given the amount of private sexual detail that emerged in the public sphere: in print, on the Internet, on TV and radio. It was certainly a gift to academics: Lauren Berlant and Lisa Duggan's *Our Monica, Ourselves* (2001) has chapters called 'The First Penis Impeached', 'The President's Penis' and 'Loose Lips'.[25] *The Starr Report Disrobed* (2000), by Fedwa Malti-Douglas, is a witty, brilliant dissection of the *Starr Report*, the evidence produced against Clinton.[26] The fact that the sexual activities of a president could become so central to US politics and be of such obsessive concern to the mass media speaks to the sexualization of modern Western society that forms the context to the subject matter of this book.[27] Thus the literal political pornography of the Clinton/ Lewinsky scandal, where the president's penis and semen (on Lewinsky's blue, Gap dress) were discussed publicly, when we heard about phone sex, oral sex in the White House bathroom and while the president was on the telephone, presidential masturbation and what happened to the president's cigar, and when deleted private emails of a sexual content and recorded phone conversations were recovered and used as evidence, collated in the published *Starr Report* (named after the independent counsel, Kenneth Starr).[28] Linda Williams has observed that 'watching politics in the late nineties' was almost like 'watching pornography in the early seventies'.[29] As if to merge metaphor and materiality, porn movies appeared in 1998 on the Clinton/Lewinsky theme, including *Scenes from the Oral Office* and *Deep Throat V: The Quest: Slick Willy Rides Again*, with one scene where an intern is placed in a huge cocktail glass filled with jelly beans.[30] Malti-Douglas has amusingly discussed ripples at the everyday level of consumer culture with the supermarket product 'Monica's Down On Your Knees Hot Sauce'.[31]

However, the interesting thing about all this academic musing, this intelligent comment and cultural critique, is that the issue of sex addiction was almost never raised. Clinton, despite the list of his indiscretions, was not described as a sex addict. The only mention in *Our Monica, Ourselves*, and it was in passing, was in an analysis of Clinton represented as a 'white trash' president and in terms of a wider inability to control himself – a mere two pages.[32] Sex addiction, Clinton's or anyone else's, it should be noted, is not referred to in the *Starr Report*.

The same cannot be said of more popular discourse. Here Clinton is indeed one of the celebrity names associated with this claimed sexual malady. Nigel Hamilton's biography *Bill Clinton: An American Journey: Great Expectations* (2003) simply assumes the president's sexual addiction.[33] The influential *Newsweek* investigative journalist Michael Isikoff reported that he had been told by an alleged occasional sexual contact of Clinton that he had confessed his addiction to her in bed in a hotel room in 1988. She said that she was a sex addict at the time, attending a sex addicts' anonymous group, and raised the subject with him: 'Did you ever think *you* were a sex addict?' He replied: 'I know I am – and I've tried to overcome it...But it's so hard. Women are everywhere, and for some reason they seem to want me.'[34] The legal analyst and political commentator Jeffrey Toobin has claimed that long before the Lewinsky affair Isikoff had become convinced that Clinton was a 'sex addict...that virtually all of his problems stemmed from this vital flaw'.[35] Later, in 2007, when former president Gerald Ford's off-the-record musings were published, the press seized on the Fords' conviction that Clinton was 'sick – he's got an addiction', 'I am convinced that Clinton has a sexual addiction.'[36] Given Betty's (and therefore Gerald's) experiences with addiction, the Fords' observations were given more weight than they would have been if they had been proclaiming on many other subjects, and the issue of Clinton's sex addiction was revived again.[37]

There is evidence, then, that the theme of Clinton's sex addiction formed a strand of what Jeremy Varon has termed the media spectacle of the Clinton/Lewinsky affair.[38] The therapists seized upon the moment. While not actually declaring him an addict, it is significant that Patrick J. Carnes and Kenneth M. Adams's *Clinical Management of Sex Addiction* (2002), an edited primer of sex addiction treatment, cited this archetypal example of compartmentalizing and concealment. 'It would not be appropriate to make the determination that Clinton's behaviors indicate the presence of addiction', wrote Carnes and his co-author Marie Wilson; 'however, we are using this chain of events to illustrate an almost textbook example of one individual's complex process of denial and gradual disclosure'.[39] This was a telling disclaimer. The power resides in the 'however' (why mention him in the first place?) that allows them to use Clinton as prototypical, although, as we will see of other celebrity cases studies, there is little to suggest that he was anything more than a powerful man whose status and position afforded him sexual access to a range of women. Somewhat less circumspectly and several years later, Susan Cheever noted in her own sex addiction memoir that Carnes – whom she interviewed for the book – 'testified for Paula Jones and thinks that Bill Clinton's sex addiction moved public acknowledgement of sex addiction forward more than a decade'.[40]

There was no hesitation in Jerome D. Levin's *The Clinton Syndrome: The President and the Self-Destructive Nature of Sexual Addiction* (1998), a study by a psychotherapeutic expert in alcoholism and substance abuse.

Clinton's background as a child of addiction predisposed him biologically and socially to an addiction of his own. I will demonstrate that his sexual proclivities over a lifetime were expansive and developed the strength and persistence of a habit. Finally, I will illustrate that there were specific stresses in the president's life shortly before his alleged involvement with Monica Lewinsky that made him highly vulnerable to acting out once again his sexually addictive behavior.[41]

Clinton's sexual activity served as 'a paradigm of sexually addictive behavior'.[42] Levin contended that Clinton's (publicly reported) sexual history fulfilled his seven criteria of indicative sex addiction: (1) compulsion, (2) drive, (3) lack of control, (4) persistence, (5) damage, (6) societal disapproval and (7) acceleration.[43] The syndrome of sex addiction becomes the Clinton syndrome.

Levin's study was based not on clinical consultation of the subject of his diagnosis – though he did draw on a practice file of anonymous troubled patients that comprised a large part of the book – but rather on biographies and newspaper and magazine reports (we loop back to the previous chapter on cultural representation). Nor did it strictly conform to his seven-point diagnosis. Clinton's addiction was presented as a strange combination of genetics and environment, what Levin termed 'bio-psycho-social determinants', with his alcohol- and gambling-dependent parents passing on their 'neurochemistry' to their sons (resulting in sex addiction for Bill and drug addiction for his brother), and his relentless pursuit of women a quest to 'reconnect with his mother'.[44] Then his actions merely confirmed Levin's diagnosis. How else could one explain the reckless sexual antics? 'No man in his right mind would risk the presidency and everything he had worked so hard for to engage in a meaningless sexual encounter – unless he was caught up in a sexual addiction.'[45] It was not a high point in the history of US psychotherapeutic theory.

Rick Springfield's memoir, published in 2010, detailed a life full of sexual liaisons, starting early in his teens and continuing on during his marriage to the woman he never stopped referring to as his soul mate and the true love of his life (to whom he is still married). From the very beginning of what was a long (although not uninterrupted) career in pop/rock music Springfield had 'as much groupie sex as my road-worn penis could handle'. 'I have been as promiscuous as women have allowed me to be in my life. And I thank the worn-and-torn skin of my weary dick that they want it as much as I do.'[46] Sex was part of his definition of success. At one point he said, 'I am as driven sexually as I am career-driven' and that 'what it's really about' is 'being in a career I'm passionate about... and having sex with lots of strangers'.[47] But at no point in this memoir of a life and career of ups and downs did Springfield call himself a sex addict or seek therapy for sex addiction. He occasionally used the language of addictionology in referring to his 'habit' of casual sex or pondering the fact 'It's a hard drug to quit cold turkey, this sex thing' – but his larger perspective and interpretative framework produced another narrative.[48]

Springfield's was not only a memoir about sex but, perhaps most importantly, it was a memoir about mental illness and depression. He referred repeatedly to the/my Darkness – his depression – and revealed that he attempted suicide as a teenager because of it. Sex became a way of alleviating his fear of failure and deep-seated self-esteem issues. But Springfield did not attempt to absolve himself of blame or responsibility for his sexual behaviour (when he was cheating on a girlfriend, for example) because of this depression. He was insightful enough to know and tell us that this came – if you wanted it – with celebrity. 'Looking back, sometimes I'm amazed at my disconnect. But possibly my behavior can be excused, for a short while at least, based on the "kid in a candy store" defense.'[49] Springfield's memoir detailed his various attempts at therapy – 'so I can try to work out a solution to my disloyal behavior' – but these did not take him down the sex addiction route either.[50] In a more strident clarification he stated that 'The sexual issue had also become a habit just because I'd been doing it for so long. I never felt better from it, or higher, or less depressed, I just did it because it was "what I did." '[51] But when Springfield ended his memoir (he was in his early sixties) by saying 'The habit of a sexual path is as powerful as any habit. And I picked up a hell of a habit', it was apparent that his choice of words could open up the (re)interpretation of his story to those with vested interests.[52] The Colorado Sexual Recovery Centre's website headlined with 'Rick Springfield Opens Up about Sex Addiction' and *The Huffington Post* wrote similarly with a story on his 'Decades-Long Battle with Depression and Sex Addiction'.[53] Interestingly, Springfield told one reporter that although it was not an over-exaggeration to describe sex addiction as part of his life – it was clear that this reporter and others were doing just that – 'I don't use that word in the book because it's not to me, it's just my sexual issue...I wasn't addicted to sex...it was a habit that I fell into as a young musician.'[54]

In contrast, Russell Brand was indeed treated for sex addiction in the KeyStone Center in Philadelphia in 2005. Fame – Springfield's 'kid in a candy store' – became, in Brand's words, 'a Wonka ticket to a lovely sex factory'.[55] But despite an admission or diagnosis of sex addiction in Brand's case, it is unclear whether this treatment was a bid for career publicity or part of his comedy act. One diary entry, written during his stay there, stated that he had to write 'a victim's list – a litany of the women I've wronged as a result of my sexual addiction. I feel like Saddam Hussein trying to pick out individual Kurds.'[56] In fact Brand made the career value of the rehab experience very clear by claiming that he wrote his daily diary 'in the sort of style which suggests I knew that a couple of years later I'd be reading it out in front of a live audience (which I did when I did a stand-up show called "Better Now") and a couple of years after that transcribing it into my autobiography'.[57] The outcome was that when Brand embarked on the book-signing tour for the memoir that contained details of his sex addiction, he seized on it as an opportunity for further sexual excess:

> I am not proud of the morality employed during this indulgent time but one has to marvel at the efficiency. This operation travelled all over the world and effortlessly assimilated into any culture it encountered, New York, Sydney, Hull – it was all the same: wristbands issued, rooms filled with women in their dozens, day after day...it was a one-man, multi-woman sex epidemic.[58]

Brand's memoirs are an interesting mix of admissions of self-destruction via drugs and sex, and irreverent satire about the notion of addiction to the latter. Although he would admit to a degree of self-diagnosis of sex addiction, his main problem was with drug abuse, the sexual excess usually part and parcel of that. Like Springfield, he also had a history of depression and self-harm.[59] His management convinced him to enter rehab in the first place as they saw his career (or, rather, earning capacity) threatened, so one takes his signing of a celibacy contract and its admissions of powerlessness over sexual behaviour with a grain of salt; especially when he later tells us that 'To this day, I feel a fierce warmth for women that have the same disregard for the social conventions of sexual protocol as I do.'[60] Nonetheless, the linkage between celebrity and sex addiction (however spurious) has been an important means of publicizing the concept. So too have the memoirs of non-celebrity sex addicts.

There has been a steady increase in the publication of non-celebrity memoirs. Sex addiction is not just for celebrities – handy though that has been for publicity – and not just for those who can afford fancy treatment facilities. These sex addiction memoirs have ranged from the self-published (sometimes illiterate) ramblings of first-time authors to the well-written accounts of accomplished (or at least previously published) novelists and journalists.[61] The memoirs represent the rearguard of the sex addiction movement and are part of what Trysh Travis has called 'the territory of recovery-infused popular culture'.[62] Anyone can buy a memoir or use a workbook and spread the word. And given the estimate that at least 10 per cent of Americans are sex addicts and the role of their codependent spouses (where they have them) in 'enabling' the 'disease', then the potential market is huge. The dominance of Twelve-Step programmes in the addiction industry has worked in favour of a proliferation of people willing to tell their stories: Step 12 involves an obligation that 'Having had a spiritual awakening as the result of these steps, we tried to carry this message to other sex addicts and to practice these principles in our lives.'[63] Training to become a therapist or writing a memoir can be seen as fulfilling part of this duty.

The non-celebrity chronicles are more than just personal accounts made public in the spirit of altruism; they are harnessed to another machine – the therapy industry. While they might start as individual confessions with redemption as the goal, they actually function (as do the vignettes in more official texts) as unofficial, self-help guides to others, 'cautionary tales of sexual peril' in the service of 'healthy sexuality', and evangelical voices of sex addiction discourse.[64] Clearly written after experiencing Twelve-Step programmes for sex addiction, these books have adopted the language of addictionology, associating sex with the pursuit of the next 'high' or 'fix', 'that love-heroin sex-saturated hit'.[65] 'The amazing thing is how any addict ever stops using before he dies. The substance I used was human beings'; Michael Ryan's memoir is unambiguous, his framework is clear, 'I took out a yellow pad and wrote down what they call in twelve-step programs for sex addiction "bottom-line behavior" – behavior driven by shame and producing shame.'[66] 'Thanks to a twelve-step program for love junkies, I have stayed clear of obsessive harmful relationships for more than two years', wrote Rachel Resnick at the start of an account of those very relationships.[67] Kelly Boykin claimed sex as her drug, 'just as meth is to an addict'.[68] Jake Porter made a similar assertion: as 'marijuana is the gateway to narcotics...porn is the gateway to sex addiction...After I started watching X-rated videos, looking at an issue of *Playboy* was like a heroin junkie smoking a joint.'[69] L. J. Schwartz compared his sex addiction with alcoholism: 'I would have traded my disease for theirs. They only had to stop drinking. I had the "keeper", the ultimate disease.'[70] (Tim Robbins's character espouses the same sentiment in the film *Thanks for Sharing*, which we discussed in the previous chapter, and it is a sentiment directly from the sex addiction literature.) As Helen Keane has argued, this strategy of analogizing sex addiction with alcoholism and drug addiction represented a bold claim for its existence as a biological disorder, but the language of the memoirs, like the therapists' texts, 'demonstrates a move back to a metaphorical level of meaning'.[71]

As well as employing the language of addictionology many of the memoirs encourage an interactive and intertextual dimension in the service of therapy. Sue William Silverman's memoir morphed continuously with the addiction workbooks she was given in therapy; we (the reader) attend Sex Addicts Anonymous meetings with her, and she includes a copy of a questionnaire aimed to determine whether the 'user' is a sex addict.[72] The referential mode continued with *The Sex Addiction Workbook* (2003) and other therapeutic texts promoting Silverman's work.[73] After terminating her marriage to a sex addict, Emma Dawson gained degrees in social work and published her memoir *My Secret Life with a Sex Addict* (2001), which doubled as a therapeutic text, with exercises at the end of each chapter and textbook discussions peppered throughout.[74] Yant, also the wife of a sex addict, used her memoir to perform a wider purpose – to help identify the 'co-addict'. 'Do you sometimes look at other families, imagine that they are "normal", and wish your relationship could be happy like theirs?', 'Do you withdraw emotionally, have your mind on other things during sex, or feel empty afterwards?', she asked. These leading questions were then coupled with material taken from her research into addiction, referencing websites, their questionnaires and other intertextual interludes.[75] Peter Pelullo recounted and paraphrased his visits to specialists and therapists, and quoted directly from brochures on addiction and child abuse.[76]

The memoirs might be windows into the subjectivities of sex addicts but they have provided anything but clarity in defining sex addiction as a concept. Cheever's memoir doubled as a research text. She interviewed specialists in the field, and clearly hoped to deliver insight into sex addiction alongside her own personal revelations. Yet she did not really seem to be a sex addict and nor did she offer any meaningful definition of the 'disorder'. Cheever embraced the addictionologist's tendency to detect addicts everywhere: 'Every day there are stories about sex and love addiction in the newspaper, but they are rarely reported that way.'[77] Her famous father, the writer John Cheever, was, of course, retrospectively (and posthumously) classified as a sex addict.[78]

The sheer variety of sexual behaviours deemed problematic in the memoirs represents the conceptual vagaries and diagnostic inclusivity inherent in the idea of sex addiction, as well as its growing influence on the public imagination. They have ranged from tales of adolescent 'promiscuity', a previously undersexed serviceman's anxiety over his use of prostitutes, authors with high sex drives and relationship breakdowns, right through to the more extreme and unsettling memoirs of childhood sexual abuse that, it was claimed, led to later years spent in compulsive sexual behaviour.[79] Kelly Boykin was molested by her father from the age of three and found herself pondering whether she was a sex addict given her pronounced enjoyment of casual sex in adulthood. Although she decided she was a sex addict '*because* of the abuse', she also asked, less certainly, 'I'm a full-grown adult. Shouldn't I have the freedom to make those choices without feeling like I'm losing a battle? Maybe I'm just not clear in my definition of sex addict versus consensual sex between willing partners.'[80]

Interestingly, of the more than thirty accounts covered here, some cannot strictly be called sex addiction memoirs because their authors include no such admission or employment of the label. Their sexual behaviour has been deemed of interest by those behind the workings of search engines or book classification/retail websites for those seeking 'sex addiction memoirs' because it involved explicit and usually casual acts or personal anxieties (both sexual and non-sexual), or because their authors had other addictions (and lots of sex!).[81] Krissy Kneen's erotic memoir covered her bisexuality, obsessive sexual thoughts, casual sexual encounters, crushes, love of Internet porn and frequent masturbation. It was a largely positive account of her sexual self, not a diatribe against disorder or problems with self-control. When her friend called her a sex addict – the only time in the entire work that this was mentioned – she was somewhat at a loss: 'I feel myself unpicked; and when I am seamless there is nothing left of me but sex. I have been pathologized.'[82] But Kneen's insight into this process has been the exception. 'In the threatening world constituted by sex addiction texts', Keane has argued, 'sexual experimentation and exploration outside monogamous coupledom is perilous, even lethal, and a search for sexual excitement can only lead to heartbreak, shame, and sickness'.[83]

Unlike many claimed medical disorders, sex addiction has self-diagnosis as an important strand. Many sex addicts have been either self-defined or labelled as such by offended partners or loved ones. Ricki Lake's feature on female sex addicts began each section with the worried complaint of a friend or family member ('My daughter's a sex addict and I am very

afraid for her life'). That was the format: first the concerned
loved one, then the alleged sex addict.[84] In his memoir Ryan
Capitol recommended reading books by Patrick Carnes 'for
any of those people who are having the feelings of a significant other who is controlling in bed, or if that same person
spends more time alone than with others'.[85]

> Does your partner spend an inordinate amount of time think-
> ing about sex? Has your relationship been damaged by his
> sexual activities? Are there times when his sexual urges,
> thoughts or images seem to control him? If so, he – or she –
> may not be merely an untrustworthy cad but an addict in need
> of psychiatric help.

That was the opening of an article in Britain's newspaper *The
Guardian* in 2003, which ended with links to sex addiction
treatment organizations and therapists.[86]

Even a superficial glance at the various published case
studies of claimed sex addiction indicates that amateur diagnosis has been a significant factor in this blurred area between
medicine and popular culture. When the journalist Laura
Barnett asked recovering 'sex addicts' about the film *Shame*
there was little hesitation in their diagnoses. 'The film never
states directly that it's about *sex* addiction, but it very clearly
is', said Richard, aged 56, who had attended SAA for five
years. 'The film's title is incredibly accurate. I've struggled
with sex addiction for many years; I finally sought help last
year, and now I have a huge sense of shame about the things
I've done', stated Stephen, aged 61. Sarah, aged 38, another
member of SAA, thought that there were several sex addicts
in the film. Brandon's sister Sissy was 'pretty much a classic
sex addict'. 'Then there are the women Brandon sleeps with:
I'm not saying they're all sex addicts, but none of them is
displaying healthy sexual behaviour.'[87]

Many of the examples given by the clinical psychologist
Ley in his critique of sex addiction refer to relatives – hus-
bands, wives, a mother – who first raised the possibility that
their loved one's perceived, problematic sexual practices were
those of a sex addict.[88] Hence Tom's wife Christie's response
to his homosexual cruising at adult bookstores: 'That's addiction, right? He's addicted to this, to going to these creepy

places and having sex.'[89] Thus Jason's second wife's procla-
mation that he 'was a sex addict', and Cheryl's husband Phil's
anxiety 'that her infidelity was sign of sex addiction'.[90]

As noted in Chapter 3, sex addiction has included partners
as well as addicts and has thus generated another literature
of guides for co-addicts, some of which have been published
by Carnes's Gentle Path Press.[91] The commercial potential of
sex addiction has increased with its therapeutic extension to
include the partners (and families) of sex addicts. There are
no innocent bystanders in the sex addiction business, rather
codependents, enablers, or victims of post-traumatic stress.
The logic is that 'two sick people' find each other – the sex
addict and the co-addict – and that they need separate therapy
for their own diseases. Then, because there is no cure for their
disease, 'the best he or she can hope for is remission. Remission, as with cancer, is achieved when there are no longer any
relapses.'[92] Dawson's memoir *My Life with a Sex Addict*
'provide[s] special focus on the plight of the partner of the
sexual addict' and helps readers ascertain whether they too
may be 'collaborating in an emotionally abusive relationship
with a sex addict'.[93] Such enabling or 'collaboration' includes
'high stress in the home', 'denying there is anything wrong',
'increasing financial problems', 'alibis, excuses, and justification to others' and 'unusual dreams'.[94] Yant also 'learned' at
couples' counselling sessions (following her husband's admission of sex addiction) 'that I was responding as a classic
co-sex addict'.[95]

Although therapists Barbara Steffens and Marsha Means
have critiqued the notion of the co-addict and called for a
'paradigm shift' in the labelling of the addict's partner, they
did not question the seriousness of sex addiction and have
endorsed both the efficacy of the Twelve-Step programme and
the usual therapy options. For them, the suffering of the
spouses of addicts was best treated as a form of post-traumatic
stress disorder (PTSD).[96] This was what Maurita Corcoran
was diagnosed with. She found it difficult to deal with her
anger after discovering her husband had cheated on her
during the entirety of their fourteen-year marriage and – at
the insistence of her husband (!!) and therapist – began a
serious journey of 'spiritual and emotional recovery'. This
saw her attending AA meetings for spouses (there were no

SA meetings in her area or even in existence that she was aware of) two or three times a week for the first three years of her recovery, attending at least two expensive in-treatment programmes, and joining eight retreats.[97] When she attended The Meadows treatment facility for a five-week, in-patient programme she found herself subjected to drug and blood tests, and was admitted to their 'acute care' division.[98] Whether as co-addiction or PTSD, what these approaches have in common is their insistence on the reality of the sexual disorder being experienced. Whether suffering from co-addiction or stress, partners find themselves requiring psychological and physical help. And whatever the model, the sex addiction therapy industry is there to administer that help.

Historians may be sceptical, but a perceived condition, once located by those who believe in its aetiology and the possibility of its cure, can then be treated by experts who also believe in its existence. As Stephen B. Levine has expressed it, 'Whatever the concerns about the validity of the concept of sexual addiction, the diagnosis is well rooted in the public's mind and has seeming clarity for individuals and institutions that provide treatment.' The concept, therefore, was 'useful'.[99] A more critical response to the phenomenon might be to think in terms of what Robert Aronowitz has termed 'feedback loops between consumers and producers'. Once a type of behaviour was assessed as a medical problem in a consumer society, it could unleash highly profitable 'consumer-oriented health restoring responses'. 'These responses', wrote Aronowitz, 'have their own economy shaped by the perceived needs of the addicted as well as the actions of the promoters of different programs, health care professionals, and third party payers'.[100] Aronowitz was referring to the more general framing of addiction as a health problem, and had in mind video-poker addiction, but sex addiction has drawn on sexual consumerism as well as medical consumerism – a potent combination.

Keane (with Michel Foucault in mind) has commented perceptively on the inner contradictions of sex addiction. It is a discourse that speaks sex while condemning so many aspects of that sex. 'Rather than repressing sexual expression...sex addiction encourages individuals to develop a habit of obsessive attentiveness to their sexual desires.'[101] 'Part of my journey to healing was through journaling', wrote Boykin in her memoir *Confessions of a Sex Addict*; 'Because I had already labeled myself a sex addict, I initially wrote about the sex act, itself. I guess I thought it was "cool" to write about all the sex I was having.'[102] Yet, as Keane has argued, the concern has been with surface appearances and shallow meanings – there was no attempt to engage with the deeper connotations of sexual desire and interaction. Boykin attempted to deconstruct the sex addict identity she had taken for herself: 'I realized that the labels we put on ourselves are actually self-fulfilling prophecies and only serve to perpetuate the negative thoughts we all carry around. I've been calling myself a sex addict because I say I'm addicted to sex.'[103] But she failed to question classic addictionology: 'In actuality, I'm addicted to the euphoric responses I get *during* sex. It's not the act alone, it's the release of endorphins that fuels me. I like the "happy rush" I get. That's the "drug" I'm addicted to.'[104] In Keane's words, 'Sexual behavior is reduced to a cipher.'[105]

However, there is another side to the 'obsessive attentive-ness' to sexual detail that Keane noted. The non-celebrity memoirs offer something quite at odds with their central premise of eliciting sympathy and offering hope and redemp-tion for those suffering the disorder of sex addiction: porno-graphic prose almost as explicit as anything on the market.[106] These sexual stories dwell on the sexual exploits that led their authors to seek therapy in the first place. Ryan's elegant *Secret Life* contains descriptions of what he wanted to do to a friend's 15-year-old daughter, disturbing details of his molestation at the age of five, his longing for his sister's friend Sharon, his secret touching of a classmate Sheila, sex in the toilet with Sally, and persistent paperboy fantasies.[107] Boykin, also a victim of childhood sexual abuse, repeatedly described the beauty of a lover's penis, revealed to the reader (and an undisclosed number of other 'readers' via her online diary) when she was 'horny as hell' – 'I have to fight the urge to fuck almost anyone with a dick' – and then thanked those readers 'who sent me offers…much appreciated'.[108] Res-nick's less than elegant *Love Junkie* – 'when the second Magnum condom breaks' – recounted numerous sexual fantasies, rough sex during menstruation, urolagnia and group sex.[109] Even her first sex addiction meeting was sexualized; she became fixated on one of the men in the programme and had sex with a woman whom she met in a 'support group for love junkies' – which occasioned further descriptions of lesbian sex.[110] (Susan Cheever said such behaviour was known as 'thirteenth-stepping': experienced addicts taking advantage of newcomers to take them beyond the Twelve Steps.[111]) Silverman's *Love Sick* lured the reader through adulterous hotel-room encounters, sex with the unnamed driver of a red Corvette, and her continuing sexual obsession with an ancillary staff member at the addiction clinic.[112] The sex addict's memoir relives the sexual history that led them to the very therapy and redemption that the memoir itself is supposed to serve. Jesse Fink said that his memoir was a 'cautionary tale of how many men use online-dating sites as vagina catalogues'.[113] Fink, a published journalist and 'undiagnosed sex addict', told a sad tale of love lost and the search to find it again, but like the memoirists cited earlier filled his account with graphic sexual descriptions.[114] He lost count of the number of women he had sex with: 'It all went by so fast', it was 'a zoetrope of female body parts'.[115]

Although many (but not all) of the memoirs have started from some sort of trauma or abuse, their tendency to explicit retellings of sexual encounters crosses into pornographic territory, or perhaps more accurately, shows us the degree to which sex and pornography have become mainstreamed in Western culture. These sexual representations are also part of what Travis has aptly called the 'promiscuous print culture' that has propelled 'recovery' into becoming a mainstream commodity.[116]

Yet the irony of sex addiction's place in the world of commercial sex seems lost on the purveyors of the various sex addiction programmes. 'Spending your money on sex supports the sex industry...The sex industry may be the largest money empire in the world. Your contributions are making it even richer and more powerful', opined the authors of *The Sex Addiction Workbook* (2003); 'You are making prostitutes and strippers out of people who could and would do something else for a living if they had a reasonable choice. You are paying people to risk their health so you can get some sexual kicks.'[117] They do not mention their role in the empire. Addiction rehabilitation can cost from $7,500 to $120,000 a month depending on the quality of the amenities.[118] Celebrity is a conscious marketing tool for 'High Profile and Celebrity Rehab Centers': Cirque Lodge in Utah (Kirsten Dunst and Lindsay Lohan), Passages in Malibu (David Hasselhoff and Stephen Baldwin), Crossroads in Antigua (Colin Farrell and Britney Spears).

> When management circumstances are deterring you or someone close to you from getting care for a problem with substance abuse or behavioral addiction, executive rehabilitation treatments will be invaluable. By pairing excellent drug abuse and behavioral addiction treatments with the freedom of occasional computer and mobile access, a businessman or woman can receive assistance while keeping relatively 'plugged in'.
>
> Frequently, modern substance abuse and behavioral addiction centers provide the excellent amenities one would only expect to find in exquisite hotels, with your enjoyment and well-being being the biggest goals. From fine linens and gym facilities to private rooms and 5-star chef-prepared meals, you can get the top-rated drug abuse and behavioral addiction treatment for yourself or someone close to you while enjoying the surroundings. If you need a hand in searching for the best-rated luxury treatment for celebrities and other high-profile types, dial our no-charge helpline as soon as you're able.[119]

Tiger Woods is said to have spent £40,000 on his six-week sex addiction treatment, and it can cost several thousand dollars just to be assessed and 'evaluated' at Pine Grove in Mississippi, where he was treated.[120] Wonderland, the Hollywood drug and alcohol addiction treatment centre for celebrities that also arranges therapy for sexual addiction, charged $48,000 and $58,000 per month respectively for shared and single rooms in 2008 when the boxer Tyson was a client.[121] Ley has demonstrated the large amounts of money involved in sex addiction treatment, seminars, workshops and various self-help resources.[122]

Sex addiction, then, is the sexual codependent of the sexualized society that its supposed sufferers so vociferously denounce. It is no coincidence that in the early days of the Sexual Addiction Self Test potential testees had to run a web-page gauntlet between links to pornography sites. As one sex addictionologist put it rather primly, 'one can only imagine the results of an Internet search when the keywords cybersex *and addiction* are entered... [m]any of the hits were contrary to promoting recovery'.[123] Sex and shame have such an endur-ing relationship that it was easy to popularize the concept of sex addiction. As a concept characterized by certain moral definitions of 'normal' sexual behaviour, there are the emo-tional concomitants of guilt and shame for those who trans-gress those confines. And we want to hear and read about sex, especially its excesses and 'disorders': redemption for some and titillation for others. Like the paradox of pornog-raphy – where condemnation is to represent repeatedly the subject of denunciation – treating these 'problems' is to par-ticipate in the vilified 'pornographication' of society, referred to earlier, of which sexual addiction is an integral part.[124] The financial incentives of both the therapy industry and the wider sexualization of Western culture have fed into and continue to feed the growth of sex addiction as a construct. Billions of dollars are spent on the representation of sex and emphasis on sex as pleasurable to human experience, and this is refracted in the millions spent on creating and treating the disorders allegedly wrought by this experience. The psycho-therapist Marty Klein, a long-term critic of the concept of sex addiction, has referred to the voyeurism surrounding the lives of alleged celebrity sex addicts and the confessions of 'recov-ering sex addicts' as 'Our Addiction to Tiger Woods' "Sex Addiction".'[125] We all like sexual stories.

Chapter 6
Diagnostic Disorder

In thirty-one years as a sex therapist, marriage counselor, and psychotherapist, I've never seen sex addiction. I've heard about virtually every sexual variation, obsession, fantasy, trauma, and involvement with sex workers, but I've never seen sex addiction.
Marty Klein, 2012[1]

At early as 1985 a group of prescient academics, including the famous Thomas Szasz, author of *The Myth of Mental Illness* (1960) and *The Manufacture of Madness* (1970), questioned television's uncritical embrace of addictionology. Their targets were the media forms discussed earlier in this book: 'Any television viewer who makes a habit of watching morning news shows, talk shows, and news-magazine shows is bound to think we are a country suffering an epidemic of psychiatric "illnesses".' The communications scholar, professor of legal studies and professor of psychiatry continued, 'This year viewers of such shows have witnessed a seemingly endless parade of psychiatric experts informing us about "compulsive gambling", "eating disorders", "anxiety disease" and even jogging, working, shopping and sex "compulsions" and "addictions". And so it goes, on and on.'[2] Though they might have been surprised how long it would go on and on, they had located the very symbiosis between the popular and the academic that is the subject of this book. Richard Vatz, Lee

Weinberg and Szasz were critiquing television presenters' lack of critique, the manner in which they never questioned the claims of the supposed 'experts' who provided them with their visual and sound bites. Their specific targets included the anchors Mike Wallace and Barbara Walters, and Phil Donahue's special on sex addiction in his programme *Donahue* where the emerging expert Patrick Carnes remained unchallenged with his claims for the new 'illness'. As they wrote of the talk show host, 'Phil Donahue has endeared himself to the American public with his style of cutting through to the heart of controversial issues, but his hard-nosed skepticism stops at the door of psychiatric disorders.'[3]

There is certainly no perceptible gap between popular perceptions of sex addiction and more learned discourse, for the concept has proven influential in both spheres. Szasz and his colleagues were concerned that scholarly debate was not reflected in televisual discourse and that the latter never interrogated the former. But what is actually more remarkable is the success and acceptance of 'sex addiction' at the academic level, where, we will argue, the concept has been received almost as unquestioningly as it has been in the television of Szasz's complaint.

The academic impact is clear. A 2010 survey in the *Journal of Sex & Marital Therapy*, using the database PsycINFO, located over 700 research and clinical articles on sex addiction and its variants, compared to just over 300 in a literature search a decade earlier.[4] A search of the same database in early 2014, arranged by the authors of this book, brought the total to nearly 2,000 records.[5] This is a cumulative record. If the same database is used to plot chronologically rather than by accumulation the upward trajectory is compelling. The number of academic publications using the terms has risen yearly from just 2 in 1960 to nearly 140 in 2013 (see Figure 10).

Yet what is fascinating about this literature is how reluctant investigators have been to question the veracity of the actual syndrome when their own investigations beg for such a challenge. Two clinical psychologists who applied a widely used mental health test to a group of patients seeking help for hypersexual behaviour found neither evidence of 'addictive tendencies' nor that they were particularly obsessive or

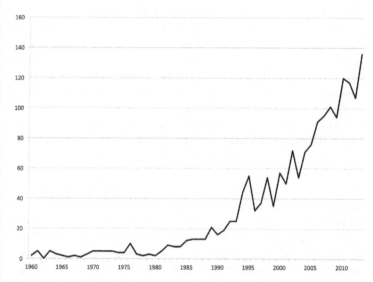

Figure 10 PsycINFO terms for sex addiction publications, 1960–2013.

compulsive. However, their conclusions were that 'hyper-sexual patients are a diverse group of individuals'.[6] Hyper-sexuality survived its lack of addictiveness, obsession or compulsiveness! As we will see, a New Zealand survey questioned the frequency of compulsive sexual behaviour but never considered its status as a concept: the article's keywords include 'sexual addiction' and 'hypersexuality'.[7]

There has been no shortage of tools of assessment of sexual compulsivity, and we have touched on some already. The *Journal of Sex & Marital Therapy* study by Joshua Hook and his team reviewed nearly twenty such measurements, both self-reporting and clinical assessing: Cognitive and Behavioral Outcomes of Sexual Behavior Scale; Compulsive Sexual Behavior Consequences Scale; Compulsive Sexual Behavior Inventory; Diagnostic Interview for Sexual Compulsivity; Garos Sexual Behavior Index; Internet Screening Test; Perceived Sexual Control Scale; Sex Addicts Anonymous Questionnaire; Sexual Addiction Scale; Sexual Addiction Screening Test (including versions for women and gay men); Sexual Compulsivity Scale; Sexual Dependency Inventory; Sexual Outlet Inventory; Sexual Symptom Assessment Scale; and the

Yale-Brown Obsessive Compulsive Scale – Compulsive Sexual Behavior.[8] We could add the Arizona Sexual Experience Scale, the Sexual Risk Behavior Scale, the Hypersexual Behavior Inventory, the Opportunity, Attachment, and Trauma Model for Sex Addiction, and the Hypersexual Disorder Screening Inventory.[9] More recently, Carnes and his colleagues have included (the perhaps aptly named) PATHOS, a simplified version of the Sexual Addiction Screening Test (SAST) and SAST Revised (SAST-R), which has raised the scary possibility of identifying a potential sex addict in less than a minute.[10] A revised assessment of tests by some of those involved in the original Hook study brought the tally of measurements of hypersexual sex to a total of 32, some of which (4) were clinical interviews but most self-reports or assessments in the form of tests or scales. This added the Cyberporn Compulsivity Scale, Cyber-Pornography Use Inventory, Hypersexual Behavior Consequences Scale, Hypersexual Disorder Diagnostic Clinical Interview, Hypersexual Disorder Questionnaire, Internet Addiction Test – Sex, Minnesota Impulse Control Inventory Questionnaire – Sexual Behavior Module, Multidimensional Sexuality Questionnaire, Pornography Consumption Effects Scale, Primary Appraisal Measure – Compulsive Sexual Behavior, and the Sexual Sensation Seeking Scale.[11] And if we include calculations against other psychiatric tests in efforts to check the viability of the original measurement, the picture becomes even more complicated, with the Beck Depression Inventory, Trait Anxiety Scale, Obsessive–Compulsive Scale, Borderline Personality Scale, Symptom Checklist-90-Revised (SCL-90-R), Mini International Neuropsychiatric Interview, NEO Personality Inventory-Revised, Freiburg Mindfulness Inventory, Maladaptive Cognitions About Sex Scale (MCAS), Shame Inventory (SI), Self-Rumination Scale (SRS), and the Self-Compassion Scale-Short Form (SCS).[12]

But how effective are these tests? It is significant that nearly 20 per cent of a sample of self-identified German sex addicts who were administered SAST-R did not qualify as sex addicts, and that among the addicts who did not report any distress at their condition (25 per cent) almost 60 per cent nonetheless met the required test score for sexual addiction. It seems an unreliable instrument for measuring an uncertain illness.[13]

The various apparatuses form an impressive medico-scientific façade. Nevertheless, the impression given, shared by those *Journal of Sex & Marital Therapy* reviewers, was of a field where a great deal of time has been devoted to measuring an assumed problem without bothering to interrogate the nature, or even the existence, of that perceived disorder. The comprehensive assessment of the various measurements of hypersexual disorder by Stephanie Womack, Hook and others was critical of their overreliance on the subjective character of the self-assessments: 'They relied on the participant to define "excessive" hypersexual thoughts, urges, and behaviors, and therefore may not accurately reflect the level of hypersexual behavior.'[14] The researchers noted the variety of definitions, the 'sometimes idiosyncratic' conceptualizations and the 'formative stage' of research on what was claimed as a syndrome.[15] They never questioned the viability of the disorder itself.

It is an unexamined maxim of sex addiction folklore that addictions live in groups. Susan Cheever's muddled memoir of sex addiction drew constantly on alcohol addiction (she was an alcoholic too) but also referred to 'the way different addictions pair with and nestle inside each other', citing money, eating and shopping disorders, as well as addiction to sex, drugs and alcohol.[16] 'I'm an alcoholic, an addict', Jennifer Ketcham began her talk at the Pasadena Recovery Center in 2012; 'I am into anything you put in front of me, whether it's human, whether it's substance.'[17] L. J. Schwartz summed himself up at the end of his memoir of sex addiction: 'I'm an ADHD [Attention Deficit Hyperactivity Disorder] adult, I have bipolar disorder, and to top it off, I'm BPD [Borderline Personality Disorder].' 'Not to take anything away from my SAA [Sex Addicts Anonymous] program. The plain, true fact is I am a sex addict.'[18] The theme is there in the popular guidebooks too. *Cybersex Unplugged* (2011), a newer workbook for cybersex addicts, moved from sexual compulsivity to other dependencies – chemical, eating, gambling, spending and working.[19] Jerome Levin, a New York psychotherapist whose practice went from treating substance abuse to treating sexual addiction, has referred, perhaps unsurprisingly, to 'a condition called *polyaddiction* or *cross-addiction*' (his emphasis), proclaiming confidently – though without evidence or specificity – that 'Of all the known people considered to be sex addicts, about 42 percent are cross-addicted to drugs and alcohol and many others are cross-addicted to food, spending, work, or gambling.'[20] A critic of the concept of sex addiction, David Ley, has summarized the situation: 'The sex addictionologists are right in a sense. We do live in an "addictive culture". The addiction lies in our society's desire to label problematic behaviors as addictive and compulsive.'[21]

Such linkages have been claimed at a less populist level as well. Early research on sex addiction detected comorbidity – hardly surprising given a culture that finds disorder everywhere. A 1990s Iowa study of thirty-six people (mostly male) who self-identified as sexually compulsive but who were not actually in treatment for their condition found that over 80 per cent of them tested for another psychiatric disorder: mood, anxiety, substance use, eating or childhood conduct disorder.[22] Nurses have long been told that other addictions may provide a clue to hidden hypersexuality. An article in *Nurse Practitioner* told primary health providers to remain alert: 'A personal history of compulsive behavior, alcohol or substance abuse, overeating or gambling are significant since co-existing addictions are common.'[23] It is over ten years since American psychiatric nurses were advised to assess substance abusers for sex addiction when presenting for treatment because 'sexual addiction often coexists with substance addiction'.[24] But a 2011 article in the journal *Evaluation & the Health Professions* explicitly linked sex addiction with tobacco, alcohol, illicit drugs, eating, gambling, Internet, love, exercise, work and shopping addictions. (Unsurprisingly, the authors reported that nearly half of the US adult population was likely to suffer from 'maladaptive signs of an addictive disorder over a 12-month period'.)[25] The 'Curbside Consultation' feature in the *American Family Physician* updated its physician readers in 2012 on very similar lines about sex addiction's concurrent disorders.[26]

The comorbidity of mental disorders has become axiomatic in sexual addiction therapy. Eric Griffin-Shelley's early guide stressed both multiple addictions and the likelihood that sufferers of the syndrome would be likely also to experience PTSD (a disorder that we saw had been added to the

DSM in 1980).[27] Far more recently, Martin Kafka's chapter on hypersexuality in a major sexual therapy text established that 'most individuals with these disorders have multiple lifetime comorbid disorders' and then provided case studies demonstrating this clustering:

> Ted's primary DSM-5 psychiatric diagnoses included: attention-deficit/hyperactivity disorder (ADHD), predominantly inattentive type; cannabis use disorder; persistent depressive disorder: late onset, with pure dysthymic syndrome, moderate; fetishistic disorder, nonliving object [an attraction to female lingerie]; other specified disruptive, impulse control, and conduct disorder[:] hypersexual disorder; pornography and masturbation.[28]

This is certainly an example of the turn to mental disorder referred to earlier.

The ever-flexible Carnes has found both a name and a syndrome for these multiple addictions: Addiction Interaction Disorder.[29] Carnes and his co-authors (or rather their staff) assessed over 1,600 patients in residential programmes, presumably at Pine Grove and/or The Meadows, and found multiple addictions (the terms used are theirs): alcoholism, substance abuse, caffeine addiction, compulsive working, high risk behaviour/danger, compulsive spending, nicotine addiction, compulsive violence/raging, addictive athleticism (exercise addiction presumably), compulsive hoarding/saving, compulsive cleaning, compulsive gambling, bulimia/anorexia.[30] Many of these were compound addictions, as the breakdown of numbers in each category was far more than the sample total. The conclusion of the study, self-referenced in a later summary of the syndrome, was

> Multiple addictions are common. Among a sample of 1,603 sex addicts, 69% of heterosexual women, and 80% of homosexual men have a lifetime prevalence of other addictive and abusive behaviors, ranging from minor to serious. In addition, 40% of heterosexual men, 40% of heterosexual women, and 60% of homosexual men engage in sexual acting out while simultaneously [not always literally, surely] involved in other addictive or abusive behaviors such as substance abuse, gambling, or eating disorders.[31]

Leaving aside the fact that these 1,604 (not 1,603) were treated for sexual disorder – sexual anorexia and sexual addiction – and were therefore not all 'sex addicts', the reliance on patient self-presenting and the miscellaneous and inclusive nature of the claimed 'addictions' raises considerable doubt about the viability of these claims for interlinkage. A doubter might also ask whether such widespread behaviour should be defined as normal rather than 'a problem', though it certainly holds out the promise of many, many clients. The pairing of sexual addiction and sexual anorexia as 'manifestations of the same problem', with claims of parallels to bulimia, stretch any conceptual meaning to breaking point – especially since the figures clearly imply that patients included sexual anorexics, sex addicts, and those suffering from both addiction and anorexia as well as all those other compulsions.[32] Carnes and his co-authors have referred to a 'confusion and blurring of issues' during the emergence of any new scientific paradigm.[33] We can certainly agree with that.

So we are already at *diagnostic vagueness*, another of the characteristics of the concept of sex addiction that irked Janice Irvine all those years ago (see our Introduction). We might expect this from the early statements establishing the new disorder. Carnes's *The Sexual Addiction* (1983), a foundational text, certainly slipped from the innocently promiscuous to the violently sexual offending in his concept of 'levels of addiction'. Thus his 'Level One' addictions included masturbation, marital sexual disjunction, heterosexual cruising, 'Centerfolds, Pornography, and Strip Shows', sex with prostitutes and, quote, 'Homosexuality'. His 'Level Two' consisted of exhibitionism, voyeurism, voyeur-exhibitionism and 'Indecent Calls and Liberties' ('Liberties' meaning unsolicited touching). Finally, 'Level Three' comprised child molesting, incest, and 'Rape and Violence' (why 'and Violence' is unclear). Carnes admitted that his levels were arbitrary but held they served to demonstrate the range of 'sexually compulsive behavior'; he reminded the reader that he could have included bestiality, sadomasochism and fetishism, which of course he did with that very mention.[34] The point is that there was no logical progression or linkage between these levels beyond Carnes's structuring. They had nothing in common – not even sex (viz. 'Rape and Violence'). Their very association, the use of the word 'level', connected hetero-sexual promiscuity with rape and child molestation and claimed the gravity of a supposed, shared addiction.

Anne Wilson Schaef, who drew heavily on Carnes, upped the ante still further, adding a fourth level of addiction and invoking, with varying degrees of gravity, 'New Age sexual freedom', autoerotic asphyxia, oral rape of infants, child prostitution rings and stolen children.[35] As Helen Keane has observed, 'A striking aspect of sex addiction is the diverse array of behaviours which are read as symptoms of the one disease.'[36]

That confusion of categories (though none quite as severe as that of Schaef) is common in the handbooks of sex addic-tion. Griffin-Shelley's description of the malady included ref-erence to a fantasizing tennis instructor, a cross-dressing seminarian, anyone practising BDSM ('a somewhat extreme example of the objectification of people that sex and love addicts practice'), incest, paedophilia, a teenager who had had sex with the family maid, a masturbating nun, and the Boston Strangler.[37] Ralph and Marcus Earle treated perpetra-tors and victims of incest and child abuse alongside hetero-sexual wives and church ministers who indulged in multiple casual sex. Though classified under the master category 'sex addiction', what conceptually could they have had in common? Arguably, many of the patients of these family psychologists would have been better off being treated for sexual abuse rather than sex addiction, whether as addicts, co-addicts, victims or victimizers.[38]

The designation 'sex addiction' has become even more inclusive post Carnes's early work. 'What may surprise novice clinicians', an update on the evaluation and treatment of sex addiction observed in the *Journal of Sex & Marital Therapy* in 2014, 'is that sex addiction patients are generally not good at sex…Therefore, in addition to addiction treatment, they need sex and conjoint therapy. Premature ejaculation, erectile dysfunction, anorgasmia, and sexual anorexia (extended periods when the addict has no sexual activity) are common.'[39] We have seen that addiction and anorexia are now routinely paired. Schaef included 'Celibacy as Sexual Addiction'.[40] Sexual compulsivity, *Cybersex Unplugged* explained, can occur 'in the absence of sexual behavior'.[41] One London psychotherapist has reputedly claimed that it was possible to be a monogamous sex addict: 'I've had a case of a man who was sex addicted to his wife. It was a problem because it was depersonalising – he turned her into an object rather than treating her as his wife.'[42]

There are many examples of diagnostic imprecision. We can see it at work in a psychiatric refresher piece in the journal *Directions in Psychiatry* in 2007 that drifted into paedophilia, incest, exhibitionism and studies of sex offenders in its discussion of the definitions and epidemiology of sexual addiction, yet with a conceptual indistinctness that by no means inhibited its suggestions for treatment.[43]

Another vivid instance occurs in the interview of Paula Hall, author of *Understanding and Treating Sex Addiction* (2012), that concludes with a list of her warning signs of those at risk of sex addiction. Feeling isolated as a teenager, hidden family issues, lack of adequate role models, controlling parents, treating sex as something shameful, and early exposure to sexuality; these are factors that could apply to just about anyone in any young population.[44] Statements such as 'it's known that early alcohol use changes the chemistry of the brain in ways that make alcoholism more likely, and it's possible that something similar could happen to a brain that is exposed to sexual images and behavior before it is ready to react to them' are too intellectually questionable even to warrant comment.[45] Similarly the reported claim by a sex addict that he had his addiction under control because he visited sex workers (the focus of his problem) but no longer had sex with them: 'I act it out by going to some dodgy place – but when I'm offered a hand job or whatever, I leave without going through with it…I get the sense of shame, but I don't participate in the sex act.' By what convoluted logic is this 'under control'?[46]

As we will see, sex addiction's search for acceptance has continued. But it has to be said that some of the published studies seem unlikely to advance this quest for professional endorsement. For example, the participants in two studies of the roles of shame and guilt in hypersexuality were users of Candeo, an online treatment programme for pornography use and masturbation, and 40–50 per cent of these users were Mormons: hardly a representative cross-section of society.[47]

The research conclusion of one of these studies that there is a 'significant' relationship between 'shame-proneness and hypersexuality' and that 'shame reduction and resolution is essential in remediating patterns of hypersexuality' does not indicate a very high level of analytical sophistication.[48] We are perplexed how the recruitment of gay and bisexual New York males with perceived compulsive sexual behaviour avoided 'self-labelling' by asking them 'Is your sex life spinning out of control? Is sex interfering with your life? Are sexual thoughts getting in the way?' How was that any different to posting 'Are You a Sex Addict?'[49] How, really, is knowledge advanced by the research finding that the triggers for sexual compulsivity in gay men include sex clubs, bars, gym steam rooms, attractive males, crystal meth, cocaine and pornography?[50] How viable is research into the role of the female partner in the reinforcement of male heterosexual sex addiction that surveys the male addicts rather than their female 'co-addicts', the actual subject of the project? Whether the co-addict nurtured or punished her partner's hypersexuality is seen purely through the perception of the addict.[51]

There are also the trademark problems of measurement. Why is the indicator of compulsivity set at 11 hours (or more) per week of reported online sexual activity?[52] Then there is the issue of the actual available data – findings at variance with the significance accorded to the perceived problem. A survey made available on the MSNBC website in 1998 actually showed how uncommon the problem of compulsivity was, even using the sexual addiction scales of measurement. Only 5 per cent of the nearly 10,000 people surveyed were defined as sexually compulsive; a mere 1 per cent were cybersex compulsive (that is, scoring high on the sexual compulsivity scale and spending more than 11 hours per week on Internet sex). And yet the overall import of the study was to stress the problem of online sexual compulsivity.[53] If 26 per cent of those receiving treatment for sexually transmitted infections in a Milwaukee health clinic stated that their desire to have sex disrupted their daily life, is that a high or a low percentage? The authors of that study saw it as an indication of sexual compulsivity.[54] Does the fact that 29 per cent of them felt that their sexual feelings were stronger than they were indicate a link between sexually transmitted infections and sexual addiction (compulsivity)?[55] And if the sexual compulsives are separated from the non-sexual compulsives in the sample, does the finding that 40 per cent of the former engaged in casual sex with one-time partners compared to the latter's 30 per cent really indicate a significant difference in sexual practice?[56] Another study of sexual compulsivity among New York gay men, lesbians and bisexual men and women claimed significance in the finding that 46 per cent of sexually compulsive men were likely to use alcohol and 39 per cent drugs with sex, compared to 39 and 32 per cent respectively for those deemed non-sexually compulsive.[57] Are the differences really indicative of a significant association between alcohol, drug use and sexually addictive behaviour? Are the sexually compulsive 'significantly more likely than the non-sexually compulsive to report engaging in the use of alcohol...and drug use with sex', which was what the authors of the study claimed?[58]

It is remarkable how concepts are clung to in the face of diagnostic dissolution. 'Research into CSB [compulsive sexual behaviour] is hindered by the lack of a generally accepted definition and reliable and valid assessment tools', wrote the authors of a paper in *Psychiatric Clinics of North America*. 'Despite these limitations, evidence indicates that CSB is relatively common in the general adult population, causes substantial personal distress, and is a source of significant psychosocial disability.'[59] A 2013 article discussing the link between compulsive sexual behaviour and HIV concluded:

> It is likely that the syndrome of CSB has a variety of different and overlapping underlying mechanisms and etiologies. That is why the term *impulsive/compulsive sexual behavior (ICSB)* might be better suited to describe this syndrome...At this point and because of its descriptive nature, this term leaves open the possibility of multiple pathological pathways and treatments...some individuals may have more problems with impulsive control, others anxiety-reduction mechanisms, others affect regulation, and still others may have more sensation-seeking dysregulation. A number of people suffering from CSB may have a number of overlapping mechanisms driving their behavior.[60]

How is this even remotely useful in understanding HIV and unprotected sex in at-risk communities? What possible logical, diagnostic coherence does ICSB have? What does the statement even mean beyond the tautological?

For all the vast literature referred to earlier, there seems little evidence either of theoretical refinement or of advances in the collection of the results of empirical research – what one scholarly article termed 'many conceptions, minimal data'.[61] A UK academic who surveyed the work on cybersex in 2001, though sympathetic to the concept of Internet sex addiction, conceded both that the empirical evidence for its existence was weak and that the 'field is still in conceptual crisis'.[62] Other academic surveys, similarly unquestioning of the actual existence of their subject, have also noted conceptual flaws. Hence Hook and others: 'the field is hampered by weak theory that identifies precisely what sexual addiction is, what its worst symptoms and consequences are, and how to make accurate diagnoses and prognoses'.[63] The Iowa study mentioned earlier concluded that 'Compulsive sexual behavior may be a clinically useful concept, but it describes a heterogeneous group of individuals with substantial psychiatric comorbidity and diverse behavioral problems.'[64] Ariel Kor and his co-authors noted definitional inconsistencies, dearth of large-scale studies and significant 'gaps' in information, including scant attention to neurobiology.[65] Even Rory Reid, whose University of California, Los Angeles, research group has conducted a DSM-5 field trial for hypersexual disorder, has been hesitant on what he has called the 'bigger question...whether the cluster of symptoms we associate with hypersexuality rise to the level of what is necessary to constitute a distinct psychiatric disorder', reporting problems with assessment, lack of knowledge about his subject's prevalence and social composition, absence of serious interrogation of the effectiveness of claimed therapies, and limited progress on the topic in the field of neurobiology – in short, the various limitations of the research in his field.[66]

Less kindly, Lennard Davis, clearly a sceptic, has referred to 'weak theories' and 'impressionistic and confused' diagnoses.[67] Charles Moser has written of 'quasi-scientific muddled thinking'.[68] David Ley has amusingly called it Valley Girl Science.[69] More seriously, Ley and two research colleagues have subjected 'pornography addiction' claims to an extensive literature review and have argued for the intellectual impoverishment of the concept (our words, not theirs). 'The theory and research behind "pornography addiction"', they write, 'is hindered by poor experimental designs, limited methodological rigor, and lack of model specification'.[70]

There are exceptions that it is tempting to say prove the rule. John Bancroft and Zoran Vukadinovic's review of 'out-of-control' sexual behaviour involved theoretical interrogation of the concepts 'sexual addiction' and 'compulsive sexual behaviour' as well as interviews of a small group (thirty-one) of self-defined sex addicts, plotted against a larger control group.[71] They were realistic about the limitations of their sample and outlined hypotheses refuted as well as those confirmed. But they raised the interesting possibility that those with out-of-control sexual behaviour who suffered from either anxiety or depression experienced heightened sexual interest (in contrast to the received opinion that such mood states diminished sexual desire, as indeed they did for the non-sexually compulsive). They posited the reasons for such increases, though we do not need to discuss them here. More significantly, however, Bancroft and Vukadinovic were critical of the 'fashionable concepts' of sex addiction and sexual compulsivity. They did question their subjects' conceptual viability. 'At this time [2004], both concepts are of uncertain scientific value.'[72] Was it merely behaviour plotted on the outer limits of normal behaviour rather than a condition inherently problematic? Was the variety of behaviours coming under its definitional orbit so vast, the range of determinants and patterns so diverse, that simple categorization was impossible?

> While acknowledging the importance to both the individual and society of patterns of sexual behavior that are out of control and have problematic consequences, we think it likely that such patterns are varied in both their etiological determinants and how they are best treated. For that reason, we consider it to be premature to attempt some overriding definition relevant to clinical management until we have a better understanding of the various patterns and their likely determinants. The concepts of compulsivity and addiction may prove to have explanatory value in some cases, but are not

helpful when used as general terms for this class of behavior problem. Until we have a better understanding of the sub-types, we prefer the general descriptive term out of control to describe sexual behavior that is unregulated for a variety of possible reasons.[73]

Predictably, the limitations of diagnosis have carried over into more practical therapy. The therapist Tracy Todd referred to a failure to consider the 'contextual complexities' of indi-vidual complaints in a rush to easy labelling, what he called the 'premature ejaculation of the sex-addict diagnosis'.[74] Hook and Reid, no hypersexual sceptics, reviewed the field of therapy and have produced a damning report of inferior methodology, inconsistent measurements, varied inclusion criteria, and failure to apply the most basic standards of good research involving randomized control trials and independent verification. (Much of their article consisted of explaining best practice.) They concluded that although some of the reported treatment outcomes were 'promising, it is unclear to what extent the treatments were helpful compared to alterna-tive interventions (or in some cases, no intervention at all)'.[75] In truth, although these researchers did not actually say so, there is little or no convincing scientific evidence that any of the treatments have been effective.

There must have been, and will remain, huge variation in local therapies. One study of sex addiction in women rather unhelpfully advised those treating them to take into account an overlap with borderline personality disorder: 'the three groups of sexually addictive/compulsives, sexually addictive/ compulsive borderlines, and nonsexually addictive/compulsive borderlines who sexually act out'.[76] Another advocated a 'good cop, bad cop' approach in therapy: 'Well, I think Bob is about the most hopeless case I have seen...Oh, I don't think it's all that bad.'[77] What do we make of the therapists who proclaimed that sex addiction was a 'spiritual longing to be connected with God', even if their focus was on sexually addicted pastors?[78] Where do we place the art therapy gone amiss when it triggered a patient's foot fetish and he left therapy in search of young women sunning their shoeless feet, or the exhibitionist who sketched a picture of an erect penis and the repeated words 'watch me, watch me' and 'I want to jack off in front of you'?[79] Would not one question the viability of any attempt to treat the homeless for sex addiction, given the gravity of all their other (real) problems?[80] Case studies in the journal *Nurse Practitioner* in 1990, included to advise healthcare workers at the ground level, had suggested 'overtly sexual response during a genital exam (moaning, arching of hips)' and sexual answers to non-sexual questions as hints of 'a compulsive sexual disorder'. Practitioners were advised to look for indirect signs of potential sexual addiction, not just in the addict themselves but in family members: depression, headaches, gastrointestinal problems might be signs of codependency. One wonders whether the 'alert primary care provider' might, in these cases, have been somewhat too attentive.[81]

On the other hand – highlighting the sort of cases that might not have been challenged under a different, less critical therapist – Tracy Todd started with the assumption that the real problem actually lay elsewhere with those who presented as sex addicts. His reported notes consisted of cases of 'supposed sexual addiction' and those whom he convinced that they were not really sex addicts.[82]

We actually know very little about the specificity of psychoanalytic treatment of sex addiction. The account by two Alberta therapists of their application of 'eastern spiritual wisdom' to a slowly recovering sex addict – 'As we sat in our chairs, he continued to feel himself clinging and contracting upon himself over the black abyss, as if he could be smashed by its murky bottom' – provides a tantalizing glimpse of the potential range of possibilities, in that particular case the Almaas Diamond Approach of self-realization.[83]

The detail and frankness of Lawrence Hatterer's early work, discussed elsewhere in this book, are in marked contrast to the brevity and opacity of many other case illustrations (where they exist). Exceptions, however, are the patient studies on sex addiction in the 1995 Workshop Series of the American Psychoanalytic Association that included significant discussion of a woman engaged in multiple extramarital relationships, and three men, one in obsessive pursuit of large penises, another in a perpetual quest for prostitutes with big breasts, and a third who was addicted to X-rated videos.[84] The studies are especially interesting for their self-reflexive analysis of the potentials of transference, presumably heightened by the sexually compulsive nature of the complaint, an issue that later addictionologists were aware of but have not explored in any great detail.[85] The female patient became convinced that her analyst, a woman, 'had sexual feelings towards her' and relayed her sexual fantasies about her therapist: 'One of these fantasies involved her sucking on my breasts and watching my face as it would become enraptured.'[86] Her therapist, Anna Ornstein, detected that the addictive nature of the woman's sexual activities became mirrored in an obsession with her psychoanalyst. Similarly one of Wayne Myers's male patients had dreams about him; 'In these, I was frequently seen as a potential sexual partner.' Others were dependent on him: 'I don't want to lose you.'[87] Also notable is the therapist's admission that years of treatment 'only effected modest changes'. The three men still engaged in their respective pursuit of large penises and breasts and X-rated tapes. The 'intensity and frequency' of their actions had 'markedly diminished' but the behaviour itself persisted.[88]

It is hard to see how 'hypersexuality' has any descriptive value for the variety of sexual 'problems' assessed. The case vignettes from a Toronto study (2013), provided to illustrate the range of hypersexuality referrals at a large city hospital's sexual behaviours clinic, included men who were attracted to the transgendered (she-males); those who spent undue time masturbating to pornography ('several hours per day'), termed 'avoidant masturbation' by the clinicians; gay men who similarly indulged in 'low-investment sexual behaviors' such as visiting bath houses, using online contact sites, and 'engaging in sexual activity with very many partners' (in other words, being promiscuously gay); the 'Chronic Adulterers' whose affairs were often a reflection of marital breakdown; those who self-presented as sex addicts but whose sexual behaviour was actually quite normal (the clinicians called them, appropriately, those afflicted with 'Sexual Guilt'); those, dubbed 'The Designated Patient', whose referral was instigated not so much by their own self-reproach as by the sexual conservatism of a family member; and finally – it is a long list – patients whose disorder was probably something other than hypersexuality. Though James Cantor and his colleagues provided the data to argue that this diversity demonstrated that presenting for hypersexuality 'may represent entirely unrelated phenomena', it also indicates the range of behaviour even contemplated as addictive, compulsive or hypersexual. This study suggests too – given the number of sex addicts who were not really sex addicts – that many of those who presented or self-presented, for whatever reason, would have been classified as hypersexual by less vigilant clinicians, but also that classifications must vary from therapist to therapist (the Toronto inclusion of attraction to the transgendered and multiple gay sex as disorders seems idiosyncratic).[89]

Treatment has proceeded despite Bancroft and Vukadinovic's warnings about clinical management. A New Zealand sex therapist began her report by actually citing their argument as 'not particularly helpful' to clinicians and advocating a practice-generated model rather than theory determining therapy.[90] She was aware of the fuzziness of the disorder but treated it nonetheless. However, it is difficult to conceive how her case study of the sex addict Bob, a committed Christian, masturbator and practitioner of sex with animals, who had been sexually abused as a child – with 'forced manual and oral stimulation and anal rape with various combinations of his father, older brother, this brother's friends and sheep' – was in any way archetypal of the prehistory of most of those suffering from 'out of control sexual behavior' (OOCSB).[91]

Amidst all this scientific imprecision sits sexual addiction's quest for inclusion in the DSM. One of the more recent developments in sexual addiction's short history is the way in which its various forms – sexual addiction, sexual desire dysregulation, sexual impulsivity, sexual compulsivity and paraphilia-related disorder – have morphed into a new sexual malady, 'Hypersexual Disorder', still (in 2014) seeking recognition, given that it was unsuccessful in DSM-5 (2013).[92] There is a sense in which hypersexuality has replaced (old fashioned) sex addiction: an article in the journal *Sexual and Relationship Therapy* simply incorporated nymphomania, satyriasis and sexual addiction into the prehistory of the master category 'hypersexuality'.[93]

So it could be argued that hypersexual disorder's proposed diagnostic criteria are merely those of sexual addiction with a more refined gloss and/or greater statistical panoply. Beneath the standardized weighting, structure correlations, subscales and scores of the *Sexual and Relationship Therapy* piece on hypersexuality lurk its not so modish keywords: sex addiction, sexual compulsivity and psychopathology.[94]

All the elements of Martin Kafka's proposal for the inclusion of 'hypersexual disorder' in DSM-5 would have been in keeping with the earliest discourses of sexual addiction: the arbitrary designation of a period of at least six months of 'recurrent and intense sexual fantasies, sexual urges, or sexual behavior' and the associated (and equally arbitrary) meeting of three or more of the five criteria involving time lost in pursuit of sexual gratification (later modified to four or more), repetitive sexual engagement, loss of sexual control, disregard for others, and use of sex for relief from the stresses and anxieties of everyday life. So too would the diagnostic specification of a wide range of perfectly normal activities rendered abnormal by their intensity and frequency: masturbation, use of pornography, casual sex ('Sexual behavior with consenting adults'), cybersex, telephone sex, resort to strip clubs and (that catch-all) 'Other'.[95] All are reminiscent of the nosology of sex addiction. It is not surprising that the editor-in-chief of the journal *Sexual Addiction & Compulsivity* admitted that he continually referred to sexual addiction when he should have said hypersexual disorder.[96] As for quantification, the hypersexual disorder literature resorts to a Kinsey-like counting of orgasms: 'From these clinically defined data, hypersexual desire in adult males was defined as a persistent TSO [total sexual outlet] of 7 or more orgasms/week for at least 6 consecutive months after the age of 15 years [later revised to 18 years].'[97]

The critiques of hypersexuality disorder as a disorder were the same as those of sexual addiction. Why is time spent on sexual matters necessarily unproductive or less important than on other activities? What is wrong with using sex to cope with the stresses of everyday life? When does a high level of sexual activity move from the normal range to pathology? Research from the University of British Columbia, Vancouver, involving an online survey of more than 11,000 Canadian and US respondents, found that 'dysregulated sex' (sexual addiction and its variants) may merely have indicated the distress associated with 'elevated sexual desire'.[98] As Jason Winters, one of the research team, warned of hyper-sexual disorder's move for DSM accreditation, 'Dysregulated sexuality may simply be a marker of high sexual desire'.[99] What is excessive anyway? Forty-four per cent of Winters's male respondents and 22 per cent of his female participants reported the seven or more orgasms a week that would render them hypersexual by Kafka's criteria.[100] One is reminded of an early warning by two Australian psychologists: 'The real danger in labeling hypersexuality is that we do not know what constitutes excessive sexual behavior, and yet we are applying a label which may have pathological symptoms inappropriately associated with it.'[101] What of the claimed distress, harm and impairment that are the result of the sexual activity?[102] As Moser posed it,

> The question is: Whose distress? Is it the individual's distress? Is it the distress of the spouse, who is dragging the 'patient' to a psychiatrist...Is it the distress from living without the type or quality of sex actually desired? Is it the distress at not being able to live up to societal expectations?[103]

How essential is distress anyway? It is intriguing that the aforementioned study of self-proclaimed German sex addicts (biased in favour of Internet users) found that 25 per cent did not feel distressed by their hypersexual activity. And although the researchers did not draw attention to it, their figures for 'functional impairment' were very low. Reworking their figures, of the total sample of 349 self-identified sex addicts 81 per cent did *not* feel impacted occupationally, 83 per cent with regards to their family life, 74 per cent socially, 84 per cent financially and 87 per cent in terms of their health. The only category of functional impairment of any significance reported by this group was relationship with their partners, with 56 per cent reporting an impact and 44 per cent not. These were remarkably non-distressed and non-impaired sex addicts.[104]

Was there a genuine risk that diagnosis of hypersexuality could mask the patient's real disorder (after all, addictionolo-gists stress the clustering of disorders)? Might treatment for sexual dysfunction not be the most appropriate solution? In fact, might the therapist be treating the effects of another disorder in the name of hypersexual disorder or sexual addiction and therefore never treat the problem itself? An early study of members of SAA in Michigan in the 1990s found that almost 80 per cent of those attending these sex addiction self-help groups said that they had been psychiatrically diagnosed for another mental illness, depression being the most common.[105] Moser has argued that the addictionologists' stress on multiple addictions and clustering actually works against their own thesis. If hypersexual disorder is a viable diagnosis, it should exist on its own rather than as part of a constellation of other psychiatric complaints. 'Is it a disorder or a symptom of another disorder?'[106] As we have mentioned elsewhere, we may not be discussing a disorder at all, at any level; the number of 'sex addicts' who claim to have experienced some form of sexual abuse raises the possibility that that trauma should be treated rather than any form of compulsive sexual behaviour.

And what about the shifting measurements: three or more versus four or more criteria; age 15 as opposed to age 18; seven orgasms a week against a five-per-week gauge? What is so magical about that 6 months' duration as a defining term?[107]

Sex addiction's quest for legitimation has been persistent. Its bid for ultimate recognition – that of the American Psychiatric Association and its DSM – has proven elusive, apart from a brief moment in DSM-III-R in 1987 in what has transpired to be a historical aberration. Even then, it was literally a mention rather than accreditation, example two in three examples of 'Other Sexual Disorders: 302.90: Sexual Disorder Not Otherwise Specified': 'distress about a pattern of repeated sexual conquests or other forms of nonparaphilic sexual addiction, involving a succession of people who exist only as things to be used'.[108] Sexual addiction is not in that *Manual*'s index.

It has been more successful with *Kaplan & Sadock's Comprehensive Textbook of Psychiatry*, the standard primer for training psychiatrists in medical schools throughout the US and influential in the discipline internationally. Sexual addiction was not in the fourth (1985) and fifth (1989) editions of *Kaplan & Sadock*, which favoured the older terms 'erotomania', 'nymphomania' and 'satyriasis', though they did briefly discuss 'hypersexuality' as an uncommon problem associated with disease (rarely), drug use and hormone therapy. (There was no suggestion that it was a significant problem.) However, sex addiction did appear in the sixth (1995) edition in its own section, 'Sex Addiction', under the broader heading 'Sexual dysfunction and sexual disorder not otherwise specified' (in deference to DSM categories).[109] It was discussed too in the seventh (1999) edition, with minor changes to the earlier version, including a different cited case study and use of the heading 'Compulsive Sexual Behavior' rather than 'Sex Addiction':

> The concept of compulsive sexual behavior, or sex addiction, developed over the past two decades to describe persons who compulsively seek out sexual experiences and whose behavior becomes impaired if they cannot gratify their sexual impulses. The concept of sex addiction derived from the model of addiction to such drugs as heroin, or addiction to behavioral patterns, such as gambling...DSM-IV does not use the terms *sex addiction* or *compulsive sexual behavior*, nor is this disorder universally recognized or accepted. Nevertheless, the person whose entire life revolves around sex-seeking behavior and activities, who spends an excessive amount of time in such behavior, and who often tries to stop such behavior but cannot do so is well known to clinicians. Such persons show repeated and increasingly frequent attempts to have a sexual experience, and deprivation evokes symptoms of distress.[110]

Virginia Sadock, the author of the piece and one of the co-editors of the *Textbook*, discussed diagnosis (lack of control, persistent desire, ineffectual guilt and deterioration of social functioning), behavioural patterns ('promiscuous and uncontrolled' sexual behaviour), comorbidity (she claimed an up-to-80-per cent correlation between sex addiction and 'substance-use disorders') and management (the Twelve-Step programmes, psychotherapy and pharmacotherapy, including the rarely used Depo-Provera). She provided a table of signs of sexual addiction taken from Carnes's *Don't Call It Love* (1991) and a brief case study of a chronic masturbator who was treated by 'insight-orientated psychotherapy, group work with other sex addicts, couple therapy, and the use of a specific serotonin reuptake inhibitor, both to treat his depression and for its side effect of decreasing libido'.[111] In other words, sexual addiction had moved from absence in an influential text to acknowledgement as a sexual disorder treatable by psychiatry. Its presence thereafter seemed secure (whatever the verdict of the DSM). The eighth (2005) edition had a whole section, 'Sexual Addiction', by Patrick Carnes himself.[112] The ninth (2009) edition retains a section on sexual addiction, this time by Aviel Goodman, which begins – contra this book's theme – by stating that it is 'not a modern invention or a product of 20th-century culture'.[113]

Neither hypersexual disorder nor sexual addiction has made the terminology of the WHO ICD-10, the World Health Organization's International Classification of Diseases. Its 2014 iteration, ICD-10-CM, includes the categories Excessive Sexual Drive and (rather quaintly) Nymphomania, and Satyriasis under the classification F52.8, 'Other sexual dysfunction not due to a substance or known physiological condition'.[114] It is possible too that those treating sex addiction could classify it under F52.9, 'Unspecified sexual dysfunction not due to a substance or known physiological condition': Sexual Dysfunction Not Otherwise Specified. But this is hardly taxonomic endorsement.

'Hypersexuality disorder is the strangest of constructs', blogged Professor Allen Frances, the head of the task force for the previous *Diagnostic and Statistical Manual of Mental Disorders* (DSM-IV) in the 1990s, but by 2010 a fierce and energetic critic of DSM-5:

> The Work Group explicitly states that it is not meant to be equated with 'Sexual Addiction' (which apparently, and fortunately, was rejected by the DSM5 group working on the 'addictions') – but then goes on to base its proposed definition exclusively on items that are borrowed directly from those used to define substance dependence. The fundamental problem with 'hypersexuality' is that it represents a half baked, poorly conceptualized medicalization of the expected variability in sexual behavior. The authors have not thought through how difficult it is to distinguish between ordinary recreational sexual misbehavior (which is very common) and sexual compulsion (which is very rare)...Sexual misbehavior should be considered 'sexual addiction' only when it is

compulsive, no longer pleasure-driven, and continues despite
great costs that obviously outweigh any gain.[115]

Though sexual disorders were not his area of specific academic expertise, Frances was able to summarize the dangers
of this sexual classification.

> The authors are trying to provide a diagnosis for the small
> group whose sexual behaviors are compulsive – but their label
> would quickly expand to provide a psychiatric excuse for the
> very large group whose misbehaviors are pleasure-driven, rec-
> reational, and impulsive. The offloading of personal respon-
> sibility in this way has already captured the public and media
> fancy and would spread like wildfire. Making an official
> mental disorder category of 'hypersexuality' would also have
> serious unintended forensic consequences in the evaluations
> of sexually violent predators (SVP).[116]

Hypersexuality was sexual addiction in a new guise. It was
poorly researched as a category – he referred in the same piece
to 'a veneer of research support'.[117] It had blurred boundaries:
how really did one distinguish promiscuity from disorder? It
had potentially unhelpful popular/media appeal. And, most
compellingly for Frances, given his experience of DSM-IV,
once awarded the imprimatur of the American Psychiatric
Association the diagnosis would have unpredictable as well
as predictable consequences. A resultant rise in diagnosed sex
addicts, treatment centres and medication was entirely expect-
able: Frances, the former chair of the Department of Psychiatry at Duke University, wrote elsewhere of a road to 'massive
over-diagnosis and harmful medication'.[118] But the history of
psychiatry had shown that there were always unimagined
repercussions, and he was especially concerned by possible
legal manipulation of psychiatric categories. His reference to
SVPs in the quote just given was to those who, under the
sexually violent predator commitment laws active in many
US states, had been detained indefinitely when classified as
suffering from a mental disorder.[119] This use of the notori-
ously vague DSM category 'Paraphilia Not Otherwise Specified' to commit rapists – a diagnosis that DSM-IV-TR
employed to indicate 'diagnostic uncertainty', a 'waste basket
diagnosis' – was no trivial matter.[120] As one commentator put

it, 'While such license may have its place in clinical settings where the major consequence of its use is the ability of the clinician to bill third-party payers, in the forensic context, the unbridled use of NOS categories may have critical consequences for case outcome.'[121] The American Psychiatric Association, the overseer of the DSMs, was opposed to the commitment laws, which they saw as threatening the integrity of psychiatry.[122] Imagine the ramifications, then, if the law could actually employ a recognized, unambiguous, legitimate, psychiatric category.[123] Hence Frances's concern about the inclusion of hypersexuality (sexual addiction) in DSM-5.

More generally, Frances was alarmed at the prospect of a surge of mental disorder through the introduction of new categories and the lowering of diagnostic thresholds.

> DSM5 would create tens of millions of newly misidentified false positive 'patients', thus greatly exacerbating the problems caused already by an overly inclusive DSM4. There would be massive overtreatment with medications that are unnecessary, expensive, and often quite harmful. DSM5 appears to be promoting what we have most feared – the inclusion of many normal variants under the rubric of mental illness, with the result that the core concept of 'mental disorder' is greatly undermined.[124]

Hypersexual disorder was part of this threatened diagnostic inflation.

A thoughtful article in *Clinical Social Work Journal* by Jerome C. Wakefield, the co-author of *Loss of Sadness* (2007), was similarly, devastatingly critical of the syndrome's inclusion in DSM-5.[125] There was no credible evidence that there was any disorder. The proposed new category 'merely provides a label that presupposes there is a dysfunction, thus assuming what has to be proved'.[126]

Ultimately, hypersexuality did not make the final cut for DSM-5. If it had, we could postulate, the ramifications would have been immense. When its inclusion seemed possible, the psychiatrist Charles Samenow anticipated a list of benefits: diagnostic legitimacy, 'increased education and advocacy', greater prominence in health training, insurance reimbursement for treatment and an influx of 'research dollars'.[127] Critics, on the other hand, as we have seen, were concerned

about the repercussions of acceptance. 'Individuals and treatment centers touting their expertise in the treatment of
"sexual addiction" have been sprouting up without standardized diagnostic criteria, studies of effectiveness, and often
without acknowledging that their treatment program is
experimental', Moser wrote in opposition to the proposed
new diagnosis; 'Adopting this proposal would validate these
ethically questionable activities.'[128]

We have argued in this book that journalists, researchers
and therapists have persisted in the use of the term without
really interrogating its viability. Imagine if it had been authen-
ticated by an influential manual that itself has been criticized
in the past for creating reified disorders – an 'unintended
epistemic prison' – and enabling research projects 'that almost
never questioned the diagnostic categories despite their lack
of validation' – and this by a former head of the National
Institute of Mental Health and, at the time that he wrote the
criticisms (2010), chair of the WHO International Advisory
Group on the Revision of ICD-10, Chapter V, and member
of the DSM-5 Task Force.[129] Take into account the impact of
sex addiction charted in this book – without an official classification and acceptance in the manual used by clinicians,
medical insurers and pharmaceutical marketers. Allow for the
aggressive tactics of the drug companies. Assume the insurance coverage for medication and therapy unlocked by DSM
endorsement. And then imagine sex addiction's counterfac-
tual magnification with the legitimation of DSM-5. It would
not have been a healthy combination.

It is certainly an anomalous state of affairs. Self-diagnosed
sex addicts seek treatment from a range of agencies and programmes for what John Giugliano, a practising psychotherapist, has termed 'a disorder that has neither a name nor an
established diagnosis'.[130] Hence this Philadelphia practitioner
could write in the same article of both the difficulties of
diagnosis *and* the treatment options available for this unclear
and controversial disorder – that he himself treats.[131] Its exci-
sion from DSM-IV did not prevent therapists from treating
perceived sex addiction under code 302.9 'Sexual Disorder
Not Otherwise Specified': 'Distress about a pattern of
repeated sexual relationships involving a succession of lovers
who are experienced by the individual only as things to be

used'.[132] Writing under the DSM-IV regime, Jennifer Schneider explained that the syndrome might also have been classified as a paraphilia or ('less commonly') an impulse control disorder. Her list of thirteen disorders that could involve excessive sexual behaviour – for example, Bipolar Affective Disorder, Post-Traumatic Stress Disorder, Obsessive-Compulsive Disorder – was included so that therapists could distinguish sexual addiction as their primary diagnosis, yet it actually demonstrated the potential for diagnostic flexibility.[133] As she and her co-author had expressed it in an earlier article to the receptive readers of the journal *Sexual Addiction & Compulsivity*, their goal was to 'demonstrate to mental health professionals that addictive sexual behaviors are indeed subsumed in various categories of the DSM-IV'.[134]

It is logical, then, that clinicians will also negotiate their way through the hypersexual-disorder-less DSM-5. The UK psychotherapist Paula Hall wrote 'we may never find a definition or diagnostic model acceptable for [the] diagnostic and statistical manual... But does that really matter?' She continued, 'we, in the sex therapy community, will remain open minded and focus our attention on the needs of clients'.[135] In response to its exclusion from DSM-5, Alexandra Katehakis, a Los Angeles practitioner and winner of a Carnes Award, as mentioned earlier, pointed out that therapists could persist in treating the problem as the addiction that they believed existed, despite the DSM-5 verdict, or they could fit their patient's symptoms into an accepted category that they knew was not a perfect match: 'a depressive disorder, an anxiety disorder, a relational problem, or a personality disorder'.[136] Martin Kafka, who had been so involved in the bid for hypersexuality disorder's acceptance and is certainly familiar with the DSM's complexities, has suggested that it now fits DSM-5's 312.89: 'Other Specified Disruptive, Impulse-Control, and Conduct Disorder', followed by the specified reason, 'hypersexual disorder'.[137] A DSM sceptic, Gary Greenberg, has mocked its diagnostic flexibility: 'I only use a handful of the codes and by now I know them by heart. At the top of my favorites list is 309.28...Adjustment Disorder with Mixed Anxiety and Depressed Mood.'[138] The DSM, he wrote, is 'a superb playbook'.[139]

The reader should note that the self-help groups have pressed on regardless of DSM decisions. When the fifty-three self-identified sex addicts who were members of the Michigan meetings of SAA were asked in the 1990s about their psychiatric diagnoses, only three (6 per cent) said that they 'had been diagnosed with a sexual disorder classified in the DSM-IV'.[140]

While there is little doubting the impact of the discourse, the strange situation of sex addiction's clinical and popular impact without the imprimatur of the American Psychiatric Association has meant a continuing search for legitimacy, an uncertainty in psychological classification. It may only be a matter of time (though the authors of this book hope not), as DSM-5 has included Gambling Disorder as its only Non-Substance-Related Disorder under the wider category 'Substance-Related and Addictive Disorders' and listed Internet Gaming Disorder among its conditions warranting further study.[141] The Society for the Advancement of Sexual Health (SASH), which grew directly out of what we have been calling the sex addiction industry as the professional organization of sex addiction therapists, has taken some encouragement from the new category 'Substance-Related and Addictive Disorders', which it wishfully shortened to 'Addiction and Related Disorders', stating in its own journal *Sexual Addictions & Compulsivity*, 'This change recognizes emerging research that supports behavioral/process addictions as being similar to substance use disorders in terms of common neurobiological mechanisms in the brain.'[142]

The door, then, seems both open and shut. It is ajar in the sense that DSM-5 has established the concept of behavioural addiction – the ever-alert Frances warned 'Watch out for careless overdiagnosis of internet and sex addiction and the development of lucrative treatment programs to exploit these new markets.'[143] (The American Society of Addiction Medicine, the professional association of physicians treating addictions, has included process addictions in its 2011 definition of addictions.[144]) Yet the door is blocked in the explicit refusal to recognize hypersexuality. The preamble to DSM-5's 'Substance-Related and Addictive Disorders' refers specifically to its exclusion of 'groups of repetitive behaviors, which some term *behavioral addictions*, with such subcategories as "sex addiction", "exercise addiction", or "shopping addiction"', explaining that 'at this time there is insufficient peer-reviewed evidence to establish the diagnostic criteria and course descriptions needed to identify these behaviors as mental disorders'.[145] But why include hoarding and skin-picking as new disorders and not hypersexuality?[146] Are their research bases and diagnostic criteria really so vastly superior? At the present (2014) the concept of sex addiction, as Lennard Davis has put it, continues to inhabit 'some interstitial space between science and culture'.[147]

Another problematic area in the history of sex addiction is the use of psychopharmacy, a subject insufficiently explored in accounts of the malady and its treatment. Pharmaceutical solutions were not mentioned in Carnes's classic sex addiction text *Out of the Shadows* (1983), which, with its theme of a direct parallel between sexual and alcohol addictions, focused on the Twelve-Steps programme of therapy.[148] Depo-Provera, lithium and Prozac were cited in his later book *Don't Call It Love* (1991), though fleetingly and inconclusively, as a way to combat withdrawal – surprising given the author's hyperbolic invocation of the aches, shakes, itches, chills and sweats of narcotic detoxification: as he quoted a multiple addict, 'I have now experienced withdrawal from four addictions, including cocaine. By far the worst withdrawal was from my sexual addiction.'[149] The subject of medication was treated tentatively. 'Speculation exists about whether medication can alleviate severe withdrawal symptoms...Because there is not yet consensus in the field, decisions are made on a case-by-case basis.'[150] The multimodality approach favoured by the father-and-son psychologists Ralph and Marcus Earle in their 1995 casebook included intensive therapy, sand-play and creative art, but seemingly no use of any pharmaceutical solution.[151]

However, given that drugs have long been used to control sex offenders and the fact that many addictionologists saw such offending as merely a point on the spectrum of sexual addiction, it was predictable that drug therapy would be recommended for more mundane behaviour.[152] We know that selective serotonin reuptake inhibitors (SSRIs) were administered to compulsive gamblers in the 1990s.[153] Moreover, the blurring of boundaries between diagnosis of

Obsessive Compulsive Disorder (OCD) and compulsive sexual behaviour meant that supposed sex addicts were treated with the serotonin reuptake blockers that were regularly administered to those suffering from OCD.[154] It was also likely, given the side effects of many medications in this pharmaceutical age, including the libido-affecting properties of antidepressant drugs, that patients might self-medicate and doctors experiment.[155] Prozac enthusiast and Providence psychiatrist Peter Kramer noticed in the early 1990s that a side effect for those on the antidepressant was trouble achieving orgasm. One of his patients, who claimed the drug made him 'feel better than well', also said that it inhibited his interest in pornography: 'on medication he felt less driven, freed of an addiction'.[156] One of the contributors to a 1995 monograph on addictive behaviour in the Workshop Series of the American Psychoanalytic Association was clearly using antidepressant medication as well as psychoanalysis in his treatment of sexual compulsion and sexually addictive behaviour.[157] John Sealy, a Californian psychiatrist who reported on the treatment of over 300 sex addicts in an in-patient unit during the 1990s, was also using SSRIs, including Prozac.[158]

Drug treatment of sexual addiction in this earlier period was marked by hit-and-miss investigation, anecdotal evidence and small-scale, non-scientific studies. Writing in 2000 for the 'next millennium', Ariel Rösler and Eliezer Witztum claimed 'an urgent need for good methodological research and carefully designed, prospective double-blind controlled studies with a large number of subjects, in order to establish whether or not SSRI medications play a beneficial role in the treatment of paraphilias'.[159] Yet this need has not really inhibited the rise of pharmacological solutions for the purported malady. Indeed later discussions of sex addiction therapy have invariably included drug treatment. Successive entries on sex addiction in more recent editions of *Kaplan & Sadock's Comprehensive Textbook of Psychiatry* have devoted increasing space to pharmacological cures: a brief mention in Carnes's chapter in 2005, a whole section by Goodman in 2009.[160] A 2007 update on the syndrome in the journal *Directions in Psychiatry*, by psychiatrists for psychiatrists, outlined the employment of a range of psychopharmacological solutions – with sometimes terrifying side effects.[161] The French authors of another summary for the *American Journal of Drug and Alcohol Abuse* in 2010 observed (like Rösler and Witztum) that they knew of 'no published large double-blind clinical trials' of the pharmacological treatment of excessive sexual behaviour, yet nonetheless outlined drug treatment, including dosages of the heavy-duty medications cyproterone acetate (CPA), a steroid, and medroxyprogesterone acetate (MPA), a progesterone derivative – both characterized elsewhere as having 'a substantial number of severe side effects'.[162] As recently as 2014, Carnes thought that 'Pharmacologic treatment can be helpful.' He and his co-authors referred to the use of medications commonly employed for bipolar disorder, attention deficit hyperactivity disorder, chemical addiction, compulsive gambling and Internet addiction disorder. They also noted that 'Sex addiction patients may require prosexual drugs to enhance sexual function', given the classification of erectile dysfunction and impaired sexual desire as part of the sexual addiction nosology discussed earlier.[163] It must have been a delicate balancing act for such clinicians.

Martin Kafka's chapter on nonparaphilic hypersexuality in the sex therapy text *Principles and Practices of Sex Therapy* (2007) endorsed what he termed 'encouraging' indications of the effectiveness of psychopharmacology.[164] He outlined his own deployment of serotonin reuptake inhibitors (Prozac, Luvox, Paxil, Celexa, Zoloft, Lexapro) and dual-action serotonin/norepinephrine medication (Effexor-XR and Cymbalta), all used to diminish sexual activity and desire (he wrote of reducing his patients' total sexual outlets per week from 5–25 times to 1–3). However, he also used psychostimulants (Ritalin, Dexedrine, Adderall, Bupropion), which had sexually activating effects, to adjust the sexual behaviour of individual cases.[165] The impression given is of both careful experimentation and diagnostic uncertainty. Kafka referred to the paucity of published data ('scant' was the word used), indecision about the optimum duration of such treatment (a year or indefinitely?) and vagueness concerning the combinations and quantities of medication, and warned of the dangers of terminating medication. He also seemed inconsistent as to whether medication should proceed in tandem with psychological counselling or only when such therapy had failed, although in his own practice (treating over 250 males) he clearly favoured the latter.[166]

It is likely that the testing – careful or not – will continue. Doctors at the Impulse Control Disorders Clinic in Los Angeles administered topiramate, an anticonvulsant, to a man who spent compulsively on sexual activities and who came to them 'requesting help with his "addiction to sex" '.[167] Two Rochester psychiatrists reported treatment of Internet sex addiction with a combination of sertraline, used for OCD and depression, and naltrexone, a morphine-receptor antagonist approved by the Food and Drug Administration for the treatment of alcoholism.[168] French clinicians writing in the US-based *Journal of Clinical Psychopharmacology* claimed to have treated the sexual addiction of a 37-year-old woman with cyproterone acetate – though how successful it really was is debatable, given the cocktail of other drugs administered for panic disorder and depression, the suicide attempt during treatment, and the episodic and dubious nature of the alleged addiction ('protracted promiscuity' at swingers' clubs).[169]

So the use of drugs, given contestable diagnoses and the likelihood (as we see it) that the ailment is fictional, makes for some worrying scenarios. One of the most disquieting, demonstrating the dangers of the disease mongering discussed at the beginning of this book, is the reported case of a South Carolina woman treated in a community health centre in the 1990s, first for Major Depressive Disorder and Borderline Personality Disorder, then for unspecified depression, Mixed Personality Disorder, Attention Deficit Disorder-Adult Type (ADD-A) and, the subject of the report, sex addiction. Her addiction was rather unreliably described: 'She engaged in sex with five men daily and two to three at a time as well as cybersex with anonymous partners and used various sexual accessories on a regular basis.' While even to non-clinicians it seems clear from the reported case summary that the patient had been sexually abused throughout her life (raped by a grandfather and by a husband) and should have been treated for that abuse, she was administered a combination of venlafaxine (an antidepressant SSRI), sodium valproate (for bipolar disorder seizures), risperidone (an anti-psychotic used for schizophrenia), paroxetine (another antidepressant) and methylphenidate (for her ADD-A: Ritalin is a methylphenidate). Though it was claimed the woman reported a diminution in her sexual cravings, it is unclear whether the reported 'control' of her addiction would have met addictionology criteria: she still engaged in cybersex.[170] The same clinician had earlier reported that Prozac had curtailed the homosexual drive of a male patient, but this psychiatrist's trademark cocktail of other drugs administered to the patient – Ritalin, Wellbutrin, Risperdal, lithium – as well as the subject's desire to curtail his homosexual activities, muddied the diagnostic waters somewhat.[171]

Mike Tyson's autobiography listed the medication that he was given during his addiction treatment, a long inventory that included (in alphabetical order) Abilify, Cymbalta, Depakote, Neurontin, Wellbutrin XL and Zyprexa.[172] Though he was no pharmacologist, and would wean himself off these drugs idiosyncratically with his 'own regimen' of Chinese herbs and cocaine, he recalled the practical effects of such multiple treatment: 'The doctors from Wonderland had me on so many meds I was totally lethargic.'[173] 'One was a mood stabilizer. Two were antidepressants. Two were mood regulators for bipolar disorder. And one was used to treat epilepsy, something I never had.'[174] Little surprise that he was listless. Abilify was indeed used to treat bipolar disorder or manic depression as well as schizophrenia and autism, Cymbalta for depression and anxiety, and Depakote for seizures and manic depression. Neurontin was the anti-epileptic drug for his nonexistent epilepsy. Wellbutrin was yet another antidepressant. And Zyprexa was used, like Abilify, for schizophrenia and manic depression.

In truth, there has been little improvement on the methodological weaknesses detected in the previous millennium. Reef Karim's 2009 presentation to the California Society of Addiction Medicine noted both the absence of specifically approved medicines for sexual compulsivity and a paucity of research data, but then went on – in a paper called 'Cutting Edge Pharmacology for Sex Addiction' – to discuss the use of a range of pharmacological treatments for that very problem.[175] A 2013 review of the literature by researchers at the University of California, Los Angeles, and George Washington University wrote damningly of 'significant methodological limitations' and 'generally compromised methodologies' in the research on pharmacology and hypersexual disorder, including an imprecision in the identification of the tested condition (disorders overlap), skewed representation in subjects, lack of randomization and control, inconsistency of dosage, failure to take into account concurrent other treatments, lack of consistency in measurement, absence of longer-term follow-up, and incomplete consideration of side effects. Ironically, they reported, the one double-blind, placebo trial approaching any statistical and methodological validity actually demonstrated little difference in the effects of the tested drug and its control.[176] A consistent problem in these studies has been the self-selective nature of the participants. (Most of Carnes's work has been based on those presenting to him as sex addicts.) The gay and bisexual men who were part of the double-blind placebo trial, as the researchers themselves noted, had an 'obvious bias toward wanting to reduce problematic sexual behaviors, and anticipating doing so could have influenced both treatment groups' (those taking the SSRI citalopram, the tested drug, and those not).[177]

The pharmaceutical companies have not embraced the disorder as they have what are claimed to be other mental illnesses: the contrast with the mass marketing of antidepressants is palpable. Perhaps this is because sex addiction does not have the sheer numbers required to engage the interest of the large drug companies and does have a clientele that, due to their socio-economic or age profile, are less likely to fall into the orbit of Medicaid or Medicare, and because of a lack of DSM recognition do not unambiguously qualify for health insurance cover anyway. The drug companies are more likely to be marketing treatments for erectile dysfunction (including enhanced sexual performance) in the form of Viagra than they are treatments for sexual addiction.[178]

If the drug companies were to become more focused on the treatment of sex addiction or hypersexuality, the outcome could be frightening. The short 'Am I a Sex Addict?' questionnaires in the quick-screening format – easily adaptable to self-testing – mimic the pharmaceutical company Pfizer's sponsored Prime-MD (Primary Care Evaluation of Mental Disorders), designed to detect what were then considered the common mental disorders – psychosomatic, depressive, anxiety, alcohol and eating – and marketed to physicians in the 1990s.[179] Prime-MD's drug-company links were unambiguous. Critics have described it as 'the Alaskan Pipeline for the pharmaceuticals, a method of gaining direct access to an immense new market'.[180] Its later iterations, the GAD (Generalized Anxiety Disorder) and PHQ (Patient Health Questionnaire) Screeners, are similar points-based, rapid diagnoses comparable to various sex addiction tests. They (GAD and PHQ) are currently (2014) available at www.pfizer.com.[181]

Historically speaking, the role of psychopharmacology in the treatment of hypersexual disorder/sex addiction is in its early stages. Yet Edward Shorter's characterization of the wider world of psychiatric drug use as the 'Wild West' certainly seems applicable to this more focused field – and to sex addiction's diagnostic and treatment regimes more generally.[182] It is a disordered disorder.

Chapter 7
Sexual Conservatism

> One of the strategies of the New Right's puritanism in sex therapy has been to set an arbitrary ideological norm for coital and orgasmic frequency. Frequency above the norm is defined as abnormal and is named *sexual addiction*.
>
> John Money, 1999[1]

'Our society is deteriorating at an alarming rate'; it was with these words that Anne Wilson Schaef began her 1987 bestseller on addicts in an addictive society.[2] A chapter in an early collection on the treatment of sex addicts referred, in similarly doom-laden vein, to a purported rise in sexually transmitted diseases, pornography, unsafe sexual practices, '[s]exually related exposés and arrests' and the availability of phone sex 'even to young children'.[3] Janice Irvine described 1980s sex addiction as a 'discourse of excess and control'; whatever the differences of approach, the variation in nomenclature of the support networks, or the order of the steps to recovery in the many manuals of advice, the focus was on 'the danger of uncontrolled sexuality'.[4] The nurse Elizabeth Kennedy responded critically to an information piece on sex addiction in the journal *Nurse Practitioner* in 1990 because she thought that, whatever the intentions of those who utilized the diagnosis, it played into the hands of conservatism:

'I am worried about the "sex addiction" movement', she wrote, 'during a period when the right wing is undermining reproductive rights, promoting censorship, using AIDS to discriminate against sexual minorities and in general portraying sex as destructive and dangerous.' The concept of sex addiction, she thought, colluded with the 'anti-sex movement'.[5]

If anything, the claims of sexual danger have intensified since sex addiction's early days. One of the features of sex addiction has been its adaptability; the way in which it responded to contemporary cultural anxieties, indeed reflected those concerns. Nowhere was this more evident than with the Internet. In the preface to his 2001 edition of *Out of the Shadows* Patrick Carnes reflected on societal shifts since the book was first published in 1983. The 'sexual landscape' had 'changed dramatically': 'First, there was the AIDS epidemic...Then there was former President Clinton and the intern Monica Lewinsky...Almost simultaneously came the cybersex revolution.'[6] And while AIDS and the Clinton affair may have indicated a cultural shift in sexual attitudes, it was the 'cybersex revolution' that seems to have had the most impact from Carnes's point of view. The new edition of *Out of the Shadows* included a chapter on cybersex addiction as well as promotion of the significantly named *In the Shadows of the Net* (2001), a book entirely devoted to cybersex addiction.[7] The Internet has been such a game changer in the history of sex addictionology that a 2013 article in *Sexual Addiction & Compulsivity* contrasted 'classic' sexual addiction with the new 'contemporary' phenomenon of 'rapid-onset sexual addiction', claimed to be a direct result of the 'explosive growth of Internet technology'.[8]

Online sex has achieved a privileged place in the checklist of sexual addiction. The Internet, advised the chapter on compulsive sex in a handbook for psychiatrists and psychologists, 'has introduced millions of people to a venue where the most explicit and varied sexual fantasies can be accessed all too easily, leading some men down the slippery slope of compulsivity'.[9] Internet sex addiction is a double addiction: to sex and to the Internet. But the checklist of 'warning signs for cybersexual addiction' – using the Internet to find online and real-life sexual partners, 'masturbating online while engaged in erotic chat', switching gender roles, viewing pornography, sharing sexual fantasies – could, in a more sex-positive context, be read as a list of the main attractions of cybersex.[10] The interpretation lies with the analyser. For the therapist of sex addiction, cybersex's 'endless variety of partners', idealized sexual encounters, 'intense orgasms from the minimal investment of a few keystrokes' and 'illusions of power and love' are indicative of sexual dysfunction: 'courtship disorder'.[11] But for others this is its precise appeal and this 'world of illusions' is not at all incompatible with 'courtship' or longer-term commitment.[12] As the progressive therapist Tracy Todd put it, 'society's definitions of healthy sexuality will continue to evolve. It is possible, indeed probable, that they will someday include cybersex and phone sex.'[13]

Marty Klein has summarized the differences between the sex-positive, sexologist clinician and therapists of the sex-negative, sex addiction movement. Twice-daily masturbation, extramarital affairs, sadomasochism, use of Internet pornography, resort to commercial sex, non-monogamy and fetishism – all were the mark of a sex addict in the sexual addiction model, whereas a clinical sexologist might diagnose such behaviour either as not necessarily a problem (the masturbation) or as sexual adventurousness (the non-monogamy).[14] David Ley has similarly selected some of the characteristics of bad sex in the sex addiction framework – masturbation, fantasy – and compared them to more positive research findings published in the *Journal of Sex Research*.[15] A New York qualitative study of men who had sex with men, and considered themselves to be sexually compulsive, found that even this group 'often implicitly identified harm reduction benefits of the internet'. The researchers, Christian Grov and others, recommended that 'health professionals might consider…a more nuanced assessment of internet use on a person's overall well-being, rather than assume that the internet primarily negatively impacts on sexual health'.[16] Ley and his colleagues have indeed argued elsewhere that high-volume use of visual sexual stimuli, interpreted negatively by addictionologists as pornography addiction, can be viewed positively in all sorts of sexually enhancing ways including reducing the likelihood of unsafe sexual contact.[17]

It should be noted that the oscillation between sexual utopia and sexual hell can occur in the same discussion – even in one that assumed that such behaviour was disordered. Amusingly, David Delmonico's alarmist account of the evils of cybersex addiction ('Not all cybersex addicts are pedophiles') contained a detailed explanation of the Internet's sexual uses, including a list of the USENET forums – for example, sex.anal, sex.bestiality, sex.enemas – and Internet Relay Chat Channels – #playroom, #BIGCLITS, #fuckmywife and so on.[18] Kimberly Young wrote that virtual sex could 'cater to any sexual desire or need imaginable', and she relayed stories of a Mormon grandmother indulging her fantasies in BDSM cybersex, and the 52-year-old nurse who found 'new sexual freedom online' as a dominatrix in a 'DomF4SubM' chat room –'for me, cybersex is the ultimate escape'.[19] But the narrative was of inevitable progression to addiction – discovery and experimentation led to escalation, compulsivity and hopelessness – and of the treatment needed to save users: 'Internet sex addiction can have devastating effects as people can now freely explore sexual fantasies that once unlocked online can be difficult to put back inside the bottle.'[20] The mixed metaphors captured the overall message. The Mormon grandmother's marriage was in trouble. The nurse's work and home life were badly affected by her liberation: 'The trouble is now I no longer want sex with my husband. I just want it from my cyberslaves. It's killing everything, my work, my marriage, but I feel helpless to stop.'[21]

It is ironic that so much of the popular success of sexual addiction as a concept – the impact of the self-diagnostic sex addiction tests, the web presence of the various treatment centres – is due to the influence of the Internet, and yet so much time and effort have gone into combating the perceived evils of what has proven to be such a useful servant. The website of the KeyStone Center (the treatment centre in Philadelphia where Russell Brand stayed) includes audio links, multimedia presentations, and links to nearly thirty other Internet sites where 'users' (in both senses of the term) can read about Carnes, the Twelve-Step philosophy and Sex Addicts Anonymous (SAA), as well as other treatment facilities and support groups for people suffering from sex addiction.[22] Carnes created the website SexHelp.com, which functions as a one-stop shop for information and links for assessment, diagnosis and therapy for the sex addict and their significant others.[23] The Internet is now the first port of call for any form of self-diagnosis.

Therapists who have employed the idea of sexual compulsivity or sexual addiction have often denied that they were anti-sex and have argued that it was the issue of lack of control that was the problem. The authors of *Cybersex Unplugged* distinguished between acceptable recreational cybersex and more problematic compulsive users.[24] Eli Coleman warned professionals away from 'overpathologizing...normal sexual behavior'.[25] Yet there is no denying a strong strand of sex-negativity in the discourse. An indication of what was considered non-normative heterosexual behaviour was provided in the examples of loss of sexual control given in *The Sex Addiction Workbook* (2003): 'frequenting prostitutes, using pornography obsessively, engaging in Internet or telephone sex, having serial affairs, frequenting massage parlors, going to strip clubs obsessively, going to bathhouses for sex, frequenting topless bars obsessively, feeling driven to have sex many times a day'.[26] Of the 152 patients in treatment for hypersexual disorder (144 of whom were male) in clinics in California, New Mexico, Pennsylvania, Texas and Utah, part of a DSM-5 field trial published in 2012, most characterized their sexual disorder in terms of pornography consumption (81 per cent) and masturbation (78 per cent). Sex with 'someone other than their monogamous partner' was another 'specifier' for hypersexuality.[27] The participants in the earlier-cited Candeo/Mormon study wanted 'to reduce, and in most cases completely eliminate pornography use. Many, but not all, would also like to reduce or eliminate masturbation.'[28]

Coleman's warning was clearly not always observed. Indeed, when Stephen Levine reviewed the cases of thirty men who had either been referred to him or self-presented for sex addiction, he found that despite the readiness of spouses (and family doctors) to attribute sexual lapses to sexual addiction, most were engaging in extramarital sex or not particularly unusual masculine behaviour: 'Many men masturbate to pornography, go to strip clubs and buy a lap dance, procure a prostitute's service, or have affairs...partner distress must be discounted as a sufficient criterion for the label.' Levine concluded that though they presented as such, 75 per cent of his patients were not sex addicts.[29]

Perhaps we should not be surprised by this essential illib-
eralism. As Charles Moser has noted, the implication behind
the diagnosis of hypersexual disorder was that there was a
'healthy amount of sex (not too much, not too little, but just
right)'.[30] A quantitative study of media and audience discourses around celebrity sex scandals (we saw the link with
alleged sexual addiction in earlier discussion) found a definite
focus on heterosexuality and adultery, with noticeable reader
judgementalism. The detected sexual frames in reader discussion of the scandals were 'conservative rather than liberal'
and 'mostly reproduce normative values around morality and
sexual conduct'.[31]

Critics of the concept of sexual addiction have always
maintained that it was sexually conservative, defining breaches
in an entirely normative moral code. An early detractor, Clark
L. Taylor, an anthropologist who had read Carnes and
attended one of his workshops, wrote of the addictionologists: 'The bottom line: They indicate sex for pleasure is
wrong.' He noted a 'general lack of sex positive affirmation',
the absence of discussion about the positive aspects of 'the
use of sex to relieve anxiety' or 'how healthy it can be to
watch people have sex or let people watch us or to enjoy
explicit sexual materials', and that one did not hear either of
those who had adjusted to AIDS or of the 'joy of multiple
partners by risk reduction'. In Carnes's philosophy, Taylor
continued, 'it becomes apparent that vanilla sex – judicious
vaginal containment in the nuptial bed – is the only truly
fulfilling, meaningful or healthy sex that exists'.[32] Lawrence
and Richard Siegel, who argued against the proposition that
sex could be addictive, pulled no punches either:

> The whole idea of 'sex addiction' is a metaphor gone amuck,
> and is borne out of a moralistic ideology masquerading as
> science. It is a concept that seems to serve no other purpose
> than to relegate sexual expression to the level of shameful
> acts, except within the extremely narrow and myopic scope
> of a monogamous, heterosexual marriage.

Consideration of the questions on a sex addiction screening
test, they continued, would reveal 'a deep-seated bias against
most forms of sexual expression'.[33]

The research psychoanalyst Paul Joannides has suggested that 'Someone who has strong religious beliefs might describe himself or herself as a sex addict, when another person who has similar sexual behaviors might not think anything of the kind.' He also thought that this lower definitional threshold for sex addiction would apply to some therapists as well as their patients.[34] The large online study which compared self-identified sex addicts with those not being treated for hyper-sexuality found that, among males, the former were more likely to be religiously inclined. The researchers hypothesized that 'it is possible that a proportion of people who seek treatment for dysregulated sexuality experience increased distress due to socioethical and religious constraints on sexuality'.[35] Another survey of psychology undergraduates at two Midwest universities found that the religious were more likely both to disapprove morally of pornography and to think that they were addicted to its use.[36] And one could easily argue that the two Rochester psychiatrists who treated a man's 'Internet sex addiction' with sertraline and naltrexone for three years would have done better to have dealt with his 'conservative Christian beliefs' and conviction that his addiction was a result of 'negative influences from the devil'.[37] In other words, a link between more conservative religious influences and belief in sex addiction seems likely. A survey of self-identified partners of sex addicts (mostly women) found that they claimed that spirituality was almost as important as therapy in coping with their situation, and that prayer and spiritual reading were the main forms that this support took.[38] Carnes told Phil Donahue on his talk show in 1984 that sex addiction was linked to a background of conservative Christianity with its unhealthy attitude towards sex and that that was why the Alcoholics Anonymous-based, Twelve-Step programme with its spiritual dimension was an appropriate means of recovery.[39]

The sexual lapses of the male sex addicts of Meg Wilson's church-going community seemed relatively minor: viewing pornography and a 'nonphysical encounter with a woman' were sufficient to invoke charges of sexual compulsivity.[40] Although Maurita Corcoran's husband had at least admitted to a hundred extramarital affairs, the threshold of defined sexual addiction was lower for some of the members of her

support group. One woman had never recovered from the
one affair that her husband had had; 'getting over his death
to cancer had been easier than getting over his single affair
that had happened more than twenty years earlier'.[41]

When, in an interview with *The Guardian*'s Jon Henley,
Catherine Millet recalled the promiscuity chronicled in
The Sexual Life of Catherine M (2001), the book that
made her famous, she was careful not to invoke sexual
addiction.

> It's what I was truly good at – what I was the best at. I loved
> particularly the anonymity, the abandonment of orgies. The
> sensation that one was glorying in this unbelievable freedom,
> this transcendence. I look back on it with nothing but pleas-
> ure. It was very important to me, to my identity, my ego, but
> it wasn't an addiction. I was never a nymphomaniac. I did not
> pounce on everything that moved. I never provoked. I made
> myself available. I profited.[42]

Similarly, Helen Keane began her chapter on sex addiction
with a contrast between Benoîte Groult's novel of cross-class
sexual longing, *Salt On Our Skin* (1992), and the literature
of sex addiction. Both dealt with 'overwhelming and insistent
erotic desire', but whereas the novel celebrated this passion,
'those at the mercy of uncontrollable desires' in sex addiction
texts were 'victims of a virulent disease'.[43]

It must be shame that distinguishes the 'celebrity sex
addict', when he or she actually exists, from the celebrity who
just has lots of shameless sex. Where there is no shame there
are no diagnoses. Hence the guiltless memoirs that (apart
from a fleeting reference by Steven Tyler) contain no talk of
sexual addiction at all despite sexual behaviour that in other
life stories would be constructed and interpreted differently.[44]
Their sexual interactions, though excessive by most standards, are rarely medicalized in the manner encountered in the
pages mentioned earlier. Tyler, no stranger to rehab, resisted
the urge to pathologize: 'I had six or seven isms hung around
my neck: drug addict, alcoholic, sex addict, codependent,
family concerns, anger management...Oh yeah, I had a full
range of life issues.' He recalled that counsellors 'were constantly trying to label me and figure me out...to make me

recognize shame – feel *bad* about my bad self'.[45] Rob Lowe saw his behaviour as unrewarding but not exactly shameful.[46] Brand did not self-diagnose but let his management admit him to a clinic when they convinced him that his career would be jeopardized by his behaviour: 'ambition is the most powerful force within me,' Brand explained, 'so once people convinced me that my sexual behavior might become damaging to my career, I found it easier to think of it as a flaw that needed to be remedied'.[47] Keith Richards was relaxed and not especially interested in the sexual opportunities that fame brought.[48] Fellow Rolling Stone Bill Wyman was matter-of-fact about everything, including the sex: 'In 1965 we sat down one evening in an hotel', he recalled, 'and worked out that since the band had started two years earlier, I'd had 278 girls, Brian 130, Mick about thirty, Keith six and Charlie none'.[49]

Shame has been a recurring theme in sex addiction. It has been there in clinical research: with testing of emotions, experimentation with sexualization, the Sexual False Self Scale and the evocatively named Shame Inventory.[50] It surfaced in film – recall McQueen's *Shame* and Waters's *A Dirty Shame*. The word 'shame' occurs 274 times in P. J. Carnes and K. M. Adams's edited sex addiction text *Clinical Management of Sex Addiction* (2002).[51] The word was there from the early days. Shame and its associated metaphor of the shadow led Carnes to change the name of his first publication from *The Sexual Addiction* (1983) to *Out of the Shadows* (1983).[52] 'As sexual compulsives, we live almost continually with shame, but often are hardly aware of it'; this was the statement of a seminar on shame organized in 1990 by the primarily gay and lesbian group Sexual Compulsives Anonymous. The pamphlet that resulted from the meetings was indeed called *Secret Shame* (1991).[53] Remember the patients who self-presented to the Toronto Sexual Behaviors Clinic as sex addicts but whose sexual behaviour was entirely in keeping with sexual norms and who were not sex addicts at all; their clinicians described them as suffering from 'Sexual Guilt' or from the 'highly restrictive sexual beliefs' of a partner.[54] Todd, the sex-positive therapist, was convinced that the cursory diagnosis of sex addiction merely reinforced 'a culture of shame'.[55]

It is significant that PATHOS, the less-than-a-minute sexual addiction screening test, essentially measures shame:

1. Do you often find yourself preoccupied with sexual thoughts? (**P**reoccupied)
2. Do you hide some of your sexual behavior from others? (**A**shamed)
3. Have you ever sought help for sexual behavior you did not like? (**T**reatment)
4. Has anyone been hurt emotionally because of your sexual behavior? (**H**urt others)
5. Do you feel controlled by your sexual desire? (**O**ut of control)
6. When you have sex do you feel sad afterwards? (**S**ad)[56]

Although the devisors of the test claimed that it could 'be used to accurately detect individuals with sex addiction' and cited the high scores of those already in treatment for sex addiction compared to the lower scores of a college student sample, they were really only measuring attitudes to sex. What they termed the 'healthy' population were indeed healthy, not because they were not in treatment for sex addiction but because their attitude to sex was healthier than that of the patient sample.[57] They were not ashamed; their sexual desires did not cause regret, feelings of unworthiness, disgrace or shame.

Sexual addiction is what Klein has termed 'pathology oriented'.[58] Jerome Wakefield has referred to it mistaking 'highly culture-bound notions of morally proper sex' for 'biological normality'.[59] In the play *Sexaholics* 'Sex is dangerous', 'promiscuous sex can kill you' and 'Flagrant sex is a disease':

> All we want, Julie... All we want is to get laid. We don't even care if it kills us. We don't even care if we create unbelievably horrible new diseases that could cripple our kids for generations and generations. We don't care, sweetheart. We wanna get laid; that's it, period![60]

Jennifer Riemersma and Michael Sytsma claim that there is a new generation of rapid-onset sex addiction that is a result of 'chronic' exposure to graphic material on the Internet, a

'toxic cocktail' producing 'comorbid mood disorders, attachment ruptures, and cross-addictions'.[61] Although their article
did not provide keywords, they might have been 'pathologic',
'comorbid', 'toxic', 'worthlessness', 'trauma' and 'impaired'.[62]
Wilson's account of her husband's supposed addiction referred
continually to darkness; 'dark land', 'dark feelings' and 'the
dark of hopelessness' are all on the one page.[63] Ricki Lake's
mid-segment summary of her talk show special on sex addiction reminded her viewers 'We are looking at the dark world
of women who are addicted to sex.'[64] The 15-year-old 'sex
addict' in The Tyra Show said 'it's like I'm trapped in a dark
place...I'm a prisoner'.[65] Internet sex addicts 'are those who
use the Internet as a forum for their sexual activities because
of their propensity for *pathological* sexual expression'.[66]
Keane's characterization of sexual addiction as 'the pathology
of promiscuous desire' seems very apt.[67]

   It is important to grasp that this pathology has permeated
the various layers of sex addiction discourse and was not
confined to talk shows and workbooks. The authors of a
study of sexual compulsivity among a sample of gay, lesbian
and bisexual New Yorkers referred to the 'significant public
health ramifications' of the condition. 'The increased risk of
HIV infection for persons who experience SC [sexual com-
pulsivity] is perhaps one of the most threatening consequences, particularly for gay and bisexual men.'[68] In his
attempt to gain acceptance for his new sexual disorder,
Martin Kafka stressed similar penalties. Hypersexual disorder could result in 'severe pair-bond dysfunction, marital
discord, divorce, sexually transmitted diseases including HIV
infection, substantial financial expenditures, job loss, and
unplanned pregnancies'.[69] Rory Reid and his co-researchers
have written that 'Hypersexual patients often present with
high levels of comorbid psychopathology including mood,
anxiety, attention-deficit, and substance-related disorders.'
They suffer from 'proneness to boredom...impulsivity and
shame...interpersonal sensitivity, alexithymia, loneliness,
and low self-esteem'. They are at 'increased risk for loss of
employment, legal problems, social isolation, higher rates of
divorce...and sexually transmitted infections'.[70] (One is
reminded of Carnes's claim on a national talk show in 1984
that car accidents were common among sex addicts because

they were not focused on their driving![71]) Sexual disorder indeed.

One might expect that this conservative agenda would have surfaced in sex addiction's attitude to same-sex sexual desire and acts. There were exceptions. The early 1990s self-help organization Sexual Compulsives Anonymous (SCA) aimed to help its gay and lesbian members come to terms with their sexualities rather than rejecting them: 'Success in SCA means learning to live contentedly with our sexual identity, not transcending it – much as many of us would like to.'[72] But generally what we find in the story of same-sex sexual addiction is a rather tortured discussion of male homosexuality, a striking silence concerning lesbianism, and a permeating sexual conservatism. SCA, after all, rejected 'the nether-world of compulsive sex' and embraced same-sex monogamy.[73]

A New York sex therapist and psychologist and consultant to the Gay Men's Health Crisis reported that as early as 1982 gay men were approaching him:

> In general, these men were highly anxious about AIDS and the risk that their sexual behavior seemed to hold. They reported not feeling in control of their sexual behavior, reported having more sex than they wanted, and reported feeling victimized by their frequent sexual activity, sometimes in a variety of ways beside the risk of AIDS. Many reported spending far too much time, by their own definition, in the pursuit of sex.[74]

This could have come straight from the pages of a sexual addiction self-help manual. A Manhattan therapist in the 1980s, who was critical of the very concept of sexual compulsion, thought that AIDS had 'created a new market for the sexual compulsion movement – people are scared to death for their very survival'.[75] It was only a matter of time until the measures of sexual compulsivity were applied to gay men and such tests were used to predict 'a potential association between sexual compulsivity and HIV transmission risks'.[76]

Not just men were at risk, of course.[77] The study of gay, lesbian and bisexual New Yorkers already referred to obviously included those other than homosexual men, indeed argued for the gendered nature of sexual compulsivity.[78]

However, the assumed link between hypersexuality and male homosexuality certainly stalks the literature. Lawrence Hatterer's work with 'changing' male homosexuality formed the basis for his pioneering sex addiction therapy. Most of the addictive sexual behaviour in *Changing Homosexuality in the Male* (1970) involved same-sex sexual acts.[79] In *The Pleasure Addicts* (1980) Hatterer denied that he was arguing that 'all homosexual behavior and life-styles are addictive', drew a distinction between 'viable homosexual life-styles' and 'addictive and asocial homosexual practices', and certainly recognized homophobia as a factor in homosexual adjustment. But male, same-sex sexual interaction did form what was close to a default position in his book on the addictive process.[80] His published case histories had strong homosexual content – 'Whenever I'm near Forty Second Street, with a porno shop every twenty feet, it's like I'm in a fever. Or in those movie houses, where everyone's wandering around looking for a blow job or to get jerked off.'[81] His descriptions of addictive environments and sexual temptation were knowing maps of New York gay sex:

> Tom's history does show that it is not easy to enter homosexual society and avoid addictive milieus. The first places homosexuals chance upon or are guided to that offer anonymity, comfort, and peer support are commercial (homosexual bars, baths, movie houses, and discos) or public (cruising neighborhoods, parks, auto rest stops, urinals, transportation stations).[82]

Hatterer's justification for this focus was 'because of many homosexuals' greater vulnerability to being driven into sexual addictiveness'.[83] Yet we should remind ourselves that this was the author who had referred to 'recovered' homosexuals, 'homosexual illness' and 'dehomosexualizing the patient', and who certainly stressed the more negative aspects of homosexuality.[84] As one of his patients challenged him, 'I don't know whether you realize it, but you often talk about homosexuals as if they are some kind of inferior people.'[85]

It is difficult to avoid the impression, then, that for Hatterer (and many but not all of his patients) it was the behaviour itself that was the problem. His case histories mention his self-help group Homosexuals Anonymous as 'a group where they help gay guys who don't want to be gay'.[86] 'He said you told him tricking like we do is like...an addiction...it starts different, but when it gets to be too much of a habit it makes you spaced-out and stuff, and you're like a sex head.'[87] Hatterer's Homosexuals Anonymous appears to have been for those who were troubled by their same-sex desires.[88] Homosexuality and sexual addiction were merged in the therapeutic logic of this early addictionologist.

On the one hand, male bisexual and homosexual sexual culture has been a kind of outer limit for gauging compulsive sex. What is problematic in heterosexuality may be accepted in the world of same-sex sex. If hypersexuality – masturbation, use of pornography, 'engaging in sex with multiple anonymous partners' – is an 'exaggerated expression of more socially accepted behaviors', where does that leave such actions in gay New York where norms are 'more liberal'? If the test for compulsive sexual behaviour holds up in that environment, for those recruited from online chat rooms and outside parks and bath houses rather than from SAA meetings, then the condition seems confirmed.[89]

On the other hand, Keane has referred to same-sex desire being considered 'guilty until proven innocent' in sex addiction discourse and written that HIV/AIDS was the addictionologists' 'trump card' in their warnings of the dangers of the sexual malady.[90] As a 1989 advice book stated, 'With the devastating epidemic of AIDS transforming every casual sexual encounter into a potentially fatal one, people will certainly die as a direct consequence of sex addiction.'[91] 'The numbers of gay men seeking relief from sexually dependent behaviors have clearly risen with the advent of HIV and AIDS', wrote Robert Weiss in an influential sex addiction text in 2002; 'Long-term illness and death, relating in part to sexual behaviors, have vitalized the sexual recovery movement and brought forward tragic realities to the gay community.'[92] Indeed some accounts treat gay men as the ground zero of sexual danger. If normal sex addicts suffer from clustered disorders or Triple Diagnosis, 'Quadruple Diagnosis' is 'common' in gay men: with comorbid substance abuse, depression, sexual compulsivity and HIV/AIDS.[93] 'It is a reasonable hypothesis...that homosexual male sexual addicts would report even higher occurrences of multiple addiction than do heterosexual sexual addicts', Weiss claimed.[94] 'Estimates indicate that rates of hypersexuality are higher among gay and bisexual men (GBM)', wrote the authors of a 2013 study, 'ranging from 14% to 28% among community examples'.[95] Moreover, the symptomatic shame in the sex addiction of gay men was a double shame: ingrained shame of self as well as of sexual longings, their 'shaming and disavowed sexual histor[ies]' the more intense.[96] Not much sense of gay pride for these men.

Yet AIDS and the homosexuality with which it was so firmly linked in the 1980s and 1990s have not proven as central to the sex addiction project as one might have predicted when the initial phase of the impact of AIDS was seen as an opportunity to rethink issues of sexual control. Perhaps this was because a double standard was operating with respect to homosexual sex in matters of sex addiction. With heterosexual sex, as we have seen, almost any casual encounter could come into the territory of troublesome and addictive behaviour. This contrasts with the advice given to gay male sex addicts in *Cruise Control* (2005), which reassured the reader that

> Not everyone who engages in anonymous sex, sees prostitutes, has multiple partners, is involved in the B/D-S/M or fetish scene, or participates in public sex is a sex addict. Not everyone who has affairs, unsafe sex, or keeps sexual secrets is a sex addict: indeed most people who fit these descriptions are likely not.[97]

Sexual addiction was thought to exist for gay men – hence *Cruise Control* – but the moral parameters were vastly different, the definitional criteria varied. Weiss, the author of *Cruise Control* and founder of the Sexual Recovery Institute in Los Angeles, saw sexual addiction in gay men as hidden in a culture generally supportive of (safe) casual sex: 'a counterculture of unfettered sexual expression can also serve to enable the denial of men who are locked into destructive addictive sexual patterns'. (Weiss defined the line being crossed as the point at which 'you lose the ability to choose whether or not you are going to be sexual'.) Of course this invisibility only served to reinforce the claims to the ubiquity of the malady by industry practitioners. Without any verification, Weiss asserted that 'Approximately 10% of gay men are sex addicts.'[98]

However, this does not explain the whole picture. Addictionology has been inconsistent in its attitudes to homosexuality. The various quoted comments in the preceding pages about bath houses, Internet hooking-up, cruising, attraction to she-males and so on have implied a sense in which homosexual sex was assumed to be compulsive. This was surely what Weiss's angry interveners at a sex addiction training programme meant when they said that the concept pathologized 'gay male culture while promoting the "traditional heterosexual values of single partnership and marriage"'. Multi-partnered, casual sex was 'the birthright of gay men who had long been shamed enough for their sexual choices'.[99] Harrison's sexual behaviour in a case study presented in an issue of the *Journal of Social Work Practice* (2001), amidst dire warnings of 'genital/urinary disorders and seropositive illnesses (hepatitis and HIV infection)', consisted of anonymous movie theatre and restroom sex of a sort not at all out of keeping with gay sex in any urban environment.[100] Though Harrison was conflicted by his practice of oral sex and mutual masturbation, it is unlikely that he was helped much by the treatment regime of bibliotherapy (reading Carnes), self-hypnosis, increased church activities and avoiding subway routes with 'gay bathrooms'. The fact that he initially reduced his encounters from five to three a week, then two, then abstention for 37 days, with a 'slip' on the thirty-eighth, indicates as much.[101] Coming to terms with his sexuality might have been a more productive solution. The significant point, though, is that it was the same-sex sexual practices that were the marker of compulsive sexuality.

Yet it remains true that addictionology's preoccupation has been with heterosexual rather than homosexual loss of control. As befitting a normative discourse in a heteronormative culture, sexual addiction has been remarkably heterosexual in its predilections. The literature is curiously fixated with heterosexual sex and with the encouragement of a very restrained, confined practice of heterosexuality. As Keane has put it, 'Sex addiction discourse...repeats the valorization of conventional heterosexual intimacy as the only source of real and lasting happiness...the only possible venue for genuine relationships and genuine self-development...is the family home'.[102]

When Lars von Trier has Joe (Charlotte Gainsbourg), the nymphomaniac in *Nymphomaniac: Volume 2* (2014), tear up her prepared speech and proclaim to a meeting of female sex addicts that she is not like them, call the facilitator a member of 'society's morality police' and shock the self-help group with her pride in her perversity – 'I love my cunt and my filthy, dirty lust' – he was making a very similar point to the chapter that you have just read.[103] Sex addiction is sexually conservative.

Chapter 8
Conclusion

Tiger Woods claims to be addicted to sex. Bullshit! These are hot women he was having sex with. If he was having sex with a dead chicken, I'd say, wow, that guy is addicted to sex.

Greg Rogell, 2011[1]

To achieve a sense of perspective on the issue of sex addiction, it is instructive to consider a study of the general population carried out in New Zealand and published in 2010. It formed part of a unique longitudinal study of a cohort of more than a thousand people born in the city of Dunedin in 1972/3 and studied and surveyed (mainly on matters other than sex) at various stages in their development. The investigation of their reported sexual behaviour and attitudes targeted 940 people, the bulk of the surviving cohort interviewed at the age of 32 and willing to discuss their sexual experiences and beliefs. The advantage of this study is that it surveyed a sample of the general population rather than an unrepresentative, targeted one (Candeo's Mormons or Carnes's participants, for example). The participants were asked if, in the last 12 months, they had had 'sexual fantasies, urges or behavior' that they had felt were 'out of control'. These were called 'out of control sexual experiences' – which, it should be noted, are different to out-of-control sexual *behaviour*. They were asked whether both their out-of-control sexual experiences and their actual sexual behaviour had interfered with their lives.

What is interesting about the study is that while 13 per cent of men and 7 per cent of women reported out-of-control sexual experiences in the preceding year, very few of the total group – 4 per cent of men and 2 per cent of women – thought that it actually interfered with their lives. Most of the reported anxiety involved fantasies and urges rather than actions. Few reported that their actual behaviour affected their lives adversely (a huge part of the sexual addiction rationale): less than 1 per cent of all men and even fewer women were so affected. As the researchers concluded, 'This suggests that the clinical syndrome of out of control sexual behavior may be unlikely to occur as frequently as has been previously surmised.'[2] Though they did not state it, the disparity between the levels of reported out-of-control sexual experiences as fantasy or impulse (on the one hand) and actual sexual behaviour (on the other) may have suggested the anxiety-producing effects of sexual addiction discourse.

Or we could consider Eric Blumberg's fascinating study of forty-four highly sexual women, those who desired sex six or seven times a week or more and/or saw sex as central to their lives and considered themselves to be highly sexual. (For example, one woman's reported weekly sexual outlet was masturbating fourteen times, having ten sexual interactions with a primary partner and twenty with another contact or contacts.)[3] These women might have been considered prime candidates for a diagnosis of sex addiction. Yet it was a description not used until societal and medical attitudes were discussed: 'That was when they labeled me addicted to sex', one woman reported of her encounter with a therapist.[4] The women claimed satisfaction and pleasure from their sexuality as well as 'negative themes'.[5] But the negative aspects, apart from relationship difficulties, featured societal attitudes: the reactions of other women and a cultural discomfort with highly sexual women, including allegations of sex addiction and nymphomania. They were not the dysfunctions of the sex addict stereotype. Moreover, Blumberg, 'an experienced addictionologist', considered and rejected the label of sex addiction as 'not useful in understanding the behavior of the study participants'.

The interviewees overall expressed strong satisfaction with themselves and their sexual choices and had grown to see themselves as psychologically strong because of having to make conscious choices in this area. Their behavior in meeting their sexual desires was typically planned, deliberate, and under their complete control. The participants did not describe their sexual behavior in ways that suggested they used it to cope with life circumstances to the exclusion of other coping mechanisms.[6]

It was far from the distressed, problematic sex of defined sexual addiction.

The narrative of sex addiction's progress is, of course, not yet concluded. The story in the US seems very different from that in the UK, where, despite its media profile, sexual addiction has made little impact on the mental health provisions of the British National Health Service.[7] It is likely that the Internet will continue to play a role, especially given that cybersex addiction is but one of many examples of Problematic Internet Use (PIU).[8]

One of the more concerning developments in addictionology has been its embracing of the neurobiological and genetic turn.[9] As Ian Hacking wrote in 2007, 'There is now a steady drive to trace the medical to the biological, and the biological to the genetic.'[10] Research on neural circuits and genetic influences has taken hold in psychiatry – correlating anxiety disorders with 'neural mechanisms' and 'risk genes'.[11] It is impacting modifications to DSM-5 as we write; the latest *Manual* specifically refers to the structural influences of neuroscience and genetics.[12] And there have been highly influential calls for rethinking categories in the light of 'the most compelling current neurobiological and genetic hypotheses'.[13] 'More Than Meets the Brain: Inside Neuropsychiatry's Secrets' was the heading of a publicity email from the psychiatrist's trade publication *Psychiatric Times* that arrived in one of the authors' inboxes as we were writing this section.[14] It was entirely predictable that neuropsychiatry would impact on sex addiction studies – especially given the latter's bid for DSM recognition of hypersexual disorder. 'Do those who develop out-of-control patterns of sexual behavior have lower levels of serotonin transporter gene markers?' John Bancroft mused in 2008.[15]

Hence a 2012 article hypothesized that sex released neuronal dopamine (DA) in the nucleus accumbens (NAc) section of the brain, analogous to the inducements of drugs: 'both drug addiction and sexual addiction represent pathological forms of neuroplasticity along with the emergence of aberrant behaviors involving a cascade of neurochemical changes mainly in the brain's rewarding circuitry'.[16] The authors cogitated on the roles of individual receptor (e.g. DRD2, DRD4, AVPR1A) and transporter genes (DAT1). Yet the article's scientific methodology consisted mainly of the citing of multiple studies involving copulating mice, rabbits, prairie voles and hamsters, and extrapolations from studies of music response and psychoactive drug intake.[17] It also involved some rather clumsy imposing of genotypes on to social scenarios. For example, Amy's failure to relate to men other than sexually, her constant flirting and inability to find satisfaction in long-term fidelity: 'This may be a case where "no satisfaction" could be lack of sufficient DA D2 receptor density.' (Not that Amy's genes had been profiled.)[18] And the stripper-related problems of Roger the club owner may have had something to do with DRD2. (Not that he was tested either.) This teaming of sex addiction therapists (Stefanie and Patrick Carnes are among the co-authors) and neuroscientists does not inspire great confidence in future collaborations of this type.

It seems, then, that the rush to pair addictionology and neurobiology has outstripped the current state of knowledge (much like the critique of DSM-5's premature embrace of neuroscience). Fred Berlin was hopeful of the possibilities of the use of positron emission topography (PET scanning) to monitor the brain changes of paedophiles during sexual arousal (his area of specialization). But Berlin, the founder of the Johns Hopkins Sexual Disorders Clinic, has been far more cautious in his assessment of the general applicability of neurobiological research to sexual compulsivity, pointing out that the bulk of the science has related to animals and that human research has been very limited: 'Little is known about neurobiologic factors that may be correlated with sexual compulsivity.'[19]

It is possible, given both the focus on neurobiology and the obsession with cybersex, that another trend will be that the patients will get younger. Eric Griffin-Shelley warned in 2002, without any cited evidence, that the plight of adolescent sex addicts was worse than that of those with general mental health problems: 'Very few of them are identified, and fewer are receiving any type of care or counseling... Most sex and love addicts trace their initial acting out to adolescence or before.'[20] Jennifer Riemersma and Michael Sytsma's previously cited study of what they term the 'GenText' generation warned of what amounted to brain damage as a result of early exposure to graphic sexual material on the Internet: 'Neurochemical alterations associated with addiction profoundly influence the young adults' [sic] developing brain, and may set the young addict up for more intense and dangerous forms of sexually addictive behavior.'[21] They argued therefore – in keeping, it has to be said, with DSM's trend towards the younger patient – that 'prevention and early intervention strategies' were needed: 'Specialized treatment with child and adolescent therapists trained in sexual addiction is extremely uncommon. Yet significant numbers of children, adolescents, and young adults are in need of just such specialized treatment.'[22] Watch out for 10-year-old sex addicts.

Hacking once discussed the various elements that go into what he has termed 'making up people': the classification (the naming of the 'disorder' – his example was Multiple Personality Disorder); the people (the patients suffering from what is claimed to be the malady); the institutions (like IITAP, SASH and SAA in the case of sex addiction, though they were not his illustrations; but also, in his framework, establishments such as therapy workshops and talk show television); knowledge, both expert and popular (we saw that in the case of sex addictionology the boundaries were somewhat indistinct); and finally the experts (again a fuzzy category in the case of sex addiction, including patients themselves, psychiatrists, psychologists, media personalities, talk show hosts, filmmakers, therapists and, of course, the DSM).[23]

As the case of 'making up people' explored in our book makes clear, the interactions between the various elements vary; different categories of what are claimed to be disorders have different histories. When Peter Conrad examined the concept of medicalization in an exploratory article in 1992,

he specifically mentioned sex addiction, along with alcoholism, as examples of minimal medicalization in the sense that
their treatment as diseases (part of the concept of medicalization) was not dependent on the medical profession (he referred
to the lack of DSM endorsement) and relied rather on media
publicity and lay interests.[24] In other words, sex addiction
conformed to two of the essential elements of medicalization
identified by Conrad – a conceptual frame and appeal at a
popular, non-specialist level – but did not have the third
ingredient – institutional promulgation.[25] We have discussed
sex addiction's part in the process in preceding pages, and
Conrad might well have seen things differently had he been
writing in 2012 rather than 1992. Sex addiction has moved
from a thing named and publicized in mass culture but with
relatively little purchase in official medical culture *to* a syndrome vying for DSM endorsement, with the research culture
necessary for that bid, enthusiastic brokers, some medical
acceptance (despite the DSM) and drug treatment, and
enhanced popular recognition and media acceptance (unthink-
ing credence, we would argue). If DSM acceded and the
pharmaceutical companies showed more interest, this history
could prove very different.

   Helen Keane once wrote of the work that has gone into
constructing the syndrome of sexual addiction. It was 'not
just a matter of recognizing an already-existing pathology,
but of producing a recognizable disease entity through epis-
temological labour'.[26] Readers of this book will have some
idea of the variety and extent of this work – and of our own
labour in unpicking the very constituting of the syndrome.
We have argued that sexual addiction's strange, short story
of social opportunism, diagnostic amorphism, therapeutic
self-interest and popular cultural endorsement is marked by
an essential social conservatism. 'Sex addiction' has become
a convenient term to describe disapproved sex, what Jerome
Wakefield has termed a confusion of 'social disapproval and
morality with issues of health and disorder'.[27] We can wonder
at its reductive powers – as we saw in Chapter 4's discussion
of film. In a remarkable instance of this the addictionologist
Robert Weiss managed to make Lars von Trier's *Nymphomaniac* (2014), a film that was perversely about nymphomania,
not sex addiction, in fact consciously critical of sex addiction,

into a case study of the malady: 'sex addiction accurate'.[28] We can marvel at the survival of a category amidst all the evidence to the contrary and the stretching of its meaning beyond... well... meaning.

Mentalization-based therapy for sex addiction (MBT-SA) – 'founded on research from evolutionary science, developmental psychology, attachment theory, psychotherapeutic clinical trials, and neuroscience' – encourages therapists and their sexually addicted patients to apply social constructionism to their problem, to think reflectively, to question, challenge and 'not-know', to embrace open-mindedness, to read Stephen Levine, to actually 'problematize the very concept of "sexual addiction"'.[29] But its advocates persist (in 2014) in their acceptance of the concept of sex addiction as a condition in need of therapy, 'We theorize that sexual addiction may be influenced or characterized in part by dysfunctional mentalization.'[30] The role of the clinician is to evaluate 'the features/symptoms of the client's sexual addiction'.[31] There is little actual problematizing of the concept.

Sexual addiction's sufferers are persuaded of its existence yet are not invariably convinced to translate their thoughts into action. Rory Reid found that of sixty-seven male outpatients at a clinic specializing in hypersexuality, 70 per cent (forty-seven) were ambivalent about that treatment and only 11 per cent (seven) 'were actively engaged in modifying their behavior'. The remaining 19 per cent (thirteen) had made minor efforts, but their sexual adjustments were planned rather than actually enacted.[32] In other words, hesitation extended to almost 90 per cent of those sexually addicted.

For all the discussion, the central issue remains: sex addiction is a label without explanatory force. As a study of 'sexual compulsivity' among students at (appropriately) Alfred Kinsey's University of Indiana concluded, 'What may appear to be pathological compulsive sexual behavior to researchers and health professionals may actually be experienced as normal sexual exploration by college students.'[33] And this, though put somewhat more crudely, was Greg Rogell's point in this chapter's epigraph about Tiger Woods and the dead chicken.

Notes

1 Introduction

1 C. Palahniuk, *Choke: A Novel* (New York, 2002), p. 203.
2 G. Goodman, *Daddy's Secret Cedar Chest* (Mustang, OK, 2013), no pagination.
3 Ibid.
4 R. R. Irons and J. R. Schneider, 'Sexual Addiction: Significant Factor in Sexual Exploitation by Health Care Professionals', *Sexual Addiction & Compulsivity*, 1:3 (1994), 198–214, quote at 204.
5 A. Goodman, 'Sexual Addiction: Designation and Treatment', *Journal of Sex & Marital Therapy*, 18:4 (1992), 303–14, quote at 312.
6 G. Manley, 'Treatment and Recovery for Sexual Addicts', *Nurse Practitioner*, 15:6 (1990), 34–41, esp. Table 2 on 38; L. J. Hatterer, *The Pleasure Addicts: The Addictive Process – Food, Sex, Drugs, Alcohol, Work, and More* (Cranbury, NJ, 1980), pp. 119, 120; M. C. Quadland, 'Compulsive Sexual Behavior: Definition of a Problem and an Approach to Treatment', *Journal of Sex & Marital Therapy*, 11:2 (1985), 121–32, at 123.
7 D. Elliott, *Love Addict* (n.p., but USA, 1959); C. Aldrich, *Love Addict* (San Diego, 1966).
8 W. Donner, *The Sex Addicts* (n.p., but USA, 1964), p. 84.
9 Ibid., pp. 107, 129.
10 L. J. Hatterer, *Changing Homosexuality in the Male: Treatment for Men Troubled by Homosexuality* (New York, 1970), pp. 113 (for quote), 415.

11 A. K. Offit, *Night Thoughts: Reflections of a Sex Therapist* (New York, 1981), p. 123.

12 M. F. Schwartz and W. S. Brasted, 'Sexual Addiction', *Medical Aspects of Human Sexuality*, 19:10 (1985), 103–7.

13 D. C. Renshaw, 'Comment: What is Sexual Addiction?', *British Journal of Sexual Medicine*, 13:11 (1986), 305–6, quote at 306.

14 *Diagnostic and Statistical Manual of Mental Disorders (Third Edition – Revised): DSM-III-R* (Washington, DC, 1987), p. 296.

15 R. J. Barth and B. N. Kinder, 'The Mislabeling of Sexual Impulsivity', *Journal of Sex & Marital Therapy*, 13:1 (1987), 15–23.

16 S. R. Lieblum and R. C. Rosen (eds.), *Sexual Desire Disorders* (New York, 1988), pp. 9 ('hyperactive desire', 'sexual compulsion', 'sexual addiction'), 42–4 ('Hyperactive Sexual Desire').

17 J. Money and M. Lamacz, *Vandalized Lovemaps: Paraphilic Outcomes of Seven Cases in Pediatric Sexology* (Buffalo, NY, 1989), p. 36.

18 L. Salzman, 'The Highly Sexed Man', *Medical Aspects of Human Sexuality*, 6:1 (1972), 36–49, quote at 49; C. D. Kasl, *Women, Sex, and Addiction: A Search for Love and Power* (New York, 1989), p. ix.

19 A. W. Schaef, *Escape from Intimacy* (New York, 1989), p. 10.

20 S. R. Lieblum and R. C. Rosen, 'Introduction', in Lieblum and Rosen (eds.), *Sexual Desire Disorders*, p. 9.

21 Ibid.

22 'Issue 6 Can Sex Be an Addiction?', in R. T. Francoeur (ed.), *Taking Sides: Clashing Views on Controversial Issues in Human Sexuality* (Guilford, CT, 1989), pp. 84–97.

23 J. M. Irvine, 'Reinventing Perversion: Sex Addiction and Cultural Anxieties', *Journal of the History of Sexuality*, 5:3 (1995), 429–50, quote at 435.

24 Irvine, 'Reinventing Perversion'.

25 M. P. Levine and R. R. Troiden, 'The Myth of Sexual Compulsivity', *Journal of Sex Research*, 25:3 (1988), 347–63, quote at 349.

26 Irvine, 'Reinventing Perversion', 438.

27 Ibid., 440.

28 Irons and Schneider, 'Sexual Addiction', 206, 208, 209.

29 M. R. Lasser, 'Sexual Addiction and Clergy', *Pastoral Psychology*, 39:4 (1991), 213–35, esp. 215.

30 A. Goodman, 'Sexual Addiction', in J. H. Lowinson, P. Ruiz, R. B. Millman, and J. G. Langrod (eds.), *Substance Abuse: A Comprehensive Textbook* (Baltimore, 1997), pp. 340–54; V. A. Sadock, 'Normal Human Sexuality and Sexual and Gender Identity Disorders', in B. J. Sadock and V. A. Sadock (eds.),

Kaplan & Sadock's Comprehensive Textbook of Psychiatry, Seventh Edition, 2 vols. (Philadelphia, 2000), vol. 1, p. 1599.

31 P. J. Carnes, 'Sexual Addiction', in Sadock and Sadock (eds.), *Kaplan & Sadock's Comprehensive Textbook of Psychiatry, Eighth Edition*, 2 vols. (Philadelphia, 2005), vol. 1, pp. 1991–2001.

32 Irvine, 'Reinventing Perversion', 442; L. Williams, 'Porn Studies: Proliferating Pornographies On/Scene: An Introduction', in L. Williams (ed.), *Porn Studies* (Durham, NC, 2004), pp. 1–23. See also B. McNair, *Striptease Culture: Sex, Media and the Democratization of Desire* (New York, 2002); L. M. Ward, 'Understanding the Role of Entertainment Media in the Sexual Socialization of American Youth: A Review of Empirical Research', *Developmental Review*, 23:3 (2003), 347–88; S. Paasonen, K. Nikunen and L. Saarenmaa (eds.), *Pornification: Sex and Sexuality in Media Culture* (New York, 2007); K. C. W. Kammeyer, *A Hypersexual Society: Sexual Discourse, Erotica, and Pornography in America Today* (New York, 2008); F. Attwood (ed.), *Mainstreaming Sex: The Sexualization of Western Culture* (New York, 2010).

33 F. Attwood, 'Sexed Up: Theorizing the Sexualization of Culture', *Sexualities*, 9:1 (2006), 77–94, quote at 78.

34 See, for example, B. L. A. Mileham, 'Online Infidelity in Internet Chat Rooms: An Ethnographic Exploration', *Computers in Human Behavior*, 23:1 (2007), 11–31; N. M. Döring, 'The Internet's Impact on Sexuality: A Critical Review of 15 Years of Research', *Computers in Human Behavior*, 25:5 (2009), 1089–101; D. K. Wysocki and C. D. Childers, '"Let My Fingers Do the Talking": Sexting and Infidelity in Cyberspace', *Sexuality & Culture*, 15:3 (2011), 217–39; C. Brickell, 'Sexuality, Power and the Sociology of the Internet', *Current Sociology*, 60:1 (2012), 28–44.

35 D. Wallis, 'Just Say No', *The New Yorker*, 13 January 1997; H. Kutchins and S. A. Kirk, *Making Us Crazy: DSM: The Psychiatric Bible and the Creation of Mental Disorders* (New York, 1997), p. 12.

36 K. S. Young, 'Psychology of Computer Use: XL. Addictive Use of the Internet: A Case That Breaks the Stereotype', *Psychological Reports*, 79:3 (1996), 899–902; K. S. Young, 'Internet Addiction: The Emergence of a New Clinical Disorder', *CyberPsychology & Behavior*, 1:3 (1998), 237–44.

37 A. Cooper and I. D. Marcus, 'Men Who Are Not In Control of Their Sexual Behavior', in S. B. Levine, D. B. Risen and S. E. Althof (eds.), *Handbook of Clinical Sexuality for Mental Health Professionals* (New York, 2003), ch. 18, quote at p. 313.

38 J. P. Schneider, 'Understanding and Diagnosing Sex Addiction', in R. H. Coombs (ed.), *Handbook of Addictive Disorders: A Practical Guide to Diagnosis and Treatment* (Hoboken, NJ, 2004), ch. 7, esp. pp. 208–13, 214; R. Weiss, 'Treating Sex Addiction', in Coombs (ed.), *Handbook of Addictive Disorders*, ch. 8, esp. pp. 262–5.

39 Carnes, 'Sexual Addiction', p. 1995.

40 R. Crooks and K. Baur, *Our Sexuality* (Belmont, CA, 2011), pp. 510–13. First published in 2008.

41 T. Todd, 'Premature Ejaculation of "Sexual Addiction" Diagnoses', in S. Green and D. Flemons (eds.), *Quickies: The Handbook of Brief Sex Therapy* (New York, 2004), ch. 5, quote at p. 68.

42 R. Weiss and C. P. Samenow, 'Smart Phones, Social Networking, Sexting and Problematic Sexual Behaviors – A Call for Research', *Sexual Addiction & Compulsivity*, 17:4 (2010), 241–6.

43 S. J. Campling, 'A Review on iRecovery – iPhone/iPad Application', *Sexual Addiction & Compulsivity*, 18:3 (2011), 188–90; https://play.google.com/store/apps/details?id=com.koolappz .EP77708470001.

44 L. J. Hatterer, 'The Addictive Process', *Psychiatric Quarterly*, 54:3 (1982), 149–56, quote at 149.

45 S. Peele, *Diseasing of America* (San Francisco, 1995), pp. 140–1. First published in 1989.

46 S. R. Edwards, 'A Sex Addict Speaks', *SIECUS Report*, 14:6 (1986), 1–3, quote at 2.

47 E. S. Moskowitz, *In Therapy We Trust: America's Obsession With Self-Fulfillment* (Baltimore, 2001), p. 1.

48 Ibid., pp. 246–7.

49 Ibid., pp. 248, 252, 253.

50 Ibid., pp. 255, 307 n. 22.

51 F. Furedi, *Therapy Culture: Cultivating Vulnerability in an Uncertain Age* (London, 2004), esp. pp. 120–4.

52 H. B. Hansen and others, 'Independent Review of Social and Population Variation in Mental Health Could Improve Diagnosis in DSM Revisions', *Health Affairs*, 32:5 (2013), 984–93, quote at 984.

53 Kutchins and Kirk, *Making Us Crazy*, ch. 3. See also A. De Block and P. R. Adriaens, 'Pathologizing Sexual Deviance: A History', *Journal of Sex Research*, 50:3 (2013), 276–98, esp. 287–9.

54 *Diagnostic and Statistical Manual of Mental Disorders (Fifth Edition): DSM-5* (Washington, DC, 2013), pp. 268–70, 410–13.

55 G. d'Orsi, V. Demaio and L. M. Specchio, 'Pathological Gambling Plus Hypersexuality in Restless Legs Syndrome: A New Case', *Neurological Sciences*, 32:4 (2011), 707–9.

56 For previous DSMs, see C. Lane, *Shyness: How Normal Behavior Became a Sickness* (New Haven, 2007), p. 43. See also De Block and Adriaens, 'Pathologizing Sexual Deviance'.

57 M. Angell, *The Truth About the Drug Companies* (New York, 2004), p. 86.

58 See P. Conrad, *The Medicalization of Society: On the Transformation of Human Conditions into Treatable Disorders* (Baltimore, 2007), chs 1, 3, 6, 7. See also Kutchins and Kirk, *Making Us Crazy*, ch. 4; D. Healy, 'The Latest Mania: Selling Bipolar Disorder', *PLoS Medicine*, 3:4 (2006), 0441–4; R. Moyniham and D. Henry, 'The Fight Against Disease Mongering: Generating Knowledge for Action', *PLoS Medicine*, 3:4 (2006), 0425–8; A. Frances, *Saving Normal* (New York, 2013), ch. 5; G. Greenberg, *The Book of Woe: The DSM and the Unmaking of Psychiatry* (London, 2013), ch. 5; and J. M. Pierre, 'Overdiagnosis, Underdiagnosis, Synthesis: A Dialectic for Psychiatry and the DSM', in J. Paris and J. Phillips (eds.), *Making the DSM-5, 2013: Concepts and Controversies* (New York, 2013), ch. 8.

59 See C. Lane, 'How Shyness Became an Illness: A Brief History of Social Phobia', *Common Knowledge*, 12:3 (2006), 388–409; Lane, *Shyness*.

60 *Diagnostic and Statistical Manual of Mental Disorders (Third Edition): DSM-III* (Washington, DC, 1980), pp. 227–30; DSM-5, pp. 202–8.

61 Kutchins and Kirk, *Making Us Crazy*, p. 12.

62 See A. V. Horwitz, *Creating Mental Illness* (Chicago, 2002); Healy, 'Latest Mania'; C. B. Phillips, 'Medicine Goes to School: Teachers as Sickness Brokers for ADHD', *PLoS Medicine*, 3:4 (2006), 0433–5; Lane, *Shyness*; A. V. Horwitz and J. C. Wakefield, *The Loss of Sadness: How Psychiatry Transformed Normal Sorrow Into Depressive Disorder* (Oxford, 2007); Conrad, *Medicalization of Society*; Frances, *Saving Normal*; J. Z. Sadler, 'Considering the Economy of DSM Alternatives', in Paris and Phillips (eds.), *Making the DSM-5*, ch. 2.

63 Lane, *Shyness*.

64 Horwitz and Wakefield, *Loss of Sadness*.

65 Ibid., p. 7.

66 Horwitz, *Creating Mental Illness*, p. 213.

67 R. C. Kessler and others, 'Lifetime Prevalence and Age-of-Onset Distributions of *DSM-IV* Disorders in the National Comorbidity Survey Replication', *Archives of General Psychiatry*, 62 (2005), 593–602.

68 T. Travis, *The Language of the Heart: A Cultural History of the Recovery Movement from Alcoholics Anonymous to Oprah Winfrey* (Chapel Hill, NC, 2009), ch. 1, esp. pp. 3–4, 6.
69 Ibid., p. 17.

2 Beginnings

1 P. Hall, *Understanding and Treating Sex Addiction* (New York, 2013), Ebook, locs. 156–9.
2 M. P. Kafka, 'Hypersexual Disorder: A Proposed Diagnosis for DSM-V', *Archives of Sexual Behaviour*, 39:2 (2010), 377–400, quote at 378.
3 Ibid.
4 See H. Ellis, *Studies in the Psychology of Sex* (New York, 1936).
5 R. von Krafft-Ebing, *Psychopathia Sexualis. With Especial Reference to the Antipathic Sexual Instinct: A Medico-Forensic Study*, trans. F. S. Klaf (New York, 1998), pp. vi, 49.
6 Ibid., pp. 46–52, 322–9.
7 One of the authors has argued this at length elsewhere: K. M. Phillips and B. Reay, *Sex Before Sexuality: A Premodern History* (Cambridge, 2011).
8 Kafka, 'Hypersexual Disorder', 378.
9 Krafft-Ebing, *Psychopathia Sexualis*, p. 47.
10 Ibid., pp. 48–51.
11 Ibid., pp. 325–9.
12 Iwan Bloch, *The Sexual Life of Our Time: In its Relations to Modern Civilization* (London, 1928), p. 429. First published in 1908.
13 Ibid., p. 432.
14 Ibid., p. 429.
15 Ibid., p. 430; R. Weiss, *Sex Addiction 101: A Basic Guide to Healing from Sex, Porn, and Love Addiction* (Longboat Key, FL, 2013), Ebook, locs. 241, 770.
16 Bloch, *Sexual Life of Our Time*, p. 429.
17 Krafft-Ebing, *Psychopathia Sexualis*, p. 48.
18 Ibid., p. 51.
19 Ibid., p. 52.
20 Ibid.
21 Ibid., p. 46.
22 Ibid., pp. 324–5.
23 D. J. Ley, *The Myth of Sex Addiction* (Lanham, MD, 2012), p. 11.

24 B. Rush, *Medical Inquiries and Observations, Upon the Diseases of the Mind* (Philadelphia, 1812), p. 347.
25 Ibid., p. 350–3.
26 Ibid., p. 315.
27 W. Stekel, *Bi-Sexual Love*, trans. J. S. Van Teslaar (New York, 1950), pp. 97–172. First published in 1922.
28 Ibid., pp. 116, 141, 164.
29 Ibid., p. 97.
30 Ibid., p. 102.
31 Ibid., p. 103.
32 Ibid., p. 163.
33 A. Ellis and E. Sagarin, *Nymphomania: A Study of the Oversexed Woman* (New York, 1964), p. 29.
34 Ibid.
35 Ibid., p. 26.
36 C. Groneman, *Nymphomania: A History* (London, 2001), p. 8.
37 Ibid., p. 91.
38 A. K. Offit, *Night Thoughts: Reflections of a Sex Therapist* (New York, 1981), pp. 121, 122.
39 Groneman, *Nymphomania*, p. 142.
40 See Ellis and Sagarin, *Nymphomania*.
41 See, for example, L. Klein, *Normal and Abnormal Sex Ways* (New York, 1962); V. Morhaim, *Casebook: Nymphomania* (New York, 1964); F. S. Klaf, *Satyriasis: A Study of Male Nymphomania* (New York, 1966). See also N. A. Shiff, *Diary of a Nymph* (New York, 1961).
42 Groneman, *Nymphomania*, p. 8; J. M. Irvine, 'Reinventing Perversion: Sex Addiction and Cultural Anxieties', *Journal of the History of Sexuality*, 5:3 (1995), 429–50, esp. 430–1.
43 Irvine, 'Reinventing Perversion', 431.
44 Kafka, 'Hypersexual Disorder', 379, 381.
45 A. C. Kinsey, W. B. Pomeroy and C. E. Martin, *Sexual Behavior in the Human Male* (Philadelphia, 1948), p. 199.
46 Ibid.
47 L. Clark, 'The Insatiable Male', *Sexology*, 29:6 (1963), 415–17, quote at 416.
48 Ibid., 415.
49 Kinsey, Pomeroy and Martin, *Sexual Behavior in the Human Male*, p. 202.
50 Ibid., p. 201.
51 For changes in deviance theory, see J. M. Irvine, ' "The Sociologist as Voyeur": Social Theory and Sexuality Research, 1910–1978', *Qualitative Sociology*, 26:4 (2003), 429–56.
52 'Nymphomania', letter in *Sexology*, 19:2 (1952), 51–2.

53 'Oversexed Husband', letter in *Sexology*, 26:10 (1960), 676.
54 Editorial, 'What Causes Nymphomania?', *Sexology*, 15:9 (1949), 561–7, quote at 562.
55 'Nymphomania', letter in Sexology, 27:8 (1961), 568–9.
56 M. Hirschfeld, *Sexual Anomalies: The Origins, Nature, and Treatment of Sexual Disorders* (New York, 1956), ch. 6, quote at p. 89. First published in 1948.
57 Ibid., pp. 86–93.
58 C. Allen, *A Textbook of Psychosexual Disorders* (London, 1969), ch. 16. First published in 1962.
59 Ibid., p. 355.
60 Stekel, *Bi-Sexual Love*, pp. 145–6.
61 S. B. Levine, 'A Modern Perspective on Nymphomania', *Journal of Sex & Marital Therapy*, 8:4 (1982), 316–24, quotes at 320, 323.
62 Offit, *Night Thoughts*, p. 122.
63 S. L. Moore, 'Satyriasis: A Case Study', *Journal of Clinical Psychiatry*, 41:8 (1981), 279–81.
64 We have in mind N. Baker, *House of Holes* (New York, 2011).
65 Krafft-Ebing, *Psychopathia Sexualis*, p. 51, for both examples.
66 See, for example, H. Oosterhuis, *Stepchildren of Nature: Krafft-Ebing, Psychiatry, and the Making of Sexual Identity* (Chicago, 2000).
67 For Stoller, also mentioned by Kafka, see R. J. Stoller, *Perversion: The Erotic Form of Hatred* (London, 1986), p. 8. First published in 1975.
68 E. E. Levitt, 'Nymphomania', *Sexual Behavior*, 3:3 (1973), 13–17, quotes at 17.
69 Ibid., 13.
70 Ibid., 17.
71 Our calculations from D. W. Burnap and J. S. Golden, 'Sexual Problems in Medical Practice', *Journal of Medical Education*, 42:7 (1967), 673–80, esp. Table 2, 675.
72 A. Auerback, 'Satyriasis and Nymphomania', *Medical Aspects of Human Sexuality*, 2:9 (1968), 39–45; L. Salzman, 'The Highly Sexed Man', *Medical Aspects of Human Sexuality*, 6:1 (1972), 36–49; T. P. Detre and J. M. Himmelhoch, 'Hyperlibido', *Medical Aspects of Human Sexuality*, 7:9 (1973), 172–86.
73 V. A. Sadock, 'Sexual Addiction', in P. Ruiz and E. C. Strain (eds.), *Lowinson and Ruiz's Substance Abuse: A Comprehensive Textbook, Fifth Edition* (Philadelphia, 2011), ch. 26, at p. 393.
74 O. Fenichel, *The Psychoanalytic Theory of Neurosis* (New York, 1945), pp. 234, 384.

75 Ibid., p. 382.
76 V. W. Eisenstein, 'Sexual Problems in Marriage', in V. W. Eisenstein (ed.), *Neurotic Interaction in Marriage* (New York, 1956), ch. 7, quotes at p. 118.
77 M. S. Segal, 'Impulsive Sexuality: Some Clinical and Theoretical Observations', *International Journal of Psychoanalysis*, 44 (1963), 407–18, quote at 408.
78 S. E. Willis, 'Sexual Promiscuity as a Symptom of Personal and Cultural Anxiety', *Medical Aspects of Human Sexuality*, 1:2 (1967), 16–23, quote at 17.
79 J. Orford, 'Hypersexuality: Implications for a Theory of Dependence', *British Journal of Addiction*, 73:3 (1978), 299–310, quotes at 299. The article was adapted in Orford's *Excessive Appetites: A Psychological View of Addictions* (Chichester, 1985), ch. 6: 'Excessive Sexuality'.
80 Orford, 'Hypersexuality', 305.
81 S. Peele and A. Brodsky, *Love and Addiction* (New York, 1975), p. 13. Emphasis in original.
82 S. Peele and A. Brodsky, 'Interpersonal Heroin: Love Can Be an Addiction', *Psychology Today*, 8:3 (1974), 22–6, image on 22.
83 Peele and Brodsky, *Love and Addiction*, p. 15.
84 Ibid., p. 18. Emphasis in original.
85 Ibid., p. 55.
86 Ibid., pp. 15–16.
87 Ibid., p. 18.
88 Ibid., p. 17.
89 S. Peele, *Diseasing of America* (San Francisco, 1995), pp. 140–1. First published in 1989. For example, Benoit Denizet-Lewis uses Peele and his quote 'Addiction is our way of life' in his book *America Anonymous: Eight Addicts in Search of a Life* (New York, 2009), Ebook, p. 13. Peele later referred to Patrick Carnes as having 'picked up on our idea of sex addiction': S. Peele and A. Brodsky, *Love and Addiction* (New York, 2014), Ebook, loc. 311.
90 L. J. Hatterer and J. Ramsey, 'Are You an Addictive Personality?', *Family Circle*, 6 (1974), 138–9.
91 Ibid., 138.
92 Ibid.
93 Ibid., 139.
94 Ibid.
95 L. J. Hatterer, *The Pleasure Addicts: The Addictive Process – Food, Sex, Drugs, Alcohol, Work, and More* (Cranbury, NJ, 1980), quotes at pp. 12, 15, 188.

96 L. J. Hatterer, *Changing Homosexuality in the Male: Treatment for Men Troubled by Homosexuality* (New York, 1970), p. 63.
97 Ibid., pp. 56, 111, 185, 403, 440.
98 Ibid., p. 182.
99 Ibid., p. 197.
100 Hatterer, *The Pleasure Addicts*, p. 37.
101 Ibid.
102 Ibid., pp. 94, 99.
103 Ibid., p. 12.
104 Ibid., p. 117.
105 Ibid., p. 188.
106 Ibid., p. 189.
107 Ibid., p. 188.

3 Addictionology 101

1 Promotional quote for P. Carnes, *Out of the Shadows: Understanding Sexual Addiction* (Minneapolis, 1983).
2 P. J. Carnes and others, 'PATHOS: A Brief Screening Application for Assessing Sexual Addiction', *Journal of Addiction Medicine*, 6:1 (2012), 29–34, at 29.
3 See for example, as sole author: *The Sexual Addiction* (Minneapolis, 1983); *Out of the Shadows*; *Contrary to Love: Helping the Sexual Addict* (Minneapolis, 1989); *Don't Call It Love: Recovery from Sexual Addiction* (New York, 1991); *Counseling the Sexual Addict: Systems, Strategies and Skills* (Center City, MN, 1994); *The Betrayal Bond: Breaking Free of Exploitive Relationships* (Deerfield Beach, FL, 1997); *Facing the Shadow: Starting Sexual and Relationship Recovery* (Carefree, AZ, 2001). And, as co-author, with: L. J. Rening, *27 Tasks for Changing Compulsive, Out-of-Control, and Inappropriate Sexual Behavior* (Plymouth, MN, 1994); J. M. Moriarity, *Sexual Anorexia: Overcoming Sexual Self-Hatred* (Center City, MN, 1997); D. Laaser and M. Laaser, *Open Hearts: Renewing Relationships with Recovery, Romance and Reality* (Wickenburg, AZ, 1999); P. Carnes, D. L. Delmonico and E. Griffin, *In the Shadows of the Net: Breaking Free of Compulsive Online Sexual Behavior* (Center City, MN, 2001); K. M. Adams, *Clinical Management of Sex Addiction* (New York, 2002); and D. L. Delmonico, *Assessment of Sexual Dependency* (New York, 2006).

4 D. Goleman, 'Some Sexual Behavior Viewed as an Addiction', *The New York Times*, 16 October 1984.

5 Calculated from the Ebook version of P. J. Carnes and K. M. Adams (eds.), *Clinical Management of Sex Addiction* (New York, 2013).

6 Carnes, *Don't Call It Love*, p. 30.

7 Carnes, *Out of the Shadows*, p. v. *Out of the Shadows* was the republished title of Carnes, *The Sexual Addiction*. The contents are the same. We use *Out of the Shadows* because it is the more commonly known book and the title of two subsequent editions (1992 and 2001). Unless indicated otherwise, we use the first (1983) edition.

8 http://www.sash.net/sexual-addiction.

9 http://www.sexhelp.com/am-i-a-sex-addict.

10 Ibid.

11 See lists at http://www.sash.net/sexual-addiction.

12 Carnes, *Out of the Shadows*, p. 28.

13 Ibid., p. 37.

14 Ibid., p. 45.

15 P. Carnes, 'Sex Addiction 101: Assessment and Treatment' (2012): IITAP Material for Sex Addiction, http://www.google.co.nz/url?sa=t&rct=j&q=&esrc=s&source=web&cd=2&ved=0CC8QFjAB&url=http%3A%2F%2Fwww.iitap.com%2Fimages%2FSexAddiction101.ppt&ei=sVlMU5XJM5P98QWehYHYCA&usg=AFQjCNGe11LG8RYBiyXcnodBIig_eks-HA&bvm=bv.64542518,d.dGc.

16 R. Weiss, *Cruise Control: Understanding Sex Addiction in Gay Men*, 2nd edn (Carefree, AZ, 2013), p. 6.

17 Carnes, 'Sex Addiction 101'.

18 Carnes, *Out of the Shadows*, p. 25.

19 Weiss, *Cruise Control*, p. xv.

20 P. Carnes, *Out of the Shadows: Understanding Sexual Addiction* (Center City, MN, 2001), p. xvii.

21 Ibid.

22 Carnes, *Out of the Shadows*, pp. i–ii.

23 L. J. Hatterer and J. Ramsey, 'Are You an Addictive Personality?', *Family Circle*, 6 (1974), 138–9, quote at 138.

24 Ibid., 139.

25 Ibid.

26 Carnes, *Out of the Shadows*, pp. 136–7.

27 Alcoholics Anonymous World Services, *Alcoholics Anonymous: The Story of How Many Thousands of Men and Women Have Recovered from Alcoholism (The Big Book)*, 4th edn (New York, 2001), pp. 58–60. See also J. Parker and D. Guest, 'The Integration of Psychotherapy and 12-Step

Programs in Sexual Addiction Treatment', in Carnes and Adams (eds.), *Clinical Management of Sex Addiction*, ch. 8, p. 117.

28 J. M. Irvine, 'Reinventing Perversion: Sex Addiction and Cultural Anxieties', *Journal of the History of Sexuality*, 5:3 (1995), 429–50, quote at 432.

29 Carnes, *Don't Call It Love*, p. 220.

30 Irvine, 'Reinventing Perversion', 432.

31 http://www.recoveryzone.com/tests/sex-addiction/SAST/index .php.

32 For just a sample of the tests available, see: http://psychcentral. com/sexquiz.htm; www.freedomeveryday.org; www.sexhelp. com/am-i-a-sex-addict/sex-addiction-test; www.sash.net/am-i -a-sex-addict; www.sexualrecovery.com/resources/self-tests/ wsast.php; sexaddictionhouston.squarespace.com/storage/Addict _Test.pdf; www.doctoroz.com/quiz/are-you-sex-addict; www .copacms.com/resources/diagnostic-quizes/sexual-addiction -quiz.

33 Carnes, *Contrary to Love*, pp. 218–19.

34 Quote from https://www.recoveryzone.com/tests/sex-addiction/ SAST/SASTresults.php. For the limitations of SAST, see Carnes, *Contrary to Love*, pp. 217, 221.

35 www.sexhelp.com/am-i-a-sex-addict/sexual-addiction-risk -assessment.

36 www.recoveryzone.com.

37 Ibid.

38 www.recoveryzone.com/tests/sex-addiction/PSS/index.php.

39 Carnes, 'Sex Addiction 101'.

40 Carnes, *Don't Call It Love*, pp. 42–67.

41 Ibid., p. 42.

42 Ibid., p. 46.

43 Ibid., p. 68.

44 https://www.recoveryzone.com/tests/sex-addiction/SAST /SASTresults.php.

45 https://www.recoveryzone.com/tests/sex-addiction/SAST /images/patient_sast_score19.png.

46 https://www.recoveryzone.com/tests/sex-addiction/SAST /SASTresults.php.

47 Carnes and Adams (eds.), *Clinical Management of Sex Addiction*, Section 3 (chs 15–23).

48 R. Weiss, *Sex Addiction 101: A Basic Guide to Healing from Sex, Porn, and Love Addiction* (Longboat Key, FL, 2013), Ebook, chs 16–18.

49 K. McDaniel and S. Boggs, *Ready to Heal*, 3rd edn (Carefree, AZ, 2012), p. xii.

50 M. C. Ferree (ed.), *Making Advances: A Comprehensive Guide for Treating Female Sex and Love Addicts* (Royston, GA, 2012). See also C. Kasl, *Women, Sex and Addiction: A Search for Love and Power* (New York, 1990); K. McDaniel, *Ready to Heal: Women Facing Love, Sex and Relationship Addiction* (Carefree, AZ, 2008); T. Rodriguez, 'Sex "Addiction" Isn't a Guy Thing', *The Atlantic*, 19 November 2013: http://www.theatlantic.com/health/archive/2013/11/sex-addiction-isnt-a-guy-thing/281401.

51 M. C. Ferree, 'Females: The Forgotten Sexual Addicts', in Carnes and Adams (eds.), *Clinical Management of Sex Addiction*, ch. 16, quote at p. 240. See also M. C. Ferree, 'Making Advances: Treating Female Sex and Love Addicts', *IITAP*, March 2013: www.iitap.com/images/03_13_IITAP_NEWS_final4.pdf.

52 Ferree, 'Females: The Forgotten Sexual Addicts', p. 258.

53 Ferree, 'Making Advances', no pagination.

54 R. Weiss, 'Treating Sex Addiction', in R. H. Coombs (ed.), *Handbook of Addictive Disorders: A Practical Guide to Diagnosis and Treatment* (Hoboken, NJ, 2004), ch. 8.

55 R. Earle and G. Crow, *Lonely All the Time: Recognizing, Understanding, and Overcoming Sex Addiction, For Addicts and Co-Dependents* (New York, 1989), p. 5.

56 Carnes, *Don't Call It Love*, p. 143.

57 Ibid., p. 152.

58 M. R. Laaser, 'Recovery for Couples', in Carnes and Adams (eds.), *Clinical Management of Sex Addiction*, ch. 9, esp. pp. 122 and 130. Originally published in 1996. See websites: http://www.sanon.org; http://www.coslaa.org; http://www.cosa-recovery.org; http://www.recovering-couples.org.

59 http://www.cosa-recovery.org.

60 http://www.sanon.org/sateen/whatissateen.html.

61 Carnes, *Don't Call it Love*, p. 146.

62 D. Weiss and D. DeBusk, *Women Who Love Sex Addicts: Help For Healing from the Effects of a Relationship With a Sex Addict* (Fort Worth, TX, 1993), p. 9.

63 Ibid., pp. 17, 37.

64 Ibid., p. 185.

65 E. Griffin-Shelley, *Adolescent Sex and Love Addicts* (Westport, CT, 1994).

66 Carnes's interview with Joe Polish, 2011: http://www.youtube.com/watch?v=i1pQfGD_MQI.

67 C. K. Belous, T. M. Timm, G. Chee and M. R. Whitehead, 'Revisiting the Sexual Genogram', *American Journal of Family Therapy*, 40:4 (2012), 281–96, quote at 283.

68 C. Moser, 'Hypersexual Disorder: Searching for Clarity', *Sexual Addiction & Compulsivity*, 20:1–2 (2013), 48–58, quote at 48.

69 D. C. Renshaw, 'Promiscuity is Not a True Addiction', *Chicago Tribune*, 14 January 1991: http://articles.chicagotribune.com/1991-01-14/features/9101040818_1_dear-ann-landess-sexual-column.

70 T. P. Sbraga and W. T. O'Donohue, *The Sex Addiction Workbook: Proven Strategies to Help You Regain Control of Your Life* (Oakland, 2003), p. 2.

71 M. Herkov, 'What Is Sexual Addiction?', PsychCentral: http://psychcentral.com/lib/what-is-sexual-addiction/000748.

72 H. Keane, 'Disorders of Desire: Addiction and Problems of Intimacy', *Journal of Medical Humanities*, 25:3 (2004), 189–204, quote at 191. See also H. Keane, *What's Wrong With Addiction?* (New York, 2002).

73 P. Hall, *Understanding and Treating Sex Addiction* (New York, 2013), Ebook, locs. 162 and 334.

74 A. S. Hastings, *Treating Sexual Shame: A New Map for Overcoming Dysfunction, Abuse, and Addiction* (Northvale, NJ, 1998), p. 70. Emphasis in the original.

75 M. Herkov, 'If You Think You Have a Problem with Sexual Addiction', PsychCentral (2006): http://psychcentral.com/lib/if-you-think-you-have-a-problem-with-sexual-addiction/000750.

76 J. P. Schneider, 'Understanding and Diagnosing Sex Addiction', in Coombs (ed.), *Handbook of Addictive Disorders*, ch. 7, quote at p. 198.

77 Weiss, *Sex Addiction 101*, loc. 1088. See also locs. 311, 783, 798, 1074.

78 M. Laaser, *Healing the Wounds of Sexual Addiction* (Grand Rapids, MI, 2009), Ebook edn, loc. 158.

79 A. W. Schaef, *Escape from Intimacy: Untangling the 'Love' Addictions: Sex, Romance, Relationships* (New York, 1989).

80 M. C. Fulton, 'Breaking Through Defenses', in Carnes and Adams (eds.), *Clinical Management of Sex Addiction*, ch. 3, quote at p. 34. Originally published in 1999.

81 Hall, *Understanding and Treating Sex Addiction*, loc. 402.

82 Ibid.

83 Carnes, *Contrary to Love*, p. 189.

84 Sex Addicts Anonymous, *Sex Addicts Anonymous*, 3rd edn (Houston, TX, 2012), Ebook, loc. 2789.

85 Carnes, *Contrary to Love*, pp. 3–4.

86 M. C. Ferree, *No Stones: Women Redeemed from Sexual Addiction* (Downers Grove, IL, 2013), Ebook, p. 199.

87 *Sex Addicts Anonymous*, loc. 3614.
88 Weiss, *Cruise Control*, p. xvi.
89 Cited in J. R. Sealy, 'Dual and Triple Diagnoses: Addictions, Mental Illness and HIV Infection Guidelines for Outpatient Therapists', in Carnes and Adams (eds.), *Clinical Management of Sex Addiction*, ch. 14, quote at p. 216. Originally published in 1999.
90 Keane, 'Disorders of Desire', 193.
91 Weiss, 'Treating Sex Addiction', p. 233.
92 Carnes, *Out of the Shadows*, p. xi.
93 R. R. Warhol and H. Michie, 'Twelve-Step Teleology: Narratives as Recovery/Recovery as Narrative', in S. Smith and J. Watson (eds.), *Getting a Life: Everyday Uses of Autobiography* (Minneapolis, 1996), pp. 327–50.
94 D. Mason-Schrock, 'Transsexuals' Narrative Construction of the "True Self" ', *Social Psychology Quarterly*, 59:3 (1996), 176–92.
95 D. E. Putnam and M. M. Maheu, 'Online Sexual Addiction and Compulsivity: Integrating Web Resources and Behavioral Telehealth in Treatment', *Sexual Addiction & Compulsivity*, 7:1–2 (2000), 91–112, quote at 101.
96 McDaniel and Boggs, *Ready to Heal*, 3rd edn (2012), p. xi
97 Warhol and Michie, 'Twelve-Step Teleology'.
98 Ferree, 'Females: The Forgotten Sexual Addicts', p. 259.
99 K. M. Adams, *Silently Seduced: When Parents Make Their Children Partners (Revised and Updated)* (Deerfield Beach, FL, 2011), p. 1.
100 Carnes, *Contrary to Love*, pp. 1–2.
101 Carnes, *Out of the Shadows* (2001), p. xviii.
102 Carnes's interview with Joe Polish, 2011: http://www.youtube.com/watch?v=i1pQfGD_MQI.
103 Carnes, *Don't Call It Love*, p. 32; P. Carnes, *A Gentle Path Through the Twelve Steps* (Center City, MN, 2012), p. 8.
104 A. Katehakis, 'Affective Neuroscience and the Treatment of Sex Addiction', *Sexual Addiction & Compulsivity*, 16:1 (2009), 1–31.
105 Carnes, *Don't Call It Love*, p. 32.
106 Carnes, Delmonico and Griffin, *In the Shadows of the Net*; J. P. Schneider and R. Weiss, *Cybersex Exposed: Simple Fantasy or Obsession?* (Center City, MN, 2001); A. Cooper (ed.), *Sex and the Internet: A Guidebook for Clinicians* (New York, 2002).
107 D. Delmonico, 'Cybersex: High-Tech Sex Addiction', *Sexual Addiction & Compulsivity*, 4:2 (1997), 159–67.
108 Ibid., 161.
109 Google search, 17 June 2014.

110 Carnes, *Out of the Shadows*, p. xiii.
111 Weiss, *Sex Addiction 101*, loc. 409.
112 Carnes, *Contrary to Love*, pp. 52–102.
113 Schneider, 'Understanding and Diagnosing Sex Addiction', p. 216.
114 Carnes's interview with Joe Polish, 2011: http://www.youtube .com/watch?v=i1pQfGD_MQI.
115 A. Cooper, 'Sexuality and the Internet: Surfing into the New Millennium', *CyberPsychology & Behavior*, 1:2 (1998), 187–93; A. Cooper, D. E. Putnam, L. A. Planchon and S. C. Boies, 'Online Sexual Compulsivity: Getting Tangled in the Net', *Sexual Addiction & Compulsivity*, 6:2 (1999), 79–104; A. Cooper, D. Delmonico and R. Burg, 'Cybersex Users, Abusers, Compulsives: New Findings and Implications', *Sexual Addiction & Compulsivity*, 7:1–2 (2000), 5–29.
116 Putnam and Maheu, 'Online Sexual Addiction and Compulsivity', 91.
117 M. Herkov, 'What Is Sexual Addiction?', PsychCentral: http://psychcentral.com/lib/what-is-sexual-addiction/000748; M. Herkov, 'Symptoms of Sexual Addiction', http://psychcentral .com/lib/symptoms-of-sexual-addiction/000745; M. Herkov, 'What Causes Sexual Addiction?', http://psychcentral.com/lib/ what-causes-sexual-addiction/000744; M. Herkov, 'Sex Quiz: Am I Addicted to Sex?', http://psychcentral.com/lib/self-quiz -am-i-addicted-to-sex/000751; M. Herkov, 'Is Someone I Know Addicted to Sex?', http://psychcentral.com/lib/is-someone-i -know-addicted-to-sex/000749; M. Herkov, 'Is Sex Addiction a Recognized Disorder?', http://psychcentral.com/lib/is-sexual -addiction-a-recognized-disorder/000746; M. Herkov, 'Understanding More about Sexual Addiction', http://psychcentral. com/lib/understanding-more-about-sexual-addiction/000747; M. Herkov, 'If You Think You Have a Problem with Sexual Addiction', http://psychcentral.com/lib/if-you-think-you-have -a-problem-with-sexual-addiction/000750; M. Herkov, 'Treatment for Sexual Addiction', http://psychcentral.com/lib/treat-ment-for-sexual-addiction/000752. All these pieces appeared in 2006.
118 Numbers as of 9 June 2014.
119 C. Casanova, 'From the Gentle Path Press Editor's Desk', *IITAP*, March 2013: www.iitap.com/images/03_13_IITAP _NEWS_final4.pdf.
120 Weiss, *Cruise Control*, p. 4.
121 R. Weiss, *Cruise Control: Understanding Sex Addiction in Gay Men* (Los Angeles, 2005), p. 2, and Weiss, *Cruise Control* (2013), p. 2.

4   Cultural Impact

1 J. Díaz, *This Is How You Lose Her* (New York, 2012), pp. 175–6.
2 A. Cooper and I. D. Marcus, 'Men Who Are Not In Control of Their Sexual Behavior', in S. B. Levine, D. B. Risen and S. E. Althof (eds.), *Handbook of Clinical Sexuality for Mental Health Professionals* (New York, 2003), ch. 18, quotes at pp. 311, 316.
3 T. P. Sbraga and W. T. O'Donohue, *The Sex Addiction Workbook: Proven Strategies to Help You Regain Control of Your Life* (Oakland, 2003), foreword.
4 M. Turner, 'Female Sexual Compulsivity: A New Syndrome', *Psychiatric Clinics of North America*, 31:4 (2008), 713–27, quote at 713.
5 C. McCall, 'Should Parents Who are Sex Addicts Tell Their Children?', *Psychology Today*, 1 June 2011: www.psychologytoday.com/blog/overcoming-child-abuse/201106/should-parents-who-are-sex-addicts-tell-their-children.
6 *The Guardian*, 29 August 2008, 14 October 2008, 22 January 2010.
7 *Newsweek*, 5 December 2011.
8 D. L. Ley, 'Was the Cleveland Kidnapper a Sex Addict?', *Psychology Today*, 9 May 2013: http://www.psychologytoday.com/blog/women-who-stray/201305/was-the-cleveland-kidnapper-sex-addict. Ley was critical of the claim. See also S. J. Clark, 'Ariel Castro Claims a "Sexual Addiction"', Fox4kc.com, 1 August 2013: http://fox4kc.com/2013/08/01/ariel-castro-letter-i-am-a-sexual-predator.
9 A. R. Kates, 'Sex Addiction in Police Officers as a Result of Stress and Trauma': http://www.copshock.com/sex-addiction-in-police-officers–book-chapter.php. This is an online extract from his book *CopShock: Surviving Posttraumatic Stress Disorder (PTSD)* (2013).
10 J. Moorhead, 'Sex Addiction: The Truth About a Modern Phenomenon', *The Independent*, 2 December 2012.
11 Using the ProQuest Historical Newspapers Advanced Search. *The New York Times* is the only newspaper in this database with an unbroken, searchable run from 1970 to 2009.
12 F. Malti-Douglas, *Partisan Sex: Bodies, Politics, and the Law in the Clinton Era* (New York, 2009), p. 162.
13 B. A. Williams and M. X. Delli Carpini, 'Unchained Reaction: The Collapse of Media Gatekeeping and the Clinton–Lewinsky Scandal', *Journalism*, 1:1 (2000), 61–85, quote at 75.

14 J. Fiske, *Media Matters: Race and Gender in U.S. Politics: Revised Edition* (Minneapolis, 1996), p. 7.

15 Williams and Delli Carpini, 'Unchained Reaction'.

16 Ibid., the subtitle of their article.

17 T. Travis, *The Language of the Heart: A Cultural History of the Recovery Movement from Alcoholics Anonymous to Oprah Winfrey* (Chapel Hill, NC, 2009), p. 3.

18 J. Cloud, 'Sex Addiction: A Disease or a Convenient Excuse?', *Time*, 28 February 2011: http://content.time.com/time/magazine/article/0,9171,2050027,00.html.

19 'Sex Addiction: An Illness or an Excuse?', *Today*, 18 February 2011: http://www.today.com/video/today/41662640#41662640.

20 C. Brainard, '*Newsweek* Fetishizes an "Epidemic"', *Columbia Journalism Review*, 15 December 2011: http://www.cjr.org/the_observatory/newsweek_fetishizes_an_epidemi.php?page=all.

21 *Girlfriends*, Season 1, Episode 13: 'They've Gotta Have It', 5 February 2001.

22 *Anger Management*, Season 2, Episode 38: 'Charlie and the Sex Addict', 10 October 2013.

23 For a good history and analysis of the twentieth-century origins of the genre, see J. M. Shattuc, *The Talking Cure: TV Talk Shows and Women* (New York, 1997), quote at p. 3. But our favourite study is J. Gamson, *Freaks Talk Back: Tabloid Talk Shows and Sexual Nonconformity* (Chicago, 1998).

24 R. E. Vatz, L. S. Weinberg and T. S. Szasz, 'Why Does Television Grovel at the Altar of Psychiatry?', *The Washington Post*, 15 September 1985.

25 T. Kornheiser, 'For Your Sins and Mine, Let Me Say I'm Sorry', *The Washington Post*, 24 February 1989.

26 M. Specter, 'Marion Barry Airing His Vices: On Sally Jessy Raphael, the Ex-Mayor Tells of Sex Addiction', *The Washington Post*, 14 May 1991.

27 Ibid.

28 Shattuc, *Talking Cure*, ch. 5, esp. pp. 111, 135.

29 See TV Guide.com, Maury Episodes: http://www.tvguide.com/tvshows/maury/episodes/194938.

30 *Ricki Lake*: 'Exposed: Female Sex Addicts!', 3 March 2004.

31 For the impact of *Ricki Lake*, see Shattuc, *Talking Cure*, ch. 6; I. Hutchby, 'Confrontation as a Spectacle: The Argumentative Frame of the *Ricki Lake* Show', in A. Tolson (ed.), *Television Talk Shows: Discourse, Performance, Spectacle* (Mahwah, NJ, 2001), ch. 7.

32 *Ricki Lake*: 'Exposed: Female Sex Addicts!', 3 March 2004.

33 Ibid.

34 *Dr. Phil*: 'Suburban Dramas', 2 March 2011. See also Dr.Phil
   .com: http://www.drphil.com/shows/show/1612.
35 *Dr. Phil*: 'Secret Life of a Sex Addict', 9 September 2013. See
   also http://www.drphil.com/shows/show/2062.
36 Ibid.
37 *South Park*, Season 14, Episode 1: 'Sexual Healing', 17 March
   2010.
38 L. Hirschberg, 'First Came the Sitcom. Then Came the Murder',
   The New York Times, 29 September 2002.
39 It is true that Schrader explained Crane's obsessive quest for
   anonymous sex as an 'addictive firewall', like drugs or alcohol,
   and that it was 'a kind of odd addiction, because I don't think
   it's really about sex…it never seemed to me like it was a lot
   of fun to go through fucking strange people every single day'.
   See C. Fuchs, '"A Series of Enabling Devices": An Interview
   with Paul Schrader, *Auto Focus*', *Morphizm*, 22 October 2002.
   See also K. Jackson (ed.), *Schrader on Schrader* (London,
   2004), pp. 264–74.
40 More perceptive reviewers did not use the term. Linda Ruth
   Williams managed to convey the film's theme of 'visual sexual
   obsession' without once having to resort to the shorthand of
   'sex addict' or 'sex addiction': L. R. Williams, 'Swing High,
   Swing Low', *Sight and Sound*, 13:3 (2003), 32–3.
41 C. Lee, 'This Man is Addicted to Sex', *Newsweek*, 5 December
   2011.
42 See AFP, 'Sex Obsession in Venice with McQueen's "Shame"',
   The Independent, 5 September 2011: http://www.independent
   .co.uk/arts-entertainment/films/sex-obsession-in-venice
   -with-mcqueens-shame-2349670.html; A. O'Hehir, 'Interview:
   Steve McQueen Talks Naked Bodies and "Shame"', Salon.
   com, 1 December 2011: http://www.salon.com/2011/12/01/
   interview_steve_mcqueen_talks_naked_bodies_and_shame; N.
   James, 'Sex and the City', *Sight & Sound*, 22:2 (2012), 34–8;
   and the British Film Institute and *Sight & Sound* press conference and interviews (2011), all on: http://explore.bfi.org.uk/
   4f4bb4e5126e3.
43 *Shame* (2011: Steve McQueen).
44 James, 'Sex and the City', 34.
45 C. Lee, 'Sex Addiction and the City', *Newsweek*, 5 December
   2011.
46 S. McQueen and A. Morgan, 'Shame' [Script] (London, 2010),
   pp. 63, 70: cbsla.files.wordpress.com/2012/01/shame_script.pdf;
   Shame (2011: Steve McQueen).
47 *Shame* (2011: Steve McQueen); McQueen and Morgan,
   'Shame', pp. 5, 87.

48 *Shame* (2011: Steve McQueen). The fact that McQueen repeats this imagery later in the film when Brandon fucks a woman from behind against a floor-to-ceiling window undermines the power of its first iteration: he was obviously attached to the image.

49 McQueen and Morgan, 'Shame', pp. 47–8; *Shame* (2011: Steve McQueen).

50 McQueen and Morgan, 'Shame', p. 65.

51 Ibid., p. 66; *Shame* (2011: Steve McQueen).

52 AFP, 'Sex Obsession in Venice'.

53 'Shame Press Conference', BFI London Film Festival, 2011: http://explore.bfi.org.uk/4f4bb4e5126e3.

54 McQueen and Morgan, 'Shame', p. 72; *Shame* (2011: Steve McQueen).

55 McQueen and Morgan, 'Shame', pp. 1, 3, 9, 31, 79.

56 *Shame* (2011: Steve McQueen). Or as the script puts it rather inelegantly: 'BRANDON banging the life out of HOTEL LOVER, doggy style, tits pressed up against the glass of the window': McQueen and Morgan, 'Shame', p. 70.

57 S. Sandhu, 'Shame', *Sight & Sound*, 22:2 (2012), 77.

58 L. Barnett, 'Shame: Sex Addicts Reveal All', *The Guardian*, 10 January 2012: http://www.theguardian.com/lifeandstyle/2012/jan/10/sex-addicts-talk; P. French, 'Shame – Review', *The Observer*, 15 January 2012: http://www.theguardian.com/film/2012/jan/15/shame-steve-mcqueen-fassbender-review; Lee, 'Sex Addiction and the City'.

59 R. Weiss, 'Two New Sex Addiction Films: Are They Accurate?', *Counselor: The Magazine for Addiction Professionals*, 8 October 2013: http://blog.counselormagazine.com/2013/10/two-new-sex-addiction-films-are-they-accurate.

60 Sandhu, 'Shame', 77.

61 *Diary of a Sex Addict* (2001: Joseph Brutsman). The online reviewer FlickJunkie-2 concluded, 'This movie is the worst I have ever seen, a dubious distinction given the thousands of films I have viewed': http://www.imdb.com/title/tt0253040.

62 *I Am a Sex Addict* (2006: Caveh Zahedi); Nathan Lee, 'The Fantasies and Failings of One Man', *The New York Times*, 12 April 2006.

63 *Thanks for Sharing* (2012: Stuart Blumberg). The film was made in 2012 but released in the US in 2013.

64 Ibid.

65 Ibid.

66 R. Tucker, 'Dark Comedy Explores Sex Addiction in NYC', *New York Post*, 14 September 2013: http://nypost.com/2013/09/14/dark-comedy-explores-sex-addiction-in-nyc; *Chelsea Lately*, 'Interview with Gwyneth Paltrow', 16 September 2013.

67 *Thanks for Sharing* (2012: Stuart Blumberg).

68 See, for example, A. W. Schaef, *Escape from Intimacy: Untangling the 'Love' Addictions: Sex, Romance, Relationships* (New York, 1989).

69 R. Roper, '"Thanks for Sharing" Makes You Care About Sex Addicts', Chicago Sun-Times.com, 19 September 2013: http://www.suntimes.com/entertainment/movies/22612401 -421/thanks-for-sharing-makes-you-care-about-sex-addicts .html.

70 M. O'Sullivan, '"Thanks for Sharing" Movie Review', *The Washington Post*, 20 September 2013: http://www .washingtonpost.com/goingoutguide/movies/thanks-for -sharing-movie-review/2013/09/18/99b514f6-1bd7-11e3 -a628-7e6dde8f889d_story.html.

71 Weiss, 'Two New Sex Addiction Films'.

72 C. Palahniuk, *Choke: A Novel* (New York, 2002), p. 205.

73 Ibid., pp. 16–17, 182, 213.

74 A. Salkin, 'No Sympathy for the Sex Addict', *The New York Times*, 7 September 2008.

75 *A Dirty Shame* (2004: John Waters).

76 Ibid.

77 B. French, 'Shame on You! A Conversation with *A Dirty Shame*'s John Waters, Selma Blair, and Johnny Knoxville', *AMC Blogs*, 23 September 2004: http://blogs.amctv.com/ movie-blog/2004/09/shame-on-you-a.

78 Quoted in Salkin, 'No Sympathy for the Sex Addict'.

79 *Californication*, Season 6, Episode 2: 'Quitters', 20 January 2013.

80 *Californication*, Season 6, Episode 11: 'The Abby', 31 March 2013.

81 For reality TV, see the essays in S. Holmes and D. Jermyn (eds.), *Understanding Reality Television* (London, 2004); M. Kavka, *Reality TV* (Edinburgh, 2012); L. E. Edwards, *The Triumph of Reality TV: The Revolution in American Television* (Santa Barbara, CA, 2013); B. R. Webber (ed.), *Reality Gendervision: Sexuality & Gender on Transatlantic Reality Television* (Durham, NC, 2014).

82 D. Roy, 'Is Dr. Drew a Phony?', *Daily Beast*, 17 December 2009: http://www.thedailybeast.com/articles/2009/12/17/i-am -a-sex-addict-and-i-play-one-on-tv.html.

83 K. J. Rossi, 'Just a Girl … Sex Rehab', 13 December 2009: http://kendrajaderossi.blogspot.co.nz/2009/12/sex-rehab.html.

84 E. McCombs, 'The Only Interview That Ever Made Me Blush', *xoJane*, 24 January 2012: http://www.xojane.com/sex/sex -rehab-phil-varone-sex-addict.

85 W. Bauman, 'Exclusive Interview: Phil Varone Talks Sex Tapes, Politics and Rock n Roll', *Disarray Magazine*, 23 July 2011: http://www.disarraymagazine.com/2011/07/exclusive -interview-sex-tapes-politics.html.

86 *Sex Rehab with Dr. Drew* (2009). For an example of the porn crossover, with a click of the mouse one can view *Kendra Jade Rossi The Extreme Squirt* Scene 1: http://www.tube8.com/ hardcore/kendra-jade-rossi-the-extreme-squirt-scene-1/ 1166781/; or *Kendra Jade Fucked Up*: http://www.tube8.com/ hardcore/kendra-jade-fucked-up/357272.

87 G. Longstaff, 'From Reality to Fantasy: Celebrity, Reality TV and Pornography', *Celebrity Studies*, 4:1 (2013), 71–80.

88 L. Grindstaff, *The Money Shot: Trash, Class, and the Making of TV Talk Shows* (Chicago, 2002), esp. pp. 19–20, 115–16.

89 See M. Kavka and A. West, 'Temporalities of the Real: Conceptualising Time in Reality TV', in Holmes and Jermyn (eds.), *Understanding Reality Television*, ch. 6.

90 R. Juzwiak, 'A Sex Rehab Primer With Jill Vermeire', *VH1+Shows*, 30 October 2009: http://blog.vh1.com/2009-10 -30/a-sex-rehab-primer-with-jill-vermeire.

91 http://id.loc.gov/authorities/subjects/sh89003011.html.

92 M. Schisgal, *Sexaholics* (New York, 1995), p. 24.

93 By the libraries at either the University of Auckland or the University of Melbourne, or in the Library of Congress Online Catalog.

94 In the respective catalogues of the Libraries of the University of Auckland and the University of Melbourne.

95 The problem is by no means limited to the library catalogue. In the introduction to *Mama's Boy* (2012), author Roel van den Oever lists the sexual transgressions in *Portnoy's Complaint* as 'masturbation and sex addiction': R. van den Oever, *Mama's Boy: Momism and Homophobia in Postwar American Culture* (New York, 2012), p. 2.

96 V. A. Sadock, 'Sexual Addiction', in P. Ruiz and E. C. Strain (eds.), *Lowinson and Ruiz's Substance Abuse: A Comprehensive Textbook, Fifth Edition* (Philadelphia, 2011), ch. 26, at p. 394.

97 *SBS Insight*, Episode: 'Sex Addiction', 1 October 2013.

98 E. Jong, *Fear of Flying* (New York, 2011), pp. 180, 213. First published in 1973.

99 E. Jong, *Any Woman's Blues* (London, 1990), p. 3.

100 Ibid., p. 177.

101 Ibid., p. 99.

102 Ibid., p. 164.

103 J. M. Irvine, 'Reinventing Perversion: Sex Addiction and Cul-
    tural Anxieties', *Journal of the History of Sexuality*, 5:3 (1995),
    429–50, at 437.
104 D. Rickman, 'Erica Jong on Feminism, Sex Addiction and Why
    There is No Such Thing as a Zipless F**k', *The Huffington
    Post*, 7 November 2011: http://www.huffingtonpost.co
    .uk/2011/11/07/erica-jong-no-such-thing-as-zipless-fuck
    _n_1079222.html.

5   Sexual Stories

1 R. Lowe, *Love Life* (Sydney, 2014), Ebook, loc. 1173.
2 'Shame Press Conference', BFI London Film Festival, 2011:
  http://explore.bfi.org.uk/4f4bb4e5126e3.
3 R. Houston, 'Is Charlie Sheen a Sex Addict like Tiger Woods
  and Jesse James? Check This List', Examiner.com, 8 March
  2011: http://www.examiner.com/article/is-charlie-sheen-a-sex
  -addict-like-tiger-woods-and-jesse-james-check-this-list.
  Emphasis in original.
4 W. M. Edwards, D. Delmonico and E. Griffin, *Cybersex
  Unplugged: Finding Sexual Health in an Electronic World*
  (Lexington, KY, 2011), p. 26.
5 A. D. Burks, *Sex & Surrender: An Addict's Journey* (Houston,
  TX, 2013), Ebook, loc. 85. Emphasis in original.
6 R. L. Yant, *Pants on Fire: Leaving My Marriage to a Sex Addict
  and the Journey Back to Me* (Milwaukee, WI, 2012), Ebook,
  loc. 50.
7 *South Park*, Season 14, Episode 1: 'Sexual Healing', 17 March
  2010.
8 D. J. Ley, *The Myth of Sex Addiction* (Lanham, MD, 2012),
  pp. 113, 143, 181.
9 S. Rea, 'Some Names for Sawyer's "60 Minutes" Spot', Philly
  .com [*The Philadelphia Inquirer*], 4 February 1989: http://articles
  .philly.com/1989-02-04/news/26152284_1_mark-mcewen
  -diane-sawyer-wade-boggs; M. Specter, 'Marion Barry Airing
  His Vices: On Sally Jessy Raphael, the Ex-Mayor Tells of Sex
  Addiction', *The Washington Post*, 14 May 1991; J. Follain,
  'Berlusconi Urged to Attend Clinic for Sex Addiction', *The
  Sunday Times*, 23 August 2009: http://www.thesundaytimes
  .co.uk/sto/news/world_news/article182750.ece; D. Moore and
  B. Manville, 'Addictions & Answers: Is Ex-Congressman
  Christopher Lee a Sex Addict?', *New York Daily News*, 24
  February 2011: http://www.nydailynews.com/life-style/health/

addictions-answers-ex-congressman-christopher-lee-sex-addict
-article-1.134239; no author, 'Former Sex Addict Scott Baio
Plans Tell-All Book', Starpulse.com, 9 February 2012: http://
www.starpulse.com/news/index.php/2012/02/09/former_sex
_addict_scott_baio_plans_tel; C. Sieczkowski, 'TV Host Sex
Addiction?', *The Huffington Post*, 2 May 2013: http://www
.huffingtonpost.com/2013/05/02/tv-host-sex-addiction-david
-tutera_n_3201935.html; S. Clark, 'Anthony Weiner May
Suffer from Sex Addiction & Needs Professional Help',
Hollywood Life.com, 24 July 2013: http://hollywoodlife
.com/2013/07/24/anthony-weiner-may-suffer-from-sex
-addiction-needs-professional-help; M. Callahan, 'From
Champ to Drug and Sex Addict: Tyson Tells All', *New York
Post*, 27 October 2013: http://nypost.com/2013/10/27/mike
-tyson-reveals-drug-and-sex-addictions-in-new-memoir.
10 Azeem, 'Shocking: Perez Accuses Ozil of Being a Sex Addict
and Obsessed With Women', Mixture Sport.com, 9 September
2013: http://www.mixturesport.com/shocking-perez-accuses-ozil
-of-being-a-sex-addict-and-obsessed-with-women; no author,
'Aida Yespica (ex Miss Venezuela) Says She Never Had Sex
with Arsenal's Mesut Özil', 101 Great Goals.com, 11 September 2013: http://www.101greatgoals.com/blog/aida-yespica
-ex-miss-venezuela-says-she-never-had-sex-with-arsenals
-mesut-ozil-sportmediaset.
11 X. Brooks, 'Cannes 2014 Review: Welcome to New York –
Depardieu's Grunting Triumph Exposes More Than Just
Himself', *The Guardian*, 18 May 2014: http://www.theguardian
.com/film/2014/may/18/welcome-to-new-york-review-gerard
-depardieu-abel-ferrera-cannes; Reuters, 'Dominique Strauss-
Kahn to Sue Over Gérard Depardieu Sex Addiction Film',
The Guardian, 19 May 2014: http://www.theguardian.com/
world/2014/may/19/dominique-strauss-kahn-sues-sex
-addiction-film-gerard-depardieu.
12 Callahan, 'From Champ to Drug and Sex Addict'.
13 M. Tyson with L. Sloman, *Undisputed Truth: My Autobiography* (London, 2013), Ebook, locs. 2037–42.
14 For Wonderland, see A. Fortini, 'Letter from West Hollywood:
Special Treatment: The Rise of Luxury Rehab', *The New
Yorker*, 1 December 2008.
15 Tyson with Sloman, *Undisputed Truth*, loc. 6977.
16 Ibid., locs. 5281–4.
17 Ibid., loc. 7000.
18 Ibid., loc. 7013.
19 Ibid., loc. 7024.
20 Ibid., loc. 7028.

21 Ibid., loc. 7045.

22 For reference to Douglas's claims that these reports were inaccurate and that he sought help for his drinking, see J. Serjeant, 'David Duchovny's Sex Disorder Likened to Alcoholism', *Reuters*, 29 August 2008: http://www.reuters.com/article/2008/08/29/us-duchovny-idUSN2835847820080829.

23 R. Lowe, *Stories I Only Tell My Friends: An Autobiography* (New York, 2011), p. 254.

24 S. Ellicott, 'Addicts or Adulterers; Sexaholic', *The Times*, 4 October 1992.

25 L. Berlant and L. Duggan (eds.), *Our Monica, Ourselves: The Clinton Affair and the National Interest* (New York, 2001). See also the essay by M. St. John, 'How to Do Things with the *Starr Report*: Pornography, Performance, and the President's Penis', in L. Williams (ed.), *Porn Studies* (Durham, NC, 2004), pp. 27–49.

26 F. Malti-Douglas, *The Starr Report Disrobed* (New York, 2000).

27 See Malti-Douglas's wider discussion of the merging of sex and politics in the Clinton period: F. Malti-Douglas, *Partisan Sex: Bodies, Politics, and the Law in the Clinton Era* (New York, 2009).

28 P. Kuntz (ed.), *The Starr Report: The Evidence* (New York, 1998). There are also various online versions.

29 L. Williams, 'Epilogue', in her *Hard Core: Power, Pleasure, and the 'Frenzy of the Visible'* (Berkeley and Los Angeles, 1999), pp. 280–315, quote at p. 280.

30 St. John, 'How to Do Things with the *Starr Report*', p. 38; S. Weil Davis, 'The Door Ajar: The Erotics of Hypocrisy in the White House Scandal', in Berlant and Duggan (eds.), *Our Monica, Ourselves*, ch. 5, esp. pp. 90–4.

31 Malti-Douglas, *Partisan Sex*, pp. 110, 120–3.

32 M. McElya, 'Trashing the Presidency: Race, Class, and the Clinton/Lewinsky Affair', in Berlant and Duggan (eds.), *Our Monica, Ourselves*, ch. 9, esp. pp. 165–6.

33 N. Hamilton, *Bill Clinton: An American Journey: Great Expectations* (New York, 2003), pp. 435, 437, 451.

34 M. Isikoff, *Uncovering Clinton: A Reporter's Story* (New York, 2000), p. 242.

35 J. Toobin, *A Vast Conspiracy: The Real Story of the Sex Scandal That Nearly Brought Down a President* (New York, 1999), p. 33.

36 T. M. DeFrank, *Write It When I'm Gone: Remarkable Off-the-Record Conversations with Gerald R. Ford* (New York, 2007), pp. 148, 149.

37 Of many examples, see E. Henry, 'Book: Ford Feared Cheney Was GOP Liability, Called Clinton Sex Addict', CNN Politics .com, 29 October 2007: http://edition.cnn.com/2007/POLITICS/ 10/29/ford.book.

38 J. Varon, 'It Was the Spectacle Stupid: The Clinton-Lewinsky-Starr Affair and the Politics of the Gaze', in P. Apostolidis and J. A. Williams (eds.), *Public Affairs: Politics in the Age of Sex Scandals* (Durham, NC, 2004), pp. 232–58.

39 P. J. Carnes and M. Wilson, 'The Sexual Addiction Assessment Process', in P. J. Carnes and K. M. Adams (eds.), *Clinical Management of Sex Addiction* (New York, 2002), ch. 1, quote at p. 8.

40 S. Cheever, *Desire: Where Sex Meets Addiction* (New York, 2008), p. 66.

41 J. D. Levin, *The Clinton Syndrome: The President and the Self-Destructive Nature of Sexual Addiction* (Rocklin, CA, 1998), p. 5.

42 Ibid., p. 6.

43 Ibid., ch. 2.

44 Ibid., pp. 54, 64, 89, 90, 101. Quotes at pp. 64, 101.

45 Ibid., p. 100.

46 R. Springfield, *Late, Late at Night: A Memoir* (New York, 2010), Ebook, locs. 224, 402.

47 Ibid., locs. 2716, 3120. The ellipses are in the original.

48 Ibid., loc. 2426.

49 Ibid., locs. 3072–6.

50 Ibid., loc. 3237.

51 Ibid., loc. 4186.

52 Ibid., loc. 5064.

53 See http://www.cosexualrecovery.com/rick-springfield-opens-up -about-sex-addiction?goback=.gna_3855239.gde_3855239_ member_216337684 (posted 16 November 2012); http://www. huffingtonpost.com/2012/10/15/rick-springfield -depressed_n_1962421.html (posted 12 May 2013). See also http://www.sodahead.com/entertainment/rick-springfield -talks-about-his-sex-addiction-and-depression-do-you-think -sex-addiction-is-a-real/question-3247435 (posted 16 October 2012).

54 K. Watson, 'Rick Springfield Opens Up About Sex Addiction and Depression', SheKnows.com, 19 October 2010: http:// www.sheknows.com/entertainment/articles/819431/Rick -Springfield-opens-up-about-sex-addiction-and-depression.

55 R. Brand, *My Booky Wook: A Memoir of Sex, Drugs, and Stand-Up* (New York, 2009), p. 9.

56 Ibid., p. 344.

57 Ibid., p. 313.
58 R. Brand, *My Booky Wook 2: This Time it's Personal* (London, 2011), p. 274.
59 Brand, *My Booky Wook*, p. 328.
60 Ibid., pp. 6, 9.
61 For an example of those of lesser quality, see W. Artis III, *Memoirs of an Artist: An Unorthodox Guide into the Mind of a Sex Addict* (Kearney, NE, 2012); S. Binion, *The Corporate Rise, Fall, and Rise again of a Sex Addict, Cocaine Addict, Alcoholic, and Successful Business Man* (Victoria, BC, 2012); Burks, *Sex & Surrender*; J. Porter, *Storm Tossed: How a U.S. Serviceman Won the Battle of Sex Addiction* (Greeley, CO, 2006). Examples of the better-penned memoirs include Cheever, *Desire*; J. Fink, *Laid Bare: One Man's True Story of Sex, Love and Other Disorders* (Sydney, 2012); K. Kneen, *Affection: An Erotic Memoir* (Berkeley, CA, 2010); M. Ryan, *Secret Life: An Autobiography* (New York, 1995); S. W. Silverman, *Love Sick: One Woman's Journey Through Sexual Addiction* (New York, 2001).
62 T. Travis, *The Language of the Heart: A Cultural History of the Recovery Movement from Alcoholics Anonymous to Oprah Winfrey* (Chapel Hill, NC, 2009), p. 4.
63 Sex Addicts Anonymous, *Sex Addicts Anonymous* (Houston, TX, 2012), 3rd edn, Ebook, loc. 437.
64 H. Keane, 'Taxonomies of Desire: Sex Addiction and the Ethics of Intimacy', *International Journal of Critical Psychology*, 1:3 (2001), 9–28, quote at 12.
65 See Ryan, *Secret Life*; K. Cohen, *Loose Girl: A Memoir of Promiscuity* (New York, 2008); and, for quotes, Silverman, *Love Sick*, p. 42; R. Resnick, *Love Junkie: A Memoir* (New York, 2008), p. 117.
66 Ryan, *Secret Life*, pp. 5, 7.
67 Resnick, *Love Junkie*, p. 22.
68 K. D. Boykin, *Confessions of a Sex Addict* (no place, 2011), Ebook, loc. 868.
69 Porter, *Storm Tossed*, locs. 3069–73.
70 L. J. Schwartz, *Out of Bondage: Memoirs of a Sex Addict* (Pittsburgh, PA, 2009), Ebook, p. 80.
71 Keane, 'Taxonomies of Desire', 15.
72 Silverman, *Love Sick*, pp. 33–4, 36–7, 136–43, 159–61, 247–54.
73 T. P. Sbraga and W. T. O'Donohue, *The Sex Addiction Workbook: Proven Strategies to Help You Regain Control of Your Life* (Oakland, 2003), p. 140; M. C. Feree, *No Stones: Women Redeemed from Sexual Addiction* (Downers Grove, IL, 2013), p. 201.

74 E. Dawson, *My Secret Life with a Sex Addict: From Discovery to Recovery* (Parker, CO, 2001).

75 Yant, *Pants on Fire*, locs. 397, 424, 388, 392–424.

76 P. S. Pelullo, *Betrayal and the Beast: A True Story of One Man's Journey Through Childhood Sexual Abuse, Sexual Addiction, and Recovery* (Plymouth Meeting, PA, 2012), Ebook, locs. 2178–201, 2356, 2360, 3003.

77 Cheever, *Desire*, p. 153. For references to Carnes see pp. 19, 57–8, 66, 72, 111, 129, 135. For her meeting and discussion with Martin Kafka see pp. 113–17. She also quotes from Silverman's *Love Sick* (pp. 54, 76, 131) and Ryan's *Secret Life* (pp. 11, 51, 153).

78 Cheever, *Desire*, p. 156.

79 See for example, for adolescent promiscuity, Cohen, *Loose Girl*, and J. Garcia, *Somewhere In Between: A TRU Journey Through Sex, Drugs, Alcohol & Everything in Between* (New York, 2012); for use of prostitutes, Porter, *Storm Tossed*; for relationship breakdowns, Fink, *Laid Bare*, Resnick, *Love Junkie*, and B. Waldschmidt, *Dealing Flesh: A Good Girl's Journey Through Sex Addiction and How She Became an Authentic Woman* (no place, 2012); and, for childhood sexual abuse, Schwartz, *Out of Bondage*.

80 Boykin, *Confessions of a Sex Addict*, loc. 1033. Emphasis in original.

81 Claire Halliday's book on modern sexual culture is interspersed with her own personal experiences, but is no doubt part of this 'canon' of sex addiction memoirs because she starts her book by attending a Sex Addicts Anonymous meeting (as research). See C. Halliday, *Do You Want Sex with That?* (Melbourne, 2009). Krissy Kneen talks of the 'the narcotic effect of the idea of sex' but does not problematize it. She is a sexual person: 'I am made of sex. I feed on the thought of it.' See Kneen, *Affection*, p. 11. For the last point on other addictions see C. Christian, *Babylon Confidential: A Memoir of Love, Sex, and Addiction* (Dallas TX, 2012). Christian, an American actress best known for her role on *Babylon 5*, details her struggle with alcoholism. Sex is part of a long list of 'triggers' for her: see p. 219.

82 Kneen, *Affection*, p. 11.

83 Keane, 'Taxonomies of Desire', 12.

84 *Ricki Lake*: 'Exposed: Female Sex Addicts!', 3 March 2004.

85 R. Capitol, *Bigger Than Me: An Untold Story of Sex and Love Addiction* (Bloomington, IN, 2010), Ebook, p. 2.

86 L. Atkins, 'He's Gotta Have It', *The Guardian*, 16 September 2003: http://www.theguardian.com/lifeandstyle/2003/sep/16/healthandwellbeing.health.

87 L. Barnett, 'Shame: Sex Addicts Reveal All', *The Guardian*, 10 January 2012: http://www.theguardian.com/lifeandstyle/2012/jan/10/sex-addicts-talk.

88 Ley, *Myth of Sex Addiction*, pp. 21, 87, 114, 119, 135, 164.

89 Ibid., p. 21.

90 Ibid., pp. 119, 135.

91 M. Wilson, *Hope After Betrayal: Healing When Sex Addiction Invades Your Marriage* (Grand Rapids, MI, 2007); S. Carnes (ed.), *Mending a Shattered Heart: A Guide For Partners of Sex Addicts* (Carefree, AZ, 2011); B. Steffens and M. Means, *Your Sexually Addicted Spouse: How Partners Can Cope and Heal* (Far Hills, NJ, 2010); M. Corcoran, *A House Interrupted: A Wife's Story of Recovering from Her Husband's Sex Addiction* (Carefree, AZ, 2011).

92 For the co-sex addict idea, see Carnes (ed.), *Mending a Shattered Heart*. The quotes are taken from a book more critical of this notion of codependency: Steffens and Means, *Your Sexually Addicted Spouse*, pp. 24–5.

93 Dawson, *My Secret Life with a Sex Addict*, loc. 1443.

94 Ibid., locs. 1451–4.

95 Yant, *Pants on Fire*, loc. 380.

96 Steffens and Means, *Your Sexually Addicted Spouse*, pp. 41–2.

97 Corcoran, *A House Interrupted*. See p. 144 for her diagnosis, p. 38 for AA meetings, pp. 52 and 141 for in-patient treatment, and p. 193 for her eight retreats.

98 Ibid., pp. 141–3.

99 S. B. Levine, 'What Is Sexual Addiction?', *Journal of Sex & Marital Therapy*, 36:3 (2010), 261–75, quote at 263.

100 R. Aronowitz, 'Framing Disease: An Underappreciated Mechanism for the Social Patterning of Health', *Social Science & Medicine*, 67:1 (2008), 1–9, quote at 6.

101 Keane, 'Taxonomies of Desire', 12.

102 Boykin, *Confessions of a Sex Addict*, locs. 45–9.

103 Ibid., locs. 811–15.

104 Ibid., loc. 815. Emphasis in original.

105 Keane, 'Taxonomies of Desire', 18.

106 The memoirs should not be confused with the occasional piece of crude erotic fiction employing a sex addiction setting and scenario. For example, Pynk, *Sexaholics* (New York, 2010), is ostensibly about 'women struggling with sex addiction' (p. xi) but there is much sex and precious little evidence of any struggle.

107 Ryan, *Secret Life*, pp. 8, 16–18, 203, 218–19, 265, 323.

108 Boykin, *Confessions of a Sex Addict*, locs. 87–93, 101, 1640, 1751–8.

109 Resnick, *Love Junkie*, pp. 42, 83, 87, 89–90, 94–5, 102–3, 107, 113, 117.
110 Ibid., ch. 8.
111 Cheever, *Desire*, p. 22.
112 Silverman, *Love Sick*, pp. 15, 67–8, 171–4, 182–3, 214–15, 219–20.
113 Fink, *Laid Bare*, loc. 56.
114 Ibid., loc. 1677.
115 Ibid., loc. 642.
116 Travis, *Language of the Heart*, p. 12.
117 Sbraga and O'Donohue, *The Sex Addiction Workbook*, p. 132.
118 'Frequently Asked Questions about Addiction Rehabilitation': http://www.rehabs.com/about/frequently-asked-questions -about-addiction-rehabilitation.
119 'High Profile and Celebrity Rehab Centers': http://www.rehabs .com/about/high-profile-and-celebrity-rehab.
120 J. Henley, 'Are You Addicted to Sex?', *The Guardian*, 22 January 2010; http://www.pinegrovetreatment.com/evaluation -programhtml.
121 Fortini, 'Letter from West Hollywood'.
122 Ley, *Myth of Sex Addiction*, pp. 53–5.
123 D. L. Delmonico, 'Sex on the Superhighway: Understand-ing and Treating Cybersex Addiction', in Carnes and Adams (eds.), *Clinical Management of Sex Addiction*, ch. 15, quote at p. 245.
124 B. McNair, *Striptease Culture: Sex, Media and the Democra-tization of Desire* (New York, 2002), p. 12.
125 M. Klein, 'Our Addiction to Tiger Woods' "Sex Addiction"', *Psychology Today*, 20 February 2010: http://www.psychologytoday .com/blog/sexual-intelligence/201002/our-addiction-tiger -woods-sex-addiction.

6   Diagnostic Disorder

1 M. Klein, 'You're Addicted to What?', TheHumanist.com, 28 June 2012: http://thehumanist.com/magazine/july-august-2012/ features/youre-addicted-to-what.
2 R. E. Vatz, L. S. Weinberg and T. S. Szasz, 'Why Does Televi-sion Grovel at the Altar of Psychiatry?', *The Washington Post*, 15 September 1985.
3 Ibid.

4 J. N. Hook and others, 'Measuring Sexual Addiction and Compulsivity: A Critical Review of Instruments', *Journal of Sex & Marital Therapy*, 36:3 (2010), 227–60.

5 PsycINFO search on 27 March 2014. We are grateful to Philip Abela of the University of Auckland Library for carrying out this search. The total was 1,938 results for sex* addict*, sex* compuls*, sex* impuls*, compulsive sexual behav*, hypersexual disorder*, hypersexual*.

6 R. C. Reid and B. N. Carpenter, 'Exploring the Relationships of Psychopathology in Hypersexual Patients Using the MMPI-2', *Journal of Sex & Marital Therapy*, 35:4 (2009), 294–310.

7 K. Skegg, S. Nada-Raja, N. Dickson and C. Paul, 'Perceived "Out of Control" Sexual Behaviour in a Cohort of Young Adults from the Dunedin Multidisciplinary Health and Development Study', *Archives of Sexual Behavior*, 39:4 (2010), 968–78.

8 Hook and others, 'Measuring Sexual Addiction'.

9 M. L. Wainberg and others, 'A Double-Blind Study of Citalopram Versus Placebo in the Treatment of Compulsive Sexual Behaviors in Gay and Bisexual Men', *Journal of Clinical Psychiatry*, 67:12 (2006), 1968–73; K. R. McBride, M. Reece and S. A. Sanders, 'Predicting Negative Outcomes of Sexuality Using the Compulsive Behavior Inventory', *International Journal of Sexual Health*, 19:4 (2008), 51–62; R. C. Reid, B. N. Carpenter and T. Q. Lloyd, 'Assessing Psychological Symptom Patterns of Patients Seeking Help for Hypersexual Behavior', *Sexual and Relationship Therapy*, 24:1 (2009), 47–63; P. Hall, 'A New Classification Model for Sex Addiction', *Sexual Addiction & Compulsivity*, 20:4 (2013), 279–91; J. T. Parsons and others, 'A Psychometric Investigation of the Hypersexual Disorder Screening Inventory Among Highly Sexually Active Gay and Bisexual Men: An Item Response Theory Analysis', *Journal of Sexual Medicine*, 10:12 (2013), 3088–101.

10 P. J. Carnes and others, 'PATHOS: A Brief Screening Application for Assessing Sexual Addiction', *Journal of Addiction Medicine*, 6:1 (2012), 29–34.

11 S. D. Womack and others, 'Measuring Hypersexual Behavior', *Sexual Addiction & Compulsivity*, 20:1–2 (2013), 65–78.

12 S. C. Kalichman and D. Rompa, 'The Sexual Compulsivity Scale: Further Development and Use With HIV-Positive Persons', *Journal of Personality Assessment*, 76:3 (2001), 379–95; Reid, Carpenter and Lloyd, 'Assessing Psychological Symptom Patterns of Patients'; R. C. Reid, J. E. Bramen, A. Anderson and M. S. Cohen, 'Mindfulness, Emotional

Dysregulation, Impulsivity, and Stress Proneness Among Hypersexual Patients', *Journal of Clinical Psychology*, 70:4 (2014), 313–21; J. E. Pachankis and others, 'The Role of Maladaptive Cognitions in Hypersexuality Among Highly Sexually Active Gay and Bisexual Men', *Archives of Sexual Behavior*, 43:4 (2014), 669–83; R. C. Reid, J. Temko, J. F. Moghaddam and T. F. Fong, 'Shame, Rumination, and Self-Compassion in Men Assessed for Hypersexual Disorder', *Journal of Psychiatric Practice*, 20:4 (2014), 260–8.

13 M. Spenhoff, T. H. C. Kruger, U. Hartman and J. Kobs, 'Hypersexual Behavior in an Online Sample of Males: Associations with Personal Distress and Functional Impairment', *Journal of Sexual Medicine*, 10:12 (2013), 2996–3005, esp. 3003.

14 Womack and others, 'Measuring Hypersexual Behavior', 74.

15 Ibid., 67, 73.

16 S. Cheever, *Desire: Where Sex Meets Addiction* (New York, 2008), pp. 122–4.

17 http://www.youtube.com/watch?v=P-DzAewSJzk.

18 L. J. Schwartz, *Out of Bondage: Memoirs of a Sex Addict* (Pittsburgh, PA, 2009), Ebook, p. 180.

19 W. M. Edwards, D. Delmonico and E. Griffin, *Cybersex Unplugged: Finding Sexual Health in an Electronic World* (Lexington, KY, 2011), pp. 65–71.

20 J. D. Levin, *The Clinton Syndrome: The President and the Self-Destructive Nature of Sexual Addiction* (Rocklin, CA, 1998), p. 160.

21 D. J. Ley, *The Myth of Sex Addiction* (Lanham, MD, 2012), p. 128.

22 D. W. Black, L. L. D. Kehrberg, D. L. Flumerfelt and S. S. Schlosser, 'Characteristics of 36 Subjects Reporting Compulsive Sexual Behavior', *American Journal of Psychiatry*, 154:2 (1997), 243–9.

23 S. D. Schaffer and M. L. Zimmerman, 'The Sexual Addict: A Challenge For the Primary Care Provider', *Nurse Practitioner*, 15:6 (1990), 25–33, quote at 28.

24 C. Coleman-Kennedy and A. Pendley, 'Assessment and Diagnosis of Sexual Addiction', *Journal of the American Psychiatric Nurses Association*, 8:5 (2002), 143–51, quote at 143.

25 S. Sussman, N. Lisha and M. Griffiths, 'Prevalence of the Addictions: A Problem of the Majority or Minority?', *Evaluation & the Health Professions*, 34:1 (2011), 3–56, quote at 3.

26 G. N. Dawson and D. E. Warren, 'Curbside Consultation: Evaluating and Treating Sex Addiction', *American Family Physician*, 86:1 (2012), 74–6.

27 E. Griffin-Shelley, *Sex and Love: Addiction, Treatment, and Recovery* (Westport, CT, 1997), pp. 76–86, 90, 197–203.
28 M. P. Kafka, 'Nonparaphilic Hypersexuality Disorders', in Y. M. Binik and K. S. K. Hall (eds.), *Principles and Practices of Sex Therapy, Fifth Edition* (New York, 2014), ch. 13, quotes at pp. 287, 299.
29 P. J. Carnes, R. E. Murray and L. Charpentier, 'Bargains With Chaos: Sex Addicts and Addiction Interaction Disorder', *Sexual Addiction & Compulsivity*, 12:2–3 (2005), 79–120.
30 Ibid.
31 K. P. Rosenberg, P. Carnes and S. O'Connor, 'Evaluation and Treatment of Sex Addiction', *Journal of Sex & Marital Therapy*, 40:2 (2014), 77–91, quote at 82.
32 Carnes, Murray and Charpentier, 'Bargains With Chaos', 3, 4.
33 Ibid., 9.
34 P. Carnes, *The Sexual Addiction* (Minneapolis, 1984), ch. 2. First published in 1983.
35 A. W. Schaef, *Escape from Intimacy* (New York, 1989), pp. 30–3, 42.
36 H. Keane, 'Taxonomies of Desire: Sex Addiction and the Ethics of Intimacy', *International Journal of Critical Psychology*, 1:3 (2001), 9–28, quote at 11.
37 Griffin-Shelley, *Sex and Love*, ch. 2, quote at p. 25.
38 R. H. Earle and M. R. Earle, with K. Osborn, *Sex Addiction: Case Studies and Management* (New York, 1995).
39 Rosenberg, Carnes and O'Connor, 'Evaluation and Treatment of Sex Addiction', 85.
40 Schaef, *Escape from Intimacy*, p. 22.
41 Edwards, Delmonico and Griffin, *Cybersex Unplugged*, p. 4.
42 J. Laurance, 'Sex Addiction: The Facts from the Fruity Fiction', *The Independent*, 30 April 2008.
43 O. Vesga-Lopez, A. Schmidt and C. Blanco, 'Update on Sexual Addictions', *Directions in Psychiatry*, 27:12 (2007), 143–57.
44 J. Moorhead, 'Sex Addiction: The Truth About a Modern Phenomenon', *The Independent*, 2 December 2012.
45 Ibid.
46 Ibid.
47 S. A. Hardy, J. Ruchty, T. D. Hull and R. Hyde, 'A Preliminary Study of an Online Psychoeducational Program for Hypersexuality', *Sexual Addiction & Compulsivity*, 17:4 (2010), 247–69; R. Gilliland, M. South, B. N. Carpenter and S. A. Hardy, 'The Roles of Shame and Guilt in Hypersexual Behavior', *Sexual Addiction & Compulsivity*, 18:1 (2011), 12–29.
48 Gilliland, South, Carpenter and Hardy, 'The Roles of Shame and Guilt', 12, 15.

49 J. Morgenstern and others, 'Non-Paraphilic Compulsive Sexual Behavior and Psychiatric Co-Morbidities in Gay and Bisexual Men', *Sexual Addiction & Compulsivity*, 18:3 (2011), 114–34, quote at 117–18.

50 J. T. Parsons and others, 'Accounting for the Social Triggers of Sexual Compulsivity', *Journal of Addictive Diseases*, 26:3 (2007), 5–16.

51 P. J. Wright, 'Communicative Dynamics and Recovery from Sexual Addiction: An Inconsistent Nurturing as Control Theory Analysis', *Communication Quarterly*, 59:4 (2011), 395–414.

52 A. Cooper, D. L. Delmonico and R. Burg, 'Cybersex Users, Abusers, and Compulsives: New Findings and Implications', *Sexual Addiction & Compulsivity*, 7:1–2 (2000), 5–29, at 8.

53 Ibid.

54 S. C. Kalichman and D. Cain, 'The Relationship Between Indicators of Sexual Compulsivity and High Risk Sexual Practices Among Men and Women Receiving Services from a Sexually Transmitted Infection Clinic', *Journal of Sex Research*, 41:3 (2004), 235–41, at 237.

55 Ibid., 238.

56 Ibid., 239.

57 B. C. Kelly and others, 'Sexual Compulsivity and Sexual Behaviors Among Gay and Bisexual Men and Lesbian and Bisexual Women', *Journal of Sex Research*, 46:4 (2009), 301–8, at 306.

58 Ibid., 305.

59 J. M. Kuzma and D. M. Black, 'Epidemiology, Prevalence, and Natural History of Compulsive Sexual Behavior', *Psychiatric Clinics of North America*, 31:4 (2008), 603–11, quote at 609.

60 M. H. Miner and E. Coleman, 'Compulsive Sexual Behavior and its Relationship to Risky Sexual Behavior', *Sexual Addiction & Compulsivity*, 20:1–2 (2013), 127–38, quote at 134. Emphasis in original.

61 S. N. Gold and C. L. Heffner, 'Sexual Addiction: Many Conceptions, Minimal Data', *Clinical Psychology Review*, 18:3 (1998), 367–81.

62 M. Griffiths, 'Sex on the Internet: Observations and Implications for Internet Sex Addiction', *Journal of Sex Research*, 38:4 (2001), 333–42, quote at 339.

63 Hook and others, 'Measuring Sexual Addiction', 256.

64 Black and others, 'Characteristics of 36 Subjects', 243.

65 A. Kor, Y. A. Fogel, R. C. Reid and M. N. Potenza, 'Should Hypersexual Disorder be Classified as an Addiction?', *Sexual Addiction & Compulsivity*, 20:1–2 (2013), 27–47, quote at 40.

66 R. C. Reid, 'Personal Perspectives on Hypersexual Disorder', *Sexual Addiction & Compulsivity*, 20:1–2 (2013), 4–18, quote at 6.

67 L. J. Davis, *Obsession: A History* (Chicago, 2008), p. 185.

68 C. Moser, 'Hypersexual Disorder: Just More Muddled Thinking', *Archives of Sexual Behavior*, 40:2 (2011), 227–9, quote at 229.

69 Ley, *Myth of Sex Addiction*, ch. 3.

70 D. Ley, N. Prause and P. Finn, 'The Emperor Has No Clothes: A Review of the "Pornography Addiction" Model', *Current Sexual Health Reports*, 6:2 (2014), 94–105, quote at 94.

71 J. Bancroft and Z. Vukadinovic, 'Sexual Addiction, Sexual Compulsivity, Sexual Impulsivity, or What? Toward a Theoretical Model', *Journal of Sex Research*, 41:3 (2004), 225–34.

72 Ibid., 225.

73 Ibid., 233. Bancroft reiterated this opinion in 2008: J. Bancroft, 'Sexual Behavior that is "Out of Control": A Theoretical Approach', *Psychiatric Clinics of North America*, 31:4 (2008), 593–601.

74 T. Todd, 'Premature Ejaculation of "Sexual Addiction" Diagnoses', in S. Green and D. Flemons (eds.), *Quickies: The Handbook of Brief Sex Therapy* (New York, 2004), ch. 5, quote at p. 69.

75 J. N. Hook and others, 'Methodological Review of Treatments for Nonparaphilic Hypersexual Behavior', *Journal of Sex & Marital Therapy*, 40:4 (2014), 294–308, quote at 303.

76 S. Rickards and M. A. Laaser, 'Sexual Acting Out in Borderline Women: Impulsive Self-Destructiveness or Sexual Addiction/Compulsivity?', in P. J. Carnes and K. M. Adams (eds.), *Clinical Management of Sex Addiction* (New York, 2002), ch. 17, quote at p. 272. Originally published in 1999.

77 M. C. Fulton, 'Breaking Through Defenses', in Carnes and Adams (eds.), *Clinical Management of Sex Addiction*, ch. 3, quotes at p. 41. Originally published in 1999.

78 See M. R. Laaser and K. M. Adams, 'Pastors and Sex Addiction', in Carnes and Adams (eds.), *Clinical Management of Sex Addiction*, ch. 18, quote at p. 294. Originally published in 1997.

79 M. Wilson, 'Art Therapy: Treating the Invisible Sex Addict', in Carnes and Adams (eds.), *Clinical Management of Sex Addiction*, ch. 11, at pp. 167, 171.

80 See K. McGill, 'The Homeless and Sex Addiction', in Carnes and Adams (eds.), *Clinical Management of Sex Addiction*, ch. 20.

81 Schaffer and Zimmerman, 'The Sexual Addict', 25, 28.

82 Todd, 'Premature Ejaculation of "Sexual Addiction" Diagnoses', pp. 71, 74, 79.

83 G. Nixon and B. N. Theriault, 'Nondual Psychotherapy and Second Stage Sexual Addictions Recovery: Transforming "Master of the Universe" Narcissism into Nondual Being', *International Journal of Mental Health and Addiction*, 10:3 (2012), 368–85, quote at 380.

84 A. Ornstein, 'Erotic Passion: A Form of Addiction', in S. Dowling (ed.), *The Psychology and Treatment of Addictive Behavior* (Madison, CT, 1995), ch. 5; W. A. Myers, 'Sexual Addiction', in Dowling (ed.), *Psychology and Treatment of Addictive Behavior*, ch. 6.

85 Though see T. M. Tays, B. Garrett and R. E. Earle, 'Clinical Boundary Issues With Sexually Addicted Clients', in Carnes and Adams (eds.), *Clinical Management of Sex Addiction*, ch. 7; J. P. Schneider, 'Understanding and Diagnosing Sex Addiction', in R. H. Coombs (ed.), *Handbook of Addictive Disorders: A Practical Guide to Diagnosis and Treatment* (Hoboken, NJ, 2004), ch. 7, esp. pp. 224–5; R. Weiss, 'Treating Sex Addiction', in Coombs (ed.), *Handbook of Addictive Disorders*, ch. 8, esp. pp. 257–8.

86 Ornstein, 'Erotic Passion', p. 106.

87 Myers, 'Sexual Addiction', pp. 118, 123.

88 Ibid., p. 130.

89 J. C. Cantor and others, 'A Treatment-Oriented Typology of Self-Identified Hypersexuality Referrals', *Archives of Sexual Behavior*, 42:5 (2013), 883–93.

90 R. M. Salisbury, 'Out of Control Sexual Behaviours: A Developing Practice Model', *Sexual and Relationship Therapy*, 23:2 (2008), 131–9, quote at 132.

91 Ibid., 136.

92 M. P. Kafka, 'Hypersexual Disorder: A Proposed Diagnosis for DSM-V', *Archives of Sexual Behavior*, 39:2 (2010), 377–400.

93 Reid, Carpenter and Lloyd, 'Assessing Psychological Symptom Patterns of Patients', 48.

94 Ibid., 47.

95 Kafka, 'Hypersexual Disorder', Table 1, 379. For later modifications, see M. P. Kafka, 'The Development and Evolution of the Criteria for a Newly Proposed Diagnosis for DSM-5: Hypersexual Disorder', *Sexual Addiction & Compulsivity*, 20:1–2 (2013), 19–26; J. C. Wakefield, 'The DSM-5's Proposed New Categories of Sexual Disorder: The Problem of False Positives in Sexual Diagnosis', *Clinical Social Work Journal*, 40:2 (2012), 213–23.

96 C. P. Samenow, 'Editorial: What You Should Know about Hypersexual Disorder', *Sexual Addiction & Compulsivity*, 18:3 (2011), 107–13.

97 Kafka, 'Hypersexual Disorder', 381. Once a day does not seem especially hypersexual.

98 J. Winters, K. Christoff and B. B. Gorzalka, 'Dysregulated Sexuality and High Sexual Desire: Distinct Constructs?', *Archives of Sexual Behavior*, 39:5 (2010), 1029–43, esp. 1032–4. There were 14,396 participants, but 11,219 completed all the questionnaires (1032).

99 J. Winters, ''Hypersexual Disorder: A More Cautious Approach', *Archives of Sexual Behavior*, 39:3 (2010), 594–6, quote at 595.

100 Ibid., 594.

101 N. J. Rinehart and M. P. McCabe, 'Hypersexuality: Psychopathology or Normal Variant of Sexuality?', *Sexual and Marital Therapy*, 12:1 (1997), 45–60, quote at 59.

102 For such critiques, see Moser, 'Hypersexual Disorder: Just More Muddled Thinking', 227–9; Wakefield, 'DSM-5's Proposed New Categories', 215–18.

103 Moser, 'Hypersexual Disorder: Just More Muddled Thinking', 228.

104 Spenhoff, Kruger, Hartman and Kobs, 'Hypersexual Behavior in an Online Sample of Males', 2999.

105 D. Wines, 'Exploring the Applicability of the Criteria for Substance Dependence to Sexual Addiction', *Sexual Addiction & Compulsivity*, 4:3 (1997), 195–200, at 209. The point being made is ours and not Wines's.

106 C. Moser, 'Hypersexual Disorder: Searching for Clarity', *Sexual Addiction & Compulsivity*, 20:1–2 (2013), 48–58, quote at 52.

107 For the changing definitions, see Wakefield, 'DSM-5's Proposed New Categories', 215–18; Kafka, 'Development and Evolution of the Criteria', 19–26.

108 *Diagnostic and Statistical Manual of Mental Disorders (Third Edition – Revised): DSM-III-R* (Washington, DC, 1987), p. 296.

109 H. I. Kaplan and B. J. Sadock (eds.), *Comprehensive Textbook of Psychiatry, Sixth Edition*, 2 vols. (Baltimore, 1995), vol. 1, pp. 1311–13.

110 V. A. Sadock, 'Normal Human Sexuality and Sexual and Gender Identity Disorders', in B. J. Sadock and V. A. Sadock (eds.), *Kaplan & Sadock's Comprehensive Textbook of Psychiatry, Seventh Edition*, 2 vols. (Philadelphia, 2000), vol. 1, pp. 1598–9. Emphasis in original.

111 Ibid, vol. 1, pp. 1599–60.

112 P. J. Carnes, 'Sexual Addiction', in Sadock and Sadock (eds.), *Kaplan & Sadock's Comprehensive Textbook of Psychiatry, Eighth Edition*, 2 vols. (Philadelphia, 2005), vol. 1, pp. 1991–2001.

113 A. Goodman, 'Sexual Addiction', in B. J. Sadock, V. A. Sadock and P. Ruiz (eds.), *Kaplan & Sadock's Comprehensive Textbook of Psychiatry, Ninth Edition*, 2 vols. (Philadelphia, 2009), vol. 1, pp. 2111–27.

114 *International Classification of Diseases, Tenth Revision, Clinical Modification (ICD-10-CM), Tabular List of Diseases and Injuries* (Geneva, 2014), p. 225.

115 A. Frances, 'DSM5 and Sexual Disorders – Just Say No', *Psychology Today*, 17 March 2010: http://www.psychiatrictimes .com/articles/dsm5-and-sexual-disorders-%E2%80%94-just -say-no.

116 Ibid.

117 Ibid.

118 A. Frances, 'DSM 5 Is Guide Not Bible – Ignore Its Ten Worst Changes', *Psychology Today*, 2 December 2012: http://www .psychologytoday.com/blog/dsm5-in-distress/201212/dsm-5-is -guide-not-bible-ignore-its-ten-worst-changes.

119 See A. Frances, S. Sreenivasan and L. E. Weinberger, 'Defining Mental Disorder When It Really Counts: DSM-IV-TR and SVP/SDP Statutes', *Journal of the American Academy of Psychiatry and the Law*, 36:3 (2008), 375–84; M. B. First and R. B. Halon, 'Use of DSM Paraphilia Diagnoses in Sexually Violent Predator Cases', *Journal of the American Academy of Psychiatry and the Law*, 36:4 (2008), 443–54; R. A. Prentky, A. I. Coward and A. M. Gabriel, 'Commentary: Muddy Diagnostic Waters in the SVP Courtroom', *Journal of the American Academy of Psychiatry and the Law*, 36:4 (2008), 455–8; T. K. Zander, 'Commentary: Inventing Diagnosis for Civil Commitment of Rapists', *Journal of the American Academy of Psychiatry and the Law*, 36:4 (2008), 459–69; M. Testa and S. G. West, 'Civil Commitment in the United States', *Psychiatry* (Edgemont), 7:10 (2010), 30–40, esp. 35–6.

120 Zander, 'Commentary', 464, 465.

121 Ibid., 464.

122 Ibid., 460.

123 David Ley is currently working on the uncritical use of the concept of sex addiction in a variety of US legal proceedings. Personal communication, 29 July 2014.

124 A. Frances, 'Opening Pandora's Box: The 19 Worst Suggestions for DSM5', *Psychiatric Times*, 11 February 2010:

http://www.psychiatrictimes.com/dsm-v/content/article/
10168/1522341.

125 Wakefield, 'DSM-5's Proposed New Categories', 215–18.

126 Ibid., 216.

127 Samenow, 'Editorial: What You Should Know about Hypersexual Disorder', 110.

128 Moser, 'Hypersexual Disorder: Just More Muddled Thinking',
228–9.

129 S. E. Hyman, 'The Diagnosis of Mental Disorders: The Problem
of Reification', *Annual Review of Clinical Psychology*, 6
(2010), 155–79, quotes at 157.

130 J. R. Giugliano, 'Sex Addiction as a Mental Health Diagnosis:
Coming Together or Coming Apart', *Sexologies*, 22:3 (2013),
109–11, quote at 109.

131 J. R. Giugliano, 'Sexual Addiction: Diagnostic Problems',
International Journal of Mental Health and Addiction, 7:2
(2009), 283–94. See his entry on the SASH website: http://
www.sash.net/john-giugliano-phd.

132 *Diagnostic and Statistical Manual of Mental Disorders (Fourth
Edition): DSM-IV* (Washington, DC, 1994), p. 538.

133 Schneider, 'Understanding and Diagnosing Sex Addiction',
pp. 221–2, quote at p. 221.

134 J. P. Schneider and R. Irons, 'Differential Diagnosis of Addictive Sexual Disorders Using the DSM-IV', *Sexual Addiction &
Compulsivity*, 3:1 (1996), 7–21, quote at 8–9.

135 P. Hall, 'Sex Addiction – An Extraordinarily Contentious
Problem', *Sexual and Relationship Therapy*, 29:1 (2014), 68–
75, quote at 74.

136 A. Katehakis, 'Sex Addiction Beyond the DSM-V', *Psychology
Today*, 21 December 2012: http://www.psychologytoday.com/
blog/sex-lies-trauma/201212/sex-addiction-beyond-the-dsm-v.

137 Kafka, 'Nonparaphilic Hypersexuality Disorders', p. 285;
*Diagnostic and Statistical Manual of Mental Disorders (Fifth
Edition): DSM-5* (Washington, DC, 2013), p. 479. See also M.
Kafka, ''What Happened to Hypersexual Disorder?', *Archives
of Sexual Behavior*, first published online: 21 June 2014.

138 G. Greenberg, *The Book of Woe: The DSM and the Unmaking
of Psychiatry* (London, 2013), p. 68.

139 Ibid., p. 71.

140 D. Wines, 'Exploring the Applicability of the Criteria for Substance Dependence to Sexual Addiction', *Sexual Addiction &
Compulsivity*, 4:3 (1997), 195–200, at 209.

141 DSM-5, pp. 585–9, 795–8.

142 C. P. Samenow, 'Editorial: SASH Policy Statement (Revised):
The Future of Problematic Sexual Behaviors/Sexual Addiction',

Sexual Addiction & Compulsivity, 20:4 (2013), 255–8, quote at 255.

143 Frances, 'DSM 5 Is Guide Not Bible'.

144 D. E. Smith, 'Editor's Note: The Process Addictions and the New ASAM Definition of Addiction', *Journal of Psychoactive Drugs*, 44:1 (2012), 1–4.

145 DSM-5, p. 481.

146 Ibid., pp. 247–51, 254–7.

147 Davis, *Obsession*, p. 171.

148 P. Carnes, *Out of the Shadows: Understanding Sexual Addiction* (Minneapolis, 1983).

149 P. Carnes, *Don't Call It Love: Recovery from Sexual Addiction* (New York, 1991), p. 223.

150 Ibid., p. 224.

151 Earle and Earle, *Sex Addiction*. Though they were aware of the use of SSRIs to control 'sexual obsessions': p. 11.

152 A. Rösler and E. Witztum, 'Pharmacotherapy of the Paraphilias in the Next Millennium', *Behavioral Sciences and the Law*, 18:1 (2000), 43–56; T. Suarez and others, 'Selective Serotonin Reuptake Inhibitors as a Treatment for Sexual Compulsivity', in A. O'Leary (ed.), *Beyond Condoms: Alternative Approaches to HIV Prevention* (New York, 2002), ch. 9, esp. p. 212; V. L. Codispoti, 'Pharmacology of Sexually Compulsive Behavior', *Psychiatric Clinics of North America*, 31:4 (2008), 671–9; A. A. Assumpção and others, 'Pharmacologic Treatment of Paraphilias', *Psychiatric Clinics of North America*, 37:2 (2014), 173–81.

153 See studies cited in Suarez and others, 'Selective Serotonin Reuptake Inhibitors as a Treatment for Sexual Compulsivity', p. 211.

154 D. J. Stein and others, 'Serotonergic Medications for Sexual Obsessions, Sexual Addictions, and Paraphilias', *Journal of Clinical Psychiatry*, 53:8 (1992), 267–71.

155 R. T. Segraves, 'Antidepressant-Induced Sexual Dysfunction', *Journal of Clinical Psychiatry*, 59 (suppl. 4) (1998), 48–54. More recently, see A. Clayton, A. Keller and E. L. McGarvey, 'Burden of Phase-Specific Sexual Dysfunction With SSRIs', *Journal of Affective Disorders*, 91:1 (2006), 27–32.

156 P. D. Kramer, *Listening to Prozac* (New York, 1993), pp. x–xi, 316n, 366–7n, quote at pp. x–xi.

157 Myers, 'Sexual Addiction', pp. 118, 121, 123, 126, 128, 130.

158 J. R. Sealy, 'Psychopharmacological Intervention in Addictive Sexual Behavior', in Carnes and Adams (eds.), *Clinical Management of Sex Addiction*, ch. 13. Originally published in 1995.

159 Rösler and E. Witztum, 'Pharmacotherapy of the Paraphilias', 51.

160 Carnes, 'Sexual Addiction', p. 1997; Goodman, 'Sexual Addiction', pp. 2120–1.

161 O. Vesga-Lopez, A. Schmidt and C. Blanco, 'Update on Sexual Addictions', *Directions in Psychiatry*, 27:12 (2007), 143–57.

162 F. D. Garcia and F. Thibaut, 'Sexual Addictions', *American Journal of Drug and Alcohol Abuse*, 36:5 (2010), 254–60, esp. 258–9, quote at 258. For the side effects of these drugs, including impact on the bones, see Rösler and Witztum, 'Pharmacotherapy of the Paraphilias', 46, 47, quote at 43.

163 Rosenberg, Carnes and O'Connor, 'Evaluation and Treatment of Sex Addiction', 86, 87.

164 M. P. Kafka, 'Paraphilia-Related Disorders: The Evaluation and Treatment of Nonparaphilic Hypersexuality', in S. R. Leiblum (ed.), *Principles and Practices of Sex Therapy, Fourth Edition* (New York, 2007), ch. 15, quote at p. 467.

165 Ibid., pp. 468–9.

166 Ibid., pp. 467–70, quote at p. 467. In his contribution to the *Fifth Edition* he refers to having treated more than 500 males but his conclusions regarding psychopharmacology are the same: M. P. Kafka, 'Nonparaphilic Hypersexuality Disorders', in Y. M. Binik and K. S. K. Hall (eds.), *Principles and Practices of Sex Therapy, Fifth Edition* (New York, 2014), ch. 13, at p. 296.

167 T. W. Fong, R. De La Garza and T. F. Newton, 'A Case Report of Topiramate in the Treatment of Nonparaphilic Sexual Addiction', *Journal of Clinical Psychopharmacology*, 25:5 (2005), 512–13, quote at 513 (Letters to the Editors).

168 J. M. Bostwick and J. A. Bucci, 'Internet Sex Addiction Treated With Naltrexone', *Mayo Clinic Proceedings*, 83:2 (2008), 226–30.

169 R. Dardennes, N. Al Anbar and F. Rouillon, 'Episodic Sexual Addiction in a Depressed Woman Treated with Cyproterone Acetate', *Journal of Clinical Psychopharmacology*, 33:2 (2013), 274–6, quote at 275 (Letters to the Editors).

170 The case started in 1996 but was reported in 2005: J. L. Elmore, 'Psychotropic Medication Control of Non-Paraphilic Sexual Addiction in a Female', *Sexual and Relationship Therapy*, 20:2 (2005), 211–13, quote at 212.

171 J. L. Elmore, 'Fluoxetine-Associated Remission of Ego-Dystonic Male Homosexuality', *Sexuality and Disability*, 20:2 (2002), 149–51.

172 M. Tyson with L. Sloman, *Undisputed Truth: My Autobiography* (London, 2013), Ebook, locs. 7202–7.

173 Ibid., loc. 7178.
174 Ibid., loc. 7207.
175 R. Karim, 'Cutting Edge Pharmacology for Sex Addiction', California Society of Addiction Medicine, 14 October 2009: http://www.csam-asam.org/pdf/misc/Sex_Addiction.pdf.
176 H. Naficy, C. P. Samenow and T. F. Fong, 'A Review of Pharmacological Treatments for Hypersexual Disorder', *Sexual Addiction & Compulsivity*, 20:1–2 (2013), 139–53, quotes at 148.
177 Wainberg and others, 'Double-Blind Study of Citalopram Versus Placebo', 1972.
178 For Viagra, see M. Loe, *The Rise of Viagra: How the Little Blue Pill Changed Sex in America* (New York, 2004).
179 http://www.psy-world.com/prime-md_print1.htm.
180 H. Kutchins and S. A. Kirk, *Making Us Crazy: DSM: The Psychiatric Bible and the Creation of Mental Disorders* (New York, 1997), p. 13.
181 See *Instruction Manual: Instructions for Patient Health Questionnaire (PHQ) and GAD-7 Measures*: http://www .phqscreeners.com/overview.aspx.
182 E. Shorter, *Before Prozac: The Troubled History of Mood Disorders in Psychiatry* (Oxford, 2009), p. 209.

7   Sexual Conservatism

1 J. Money, *The Lovemap Guidebook: A Definitive Statement* (New York, 1999), p. 52.
2 A. W. Schaef, *When Society Becomes an Addict* (New York, 1988), p. 3. First published in 1987.
3 W. Lord, 'A Diagnostic Proposal with Neurochemical Underpinnings', in E. Griffin-Shelley (ed.), *Outpatient Treatment of Sex and Love Addicts* (Westport, CT, 1993), ch. 3, quotes at p. 21.
4 J. M. Irvine, 'Reinventing Perversion: Sex Addiction and Cultural Anxieties', *Journal of the History of Sexuality*, 5:3 (1995), 429–50, quotes at 430, 432.
5 E. Kennedy, 'Sexual-Addiction Diagnosis Supports Anti-Sex Movement', *Nurse Practitioner*, 16:8 (1991), 13 (Letters to the Editor).
6 P. Carnes, *Out of the Shadows: Understanding Sexual Addiction* (Center City, MN, 2001), p. xiii.
7 P. Carnes, D. L. Delmonico and E. Griffin, *In the Shadows of the Net: Breaking Free of Compulsive Online Sexual Behavior* (Center City, MN, 2001).

8 J. Riemersma and M. Sytsma, 'A New Generation of Sexual Addiction', *Sexual Addiction & Compulsivity*, 20:4 (2013), 306–22, quotes at 306.

9 A. Cooper and I. D. Marcus, 'Men Who Are Not In Control of Their Sexual Behavior', in S. B. Levine, D. B. Risen and S. E. Althof (eds.), *Handbook of Clinical Sexuality for Mental Health Professionals* (New York, 2003), ch. 18, quote at p. 311.

10 M. Griffiths, 'Sex on the Internet: Observations and Implications for Internet Sex Addiction', *Journal of Sex Research*, 38:4 (2001), 333–42, quotes at 336.

11 M. F. Schwartz and S. Southern, 'Compulsive Cybersex: The New Tea Room', *Sexual Addiction & Compulsivity*, 7:1–2 (2000), 127–44, quotes at 128, 139.

12 In contrast to alarmist accounts, see B. L. A. Mileham, 'Online Infidelity in Internet Chat Rooms: An Ethnographic Exploration', *Computers in Human Behavior*, 23:1 (2007), 11–31.

13 T. Todd, 'Premature Ejaculation of "Sexual Addiction" Diagnoses', in S. Green and D. Flemons (eds.), *Quickies: The Handbook of Brief Sex Therapy* (New York, 2004), ch. 5, quote at p. 86.

14 M. Klein, 'Sex Addiction: A Dangerous Clinical Concept', *SIECUS Report*, 31:5 (2003), 8–11.

15 D. J. Ley, *The Myth of Sex Addiction* (Lanham, MD, 2012), ch. 5.

16 C. Grov and others, 'Exploring the Internet's Role in Sexual Compulsivity and Out of Control Sexual Thoughts/Behaviour: A Qualitative Study of Gay and Bisexual Men in New York City', *Culture, Health & Sexuality*, 10:2 (2008), 107–25, quotes at 120.

17 D. Ley, N. Prause and P. Finn, 'The Emperor Has No Clothes: A Review of the "Pornography Addiction" Model', *Current Sexual Health Reports*, 6:2 (2014), 94–105.

18 D. L. Delmonico, 'Sex on the Superhighway: Understanding and Treating Cybersex Addiction', in P. J. Carnes and K. M. Adams (eds.), *Clinical Management of Sex Addiction* (New York, 2002), ch. 15, quote at p. 237.

19 K. S. Young, 'Internet Sex Addiction: Risk Factors, Stages of Development, and Treatment', *American Behavioral Scientist*, 52:1 (2008), 21–37, quotes at 22, 27–8.

20 Ibid., 23.

21 Ibid., 28.

22 www.keystonecenterecu.net.

23 www.sexhelp.com.

24 Edwards, Delmonico and Griffin, *Cybersex Unplugged*, pp. 37–9.
25 E. Coleman, 'Compulsive Sexual Behavior: What To Call It, How To Treat It', *SIECUS Report*, 31:5 (2003), 12–16, quote at 13.
26 T. P. Sbraga and W. T. O'Donohue, *The Sex Addiction Workbook: Proven Strategies to Help You Regain Control of Your Life* (Oakland, 2003), pp. 12–13.
27 R. Reid and others, 'Report of Findings in a DSM-5 Field Trial for Hypersexual Disorder', *Journal of Sexual Medicine*, 9:11 (2012), 2868–77, quotes at 2874.
28 S. A. Hardy, J. Ruchty, T. D. Hull and R. Hyde, 'A Preliminary Study of an Online Psychoeducational Program for Hypersexuality', *Sexual Addiction & Compulsivity*, 17:4 (2010), 247–69, quote at 253.
29 S. B. Levine, 'What Is Sexual Addiction?', *Journal of Sex & Marital Therapy*, 36:3 (2010), 261–75, quote at 272.
30 C. Moser, 'Hypersexual Disorder: Just More Muddled Thinking', *Archives of Sexual Behavior*, 40:2 (2011), 227–9, quote at 228.
31 H. Van Den Bulck and N. Claessens, 'Guess Who Tiger is Having Sex With Now? Celebrity Sex and the Framing of the Moral High Ground', *Celebrity Studies*, 4:1 (2013), 46–57, quotes at 54, 55.
32 C. L. Taylor, 'A Social Science Perspective of Sexual Addiction', *TAOS Newsletter*, 3:7 (1985), 28–31.
33 L. A. Siegel and R. M. Siegel, 'Sex Addiction: Semantics or Science', in W. J. Taverner and R. W. McKee (eds.), *Taking Sides: Clashing Views in Human Sexuality, Twelfth Edition* (New York, 2012), pp. 39–46, quotes at pp. 39, 43.
34 P. Joannides, 'The Challenging Landscape of Problematic Sexual Behaviors, Including "Sexual Addiction" and "Hypersexuality"', in P. J. Kleinplatz (ed.), *New Directions in Sex Therapy: Innovations and Alternatives, Second Edition* (New York, 2012), ch. 5, quote at p. 77.
35 J. Winters, K. Christoff and B. B. Gorzalka, 'Dysregulated Sexuality and High Sexual Desire: Distinct Constructs?', *Archives of Sexual Behavior*, 39:5 (2010), 1029–43, quote at 1039.
36 J. B. Grubbs and others, 'Transgression as Addiction: Religiosity and Moral Disapproval as Predictors of Perceived Addiction to Pornography', *Archives of Sexual Behavior*, first published online: 12 February 2014.
37 J. M. Bostwick and J. A. Bucci, 'Internet Sex Addiction Treated with Naltrexone', *Mayo Clinic Proceedings*, 83:2 (2008), 226–30, quotes at 226.

38 S. E. Pollard, J. N. Hook, M. D. Corley and J. P. Schneider, 'Support Utilization by Partners of Self-Identified Sex Addicts', *Journal of Sex & Marital Therapy*, 40:4 (2014), 339–48, at 343.

39 The Kinsey Institute for Research in Sex, Gender, and Reproduction, University of Indiana, Bloomington, 'Donahue Transcript, 1984, Multimedia Entertainment Inc.', p. 2.

40 M. Wilson, *Hope After Betrayal: Healing When Sex Addiction Invades Your Marriage* (Grand Rapids, MI, 2007), p. 15.

41 M. Corcoran, *A House Interrupted: A Wife's Story of Recovering from Her Husband's Sex Addiction* (Carefree, AZ, 2011), p. 89.

42 J. Henley, 'How Catherine Millet Discovered Jealousy', *The Guardian*, 29 October 2009: http://www.theguardian.com/lifeandstyle/2009/oct/29/catherine-millet-jealous.

43 H. Keane, *What's Wrong With Addiction?* (Melbourne, 2002), p. 138.

44 For example, T. Lee, M. Mars, V. Neil and N. Sixx, *Mötley Crüe: The Dirt – Confessions of the World's Most Notorious Rock Band* (New York, 2002); S. Tyler, *Does the Noise in My Head Bother You? A Rock 'n' Roll Memoir* (New York, 2011).

45 Tyler, *Does the Noise*, p. 267.

46 R. Lowe, *Stories I Only Tell My Friends: An Autobiography* (New York, 2011).

47 R. Brand, *My Booky Wook: A Memoir of Sex, Drugs, and Stand-Up* (New York, 2009), p. 9.

48 K. Richards, *Life* (New York, 2010).

49 B. Wyman, *Stone Alone: The Story of a Rock 'n' Roll Band* (London, 1990), p. 355.

50 For the clinical research, see R. C. Reid, 'Differentiating Emotions in a Sample of Men in Treatment for Hypersexual Behavior', *Journal of Social Work Practice in the Addictions*, 10:2 (2010), 197–213; R. Petrican, C. T. Burris and M. Moscovitch, 'Shame, Sexual Compulsivity, and Eroticizing Flirtatious Others: An Experimental Study', *Journal of Sex Research*, first published online: 3 December 2013; C. T. Burris and K. M. Schrage, 'Incognito Libido: Introducing the Sexual False Self Scale', *Sexual Addiction & Compulsivity*, 21:1 (2014), 42–56; R. C. Reid, J. Temko, J. F. Moghaddam and T. F. Fong, 'Shame, Rumination, and Self-Compassion in Men Assessed for Hypersexual Disorder', *Journal of Psychiatric Practice*, 20:4 (2014), 260–8.

51 Carnes and Adams (eds.), *Clinical Management of Sex Addiction*. Calculated from the Ebook version.

52 Carnes, *Out of the Shadows* (2001), p. xi.

53 Sexual Compulsives Anonymous, *Secret Shame: Sexual Compulsion in the Lives of Gay Men and Lesbians* (New York, 1991), Ebook, loc. 17.

54 J. C. Cantor and others, 'A Treatment-Oriented Typology of Self-Identified Hypersexuality Referrals', *Archives of Sexual Behavior*, 42:5 (2013), 883–93, quotes at 888–9.

55 Todd, 'Premature Ejaculation of "Sexual Addiction" Diagnoses', p. 85.

56 P. J. Carnes and others, 'PATHOS: A Brief Screening Application for Assessing Sexual Addiction', *Journal of Addiction Medicine*, 6:1 (2012), 29–34, at 31.

57 Ibid.

58 Klein, 'Sex Addiction', 8.

59 J. C. Wakefield, 'The DSM-5's Proposed New Categories of Sexual Disorder: The Problem of False Positives in Sexual Diagnosis', *Clinical Social Work Journal*, 40:2 (2012), 213–23, quote at 216.

60 M. Schisgal, *Sexaholics* (New York, 1995), pp. 29, 31.

61 Riemersma and Sytsma, 'A New Generation of Sexual Addiction', 307.

62 Ibid., 306–22.

63 Wilson, *Hope After Betrayal*, p. 12.

64 *Ricki Lake*: 'Exposed: Female Sex Addicts!', 3 March 2004.

65 *The Tyra Show*, 'Sex Rehab Clinic', 24 November 2009.

66 Griffiths, 'Sex on the Internet', 336. Emphasis ours.

67 H. Keane, 'Disorders of Desire: Addiction and Problems of Intimacy', *Journal of Medical Humanities*, 25:3 (2004), 189–204, quote at 194.

68 B. C. Kelly and others, 'Sexual Compulsivity and Sexual Behaviors Among Gay and Bisexual Men and Lesbian and Bisexual Women', *Journal of Sex Research*, 46:4 (2009), 301–8, quotes at 306.

69 M. P. Kafka, 'What Is Sexual Addiction? A Response to Stephen Levine', *Journal of Sex & Marital Therapy*, 36:3 (2010), 276–81, quote at 277.

70 R. C. Reid, J. E. Bramen, A. Anderson and M. S. Cohen, 'Mindfulness, Emotional Dysregulation, Impulsivity, and Stress Proneness Among Hypersexual Patients', *Journal of Clinical Psychology*, 70:4 (2014), 313–21, quote at 314.

71 'Donahue Transcript, 1984, Multimedia Entertainment Inc.', p. 4.

72 Sexual Compulsives Anonymous, *Secret Shame*, loc. 159.

73 Ibid., locs. 186, 193.

74 M. C. Quadland and W. Shattls, 'AIDS, Sexuality, and Sexual Control', *Journal of Homosexuality*, 14:1–2 (1987), 277–98,

quote at 287. See also M. C. Quadland, 'Compulsive Sexual Behavior: Definition of a Problem and an Approach to Treatment', *Journal of Sex & Marital Therapy*, 11:2 (1985), 121–32.

75 R. William Wedin, quoted in G. Destefano, 'The Gay Sex Addict Controversy', *Forum*, 15:4 (1986), 54–9, quotes at 57, 58.

76 J. T. Parsons and D. S. Bimbi, 'Intentional Unprotected Anal Intercourse Among Sex [sic] Who Have Sex With Men: Barebacking – From Behaviour to Identity', *AIDS and Behavior*, 11:2 (2007), 277–87; C. Grov, J. T. Parsons and D. S. Bimbi, 'Sexual Compulsivity and Sexual Risk in Gay and Bisexual Men', *Archives of Sexual Behavior*, 39:4 (2010), 940–9, quote at 941; E. Coleman and others, 'Compulsive Sexual Behavior and Risk for Unsafe Sex Among Internet Using Men Who have Sex with Men', *Archives of Sexual Behavior*, 39:5 (2010), 1045–53.

77 See S. C. Kalichman and D. Rompa, 'The Sexual Compulsivity Scale: Further Development and Use With HIV-Positive Persons', *Journal of Personality Assessment*, 76:3 (2001), 379–95.

78 Kelly and others, 'Sexual Compulsivity', 301–8.

79 L. J. Hatterer, *Changing Homosexuality in the Male: Treatment for Men Troubled by Homosexuality* (New York, 1970).

80 L. J. Hatterer, *The Pleasure Addicts: The Addictive Process – Food, Sex, Drugs, Alcohol, Work, and More* (Cranbury, NJ, 1980), quotes at pp. 120, 121.

81 Ibid., p. 205.

82 Ibid., p. 120.

83 Ibid., p. 121.

84 Hatterer, *Changing Homosexuality*, pp. viii, 63, 86, and esp. ch. 10.

85 Ibid., p. 251.

86 Hatterer, *The Pleasure Addicts*, p. 89.

87 Ibid., p. 91.

88 Not to be confused with the Pennsylvania-based, homosexual-conversion group Homosexuals Anonymous, founded in the early 1980s. For this latter group, see A. F. Ide, *Homosexuals Anonymous: A Psychoanalytic and Theological Analysis of Colin Cook and His Cure for Homosexuality* (Garland, TX, 1987). See also D. C. Haldeman, 'The Practice and Ethics of Sexual Orientation Conversion Therapy', *Journal of Consulting and Clinical Psychology*, 62:2 (1994), 221–7; J. G. Ford, 'Healing Homosexuals: A Psychologist's Journey Through the Ex-Gay Movement and the Pseudo-Science of Reparative

Therapy', *Journal of Gay & Lesbian Psychotherapy*, 5:3–4 (2002), 69–86.

89 J. Morgenstern and others, 'Non-Paraphilic Compulsive Sexual Behavior and Psychiatric Co-Morbidities in Gay and Bisexual Men', *Sexual Addiction & Compulsivity*, 18:3 (2011), 114–34, quotes at 115, 117.

90 H. Keane, 'Taxonomies of Desire: Sex Addiction and the Ethics of Intimacy', *International Journal of Critical Psychology*, 1:3 (2001), 9–28, quotes at 12, 16.

91 R. Earle and G. Crow, *Lonely All the Time: Recognizing, Understanding, and Overcoming Sex Addiction, For Addicts and Co-Dependents* (New York, 1989), p. 5.

92 R. Weiss, 'Treatment Concerns for Gay Male Sex Addicts', in Carnes and Adams (eds.), *Clinical Management of Sex Addiction*, ch. 21, quote at p. 333. Originally published in 1997.

93 J. R. Sealy, 'Dual and Triple Diagnoses: Addictions, Mental Illness, and HIV Infection Guidelines for Outpatient Therapists', in Carnes and Adams (eds.), *Clinical Management of Sex Addiction*, ch. 14, quotes at p. 217. Originally published in 1999. See also E. Cuestas-Thompson, 'Treating Quadruple Diagnosis in Gay Men: HIV, Sexual Compulsivity, Substance Use Disorder, and Major Depression – Exploring Underlying Issues', *Sexual Addiction & Compulsivity*, 4:4 (1997), 301–21.

94 Weiss, 'Treatment Concerns for Gay Male Sex Addicts', p. 336.

95 J. T. Parsons and others, 'A Psychometric Investigation of the Hypersexual Disorder Screening Inventory Among Highly Sexually Active Gay and Bisexual Men: An Item Response Theory Analysis', *Journal of Sexual Medicine*, 10:12 (2013), 3088–101, quote at 3089.

96 This seems to be the message of Weiss, 'Treatment Concerns for Gay Male Sex Addicts', quote at p. 330.

97 R. Weiss, *Cruise Control: Understanding Sex Addiction in Gay Men* (Los Angeles, 2005), p. 21.

98 Ibid., pp. 20–1.

99 Quoted in Weiss, 'Treatment Concerns for Gay Male Sex Addicts', p. 332.

100 M. Cooper and R. A. Lebo, 'Assessment and Treatment of Sexual Compulsivity', *Journal of Social Work Practice in the Addictions*, 1:2 (2001), 61–74, quotes at 63–4.

101 Ibid., 70.

102 Keane, 'Disorders of Desire', 202.

103 *Nymphomaniac: Volume 2* (2014: Lars von Trier).

8 Conclusion

1 G. Rogell, 'Eddie', in *Louie*, Season 2, Episode 9, 11 August 2011.

2 K. Skegg, S. Nada-Raja, N. Dickson and C. Paul, 'Perceived "Out of Control" Sexual Behaviour in a Cohort of Young Adults from the Dunedin Multidisciplinary Health and Development Study', *Archives of Sexual Behavior*, 39:4 (2010), 968–78, quote at 977.

3 E. S. Blumberg, 'The Lives and Voices of Highly Sexual Women', *Journal of Sex Research*, 40:2 (2003), 146–57, example from 149.

4 Ibid., 150.

5 Ibid., 151.

6 Ibid., 153–4.

7 M. D. Griffiths and M. K. Dhuffar, 'Treatment of Sexual Addiction Within the British National Health Service', *International Journal of Mental Health and Addiction*, first published online: 11 February 2014.

8 P. R. Recupero, 'The Mental Status Examination in the Age of the Internet', *Journal of the American Academy of Psychiatry and the Law*, 38:1 (2010), 15–26.

9 For a thoughtful account of the rise of neuroscience, see N. Rose and J. M. Abi-Rached, *Neuro: The New Brain Sciences and the Management of the Mind* (Princeton, 2013).

10 I. Hacking, 'Kinds of People: Moving Targets', *Proceedings of the British Academy*, 151 (2007), 285–318, quote at 310.

11 S. E. Hyman, 'The Diagnosis of Mental Disorders: The Problem of Reification', *Annual Review of Clinical Psychology*, 6 (2010), 155–79, quotes at 173. For this turn, and its problems, see J. Paris, 'The Ideology Behind DSM-5', in J. Paris and J. Phillips (eds.), *Making the DSM-5, 2013: Concepts and Controversies* (New York, 2013), ch. 3.

12 *Diagnostic and Statistical Manual of Mental Disorders (Fifth Edition): DSM-5* (Washington, DC, 2013), p. xlii.

13 Hyman, 'Diagnosis of Mental Disorders', 173.

14 'More Than Meets the Brain: Inside Neuropsychiatry's Secrets', email 11 April 2014: psychiatrictimes@email.cmpmedica-usa.com.

15 J. Bancroft, 'Sexual Behavior That is "Out of Control": A Theoretical Approach', *Psychiatric Clinics of North America*, 31:4 (2008), 593–601, quote at 597.

16 K. Blum and others, 'Sex, Drugs, and Rock 'n' Roll: Hypothesizing Common Mesolimbic Activation as a Function of Reward

Gene Polymorphisms', *Journal of Psychoactive Drugs*, 44:1 (2012), 38–55, quote at 50.

17 For an informative discussion of the use of animal models in neuroscience, see Rose and Abi-Rached, *Neuro*, ch. 3.

18 Blum and others, 'Sex, Drugs, and Rock 'n' Roll', 51.

19 F. S. Berlin, 'Basic Science and Neurobiological Research: Potential Relevance to Sexual Compulsivity', *Psychiatric Clinics of North America*, 31:4 (2008), 623–42, quote at 629.

20 E. Griffin-Shelley, 'Adolescent Sex and Love Addicts', in P. J. Carnes and K. M. Adams (eds.), *Clinical Management of Sex Addiction* (New York, 2002), ch. 22, quote at p. 341.

21 J. Riemersma and M. Sytsma, 'A New Generation of Sexual Addiction', *Sexual Addiction & Compulsivity*, 20:4 (2013), 306–22, quote at 311.

22 Ibid., 317, 318.

23 Hacking, 'Kinds of People: Moving Targets', 298.

24 P. Conrad, 'Medicalization and Social Control', *Annual Review of Sociology*, 18 (1992), 209–32, esp. 219.

25 Ibid., 211.

26 H. Keane, 'Taxonomies of Desire: Sex Addiction and the Ethics of Intimacy', *International Journal of Critical Psychology*, 1:3 (2001), 9–28, quote at 14.

27 J. C. Wakefield, 'The DSM-5's Proposed New Categories of Sexual Disorder: The Problem of False Positives in Sexual Diagnosis', *Clinical Social Work Journal*, 40:2 (2012), 213–23, quote at 215.

28 *Nymphomaniac: Volume 1* and *Nymphomaniac: Volume 2* (2014: Lars von Trier); R. Weiss, 'Thoughts on Nymphomaniac: Volume 1', *The Huffington Post*, 20 March 2014: http://www.huffingtonpost.com/robert-weiss/thoughts-on-nymphomaniac_b_5002574.html.

29 M. D. Berry and P. D. Berry, 'Mentalization-Based Therapy for Sexual Addiction: Foundations for a Clinical Model', *Sexual and Relationship Therapy*, 29:2 (2014), 245–60, quotes at 247, 248.

30 Ibid., 247.

31 Ibid., 255.

32 R. C. Reid, 'Assessing Readiness to Change Among Clients Seeking Help for Hypersexual Behavior', *Sexual Addiction & Compulsivity*, 14:3 (2007), 167–86. Quote and figures on 171, 175.

33 B. Dodge, M. Reece, S. L. Cole and T. G. M. Sandfort, 'Sexual Compulsivity Among Heterosexual College Students', *Journal of Sex Research*, 41:4 (2004), 343–50, quote at 349.

Index

Page numbers in *italics* refer to a figure or table.